# Learning DraftSight™ for Windows

## A Self-Directed Approach

**By Jason Wooden**

**ISBN: 978-1-58503-662-2**

**PUBLICATIONS**

**Schroff Development Corporation**

www.SDCpublications.com

**Schroff Development Corporation**
P.O. Box 1334
Mission KS 66222
(913) 262-2664
www.SDCpublications.com

Publisher: Stephen Schroff

**Examination Copies:**

Books received as examination copies are for review purposes only and may not be made available for student use. Resale of examination copies is prohibited.

**Electronic Files:**

Any electronic files associated with this book are licensed to the original user only. These files may not be transferred to any other party.

The author and publisher of this book have used their best efforts in preparing this book. However, the author and publisher make no warranty of any kind, expressed or implied, with regard to the material contained in this book. The author and publisher shall not be liable in any event for incidental or consequential damages in connection with the use of the material contained herein.

# Table of Contents

# Introduction: Start Here!

## Who Should Use this Text

This text has been developed specifically for today's adult learner enrolled in beginning Computer Aided Drafting (CAD) classes using DraftSight™ software[*]. However, motivated high school and college students should find the content applicable as well. Any self-directed learner desiring to gain a mastery of the software outside the classroom environment will find this text useful.

What sets this text apart from others is its ability to provide the learner with greater choices in the quest for learning CAD software. For example, every effort has been made to provide an environment which covers the two main uses of the software: Mechanical and Architectural drafting.  Although diverse, these fields are related enough such that beginning CAD skills learned in one area can be adapted to the other.  Exercises and activities found in this text are typically grouped as either Mechanical or Architectural.  The learner may decide which path to take (or do both). Skills learned in these areas as transferable to subsets of these groups as well (e.g., electrical, civil, structural, textile design, interior design, and landscape design).

## Objectives

You may find that DraftSight is very similar AutoCAD[®], which is arguably the most widely used two-dimensional (2D) CAD program in the world.  At one time learning 2D CAD was a "means and an end".  In other words, most learners enrolled in 2D CAD classes in order to obtain a job working as a drafter at a firm using the software.  However, most design firms have now adopted three-dimensional (3D) modeling software, which 2D CAD is not intended to compete with.  2D CAD's usefulness in the educational drafting laboratory has shifted. The basic principles of 2D CAD can be applied toward obtaining 3D modeling skills. All 3D features, from the simplest protrusion to the most complex loft, start out as one or more 2D sketches, and most 3D models end up being represented as 2D technical drawings.  Additionally, many hobbyists and fabrication shops find 2D CAD sufficient for their drafting needs. Therefore, the

---

[*] DraftSight™ is a trademark of Dassault Systemes. However from this point on, the trademark symbol will be omitted in this text. Note: DraftSight version V1R1.2 was contemporary at the time of the writing of this text.
*AutoCAD[®] is a registered trademark of the Autodesk[®], Inc.

objective of this text is to introduce the essentials of 2D CAD to the learner. This is an area in which DraftSight, as a tool, excels.

The learner, after completing this text and proper facilitation, should be able to create simple multi-view projections of mechanical objects, as well as plan and elevation views of architectural structures. It is assumed that the learner comes to the class with some background in drafting, including proficiency in orthographic projection, sectioning, and dimensioning practices. Where the learner does not possess these skills, the facilitator will have to offer supplementary materials. The purpose of this text is to assist in learning the DraftSight software program, not drafting skills in general.

## Philosophy

It has been said that drafting is a language. It is used to communicate a customer's requirements to the fabricator of a product which is designed to meet those requirements. CAD is a tool which expedites that communication process. 2D CAD in general is far superior to manual drafting mainly because of the ease and speed by which drawings can be created and edited. Additionally, fewer mistakes are discovered during the product fabrication process, having been revealed in the design phase instead. This is due to CAD's ability to accurately depict how parts fit and function within assemblies.

## How to use this Text

In order to best meet the needs of beginning CAD adult learners, this book has two parts. Part A, "General Skills" is exactly that. It covers the basic commands necessary to effectively create geometry using DraftSight. It is intended for the learner enrolled in a beginning DraftSight class with no prior CAD experience. Such a class would be 24-36 hours in length and typically found at a college, applied technology center or trade school. As such, it would be expedient for the facilitator to introduce the chapters herein at an average rate of one per every two-hours of class time. Those wishing to forge ahead at a more rapid pace should be encouraged to do so.

Part B, "Specialized Skills" contains optional modules that are designed to address specific learner needs. The learner should consult with the facilitator before contracting to complete the modules that would be of most benefit to the learner. Building on what was learned in Part A, the learner should be able to generate and plot production-quality multi/plan view drawings on their own at the completion of Part B.

## To the class facilitator...

As you approach the facilitation of this class, keep in mind that the adult learners present in your class are there voluntarily. Learners enroll in your class to fill a missing piece somewhere in their lives, usually related to their current or future employment. All efforts should be made to discover the learner's individual needs and address them throughout the class. A few ideas for needs assessment instruments can be found in the Appendix. If the learner has a good experience they are more likely to enroll in another adult class or training program in the future. Ideally, educators like you are in the business of creating life-long self-directed learners, not just good drafters.

## A note from the author:

My father presented me with a compass-set when I was nine-years old. From that day forward, I had a keen interest in technical drawing and suspected it would play important role in my future education and career. I took three years of drafting in high school and earned an A.A.S. in drafting from Utah State University. I then started working as a tooling designer for a firm that produced snow-grooming equipment. Later I added a B.S. in Industrial Teacher Education and a M.S. in Industrial Technology. This is where I discovered that there's one thing more enjoyable than *doing*, it's *teaching*. Currently I have nineteen years of drafting experience with a variety of manufacturing and research firms and have taught classes part-time at Utah State University and an applied technology college for five years. This text came about from recognizing a need to develop a CAD curriculum for learners who want more choice in their educational experience. The product of many years of inputs from learners and educators alike, I hope you enjoy using this text as much as I've enjoyed writing it.

## Acknowledgments

Dr. Edward M. Reeve — Utah State University
Dr. Gary Straquadine — Utah State University
Dr. Maurice Thomas — Utah State University
Dr. Kurt Becker — Utah State University
John Davidson — Bridgerland Applied Technology College

...and my family for having the patience to see this project through.

# Part A. General Skills

All learners should complete Part A to acquire basic DraftSight skills.

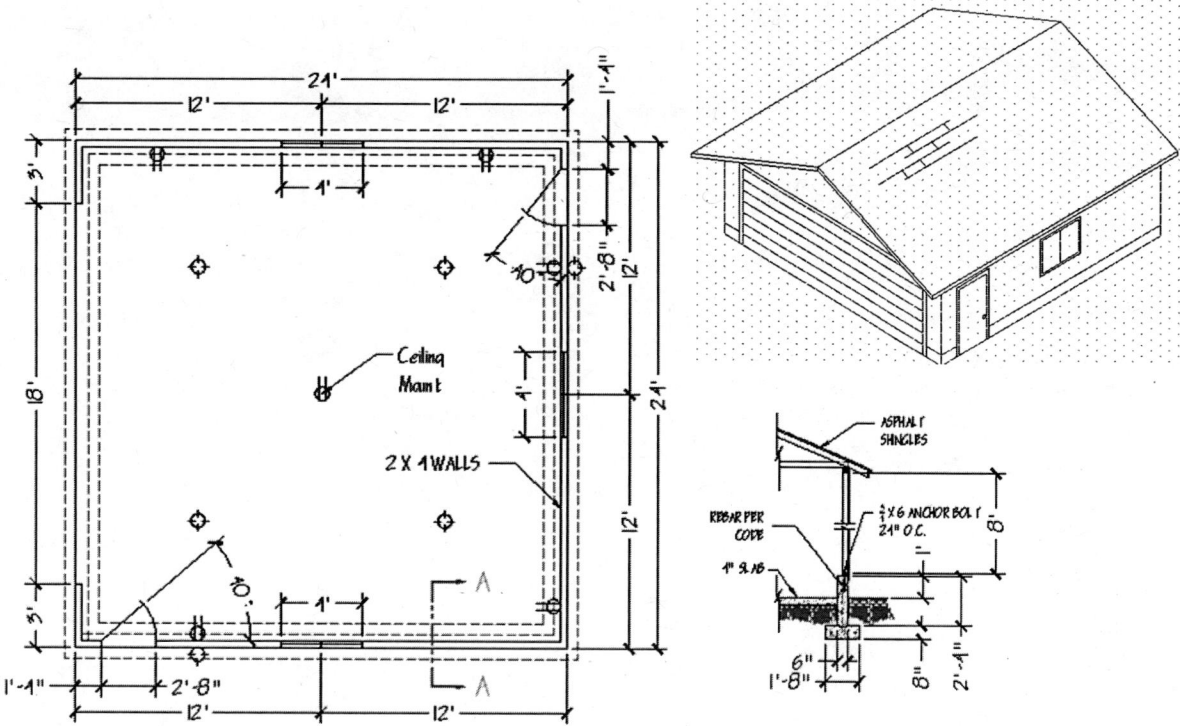

# Unit 1- Sketching and Editing

Objectives:
1. Launch DraftSight
2. Explore DraftSight's user interface
3. Open a drawing
4. Use the Pan and Zoom commands
5. Close a drawing
6. Start a new drawing

Congratulations!  If you're looking to obtain state-of-the-art two-dimensional drafting skills, you've made an excellent choice by choosing to learn DraftSight. Let's get started....

## Launching DraftSight

1. If you haven't already, turn on your computer and ask your class facilitator for assistance in logging on the system (if applicable).

2. When the Windows desktop appears, locate the **DraftSight** icon (or look for it in the **Start** menu).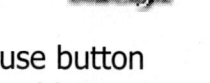

3. Position your cursor over the icon and quickly click your left mouse button twice (see below).  This called a "**double-click**".  DraftSight should start in a few moments.

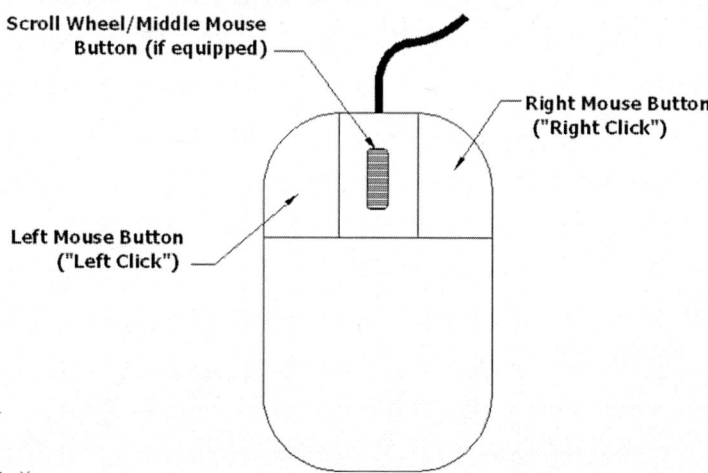

7

## The DraftSight user interface

What you should see after launching DraftSight: (Your screen probably won't look exactly like this one, but it'll be close enough.)

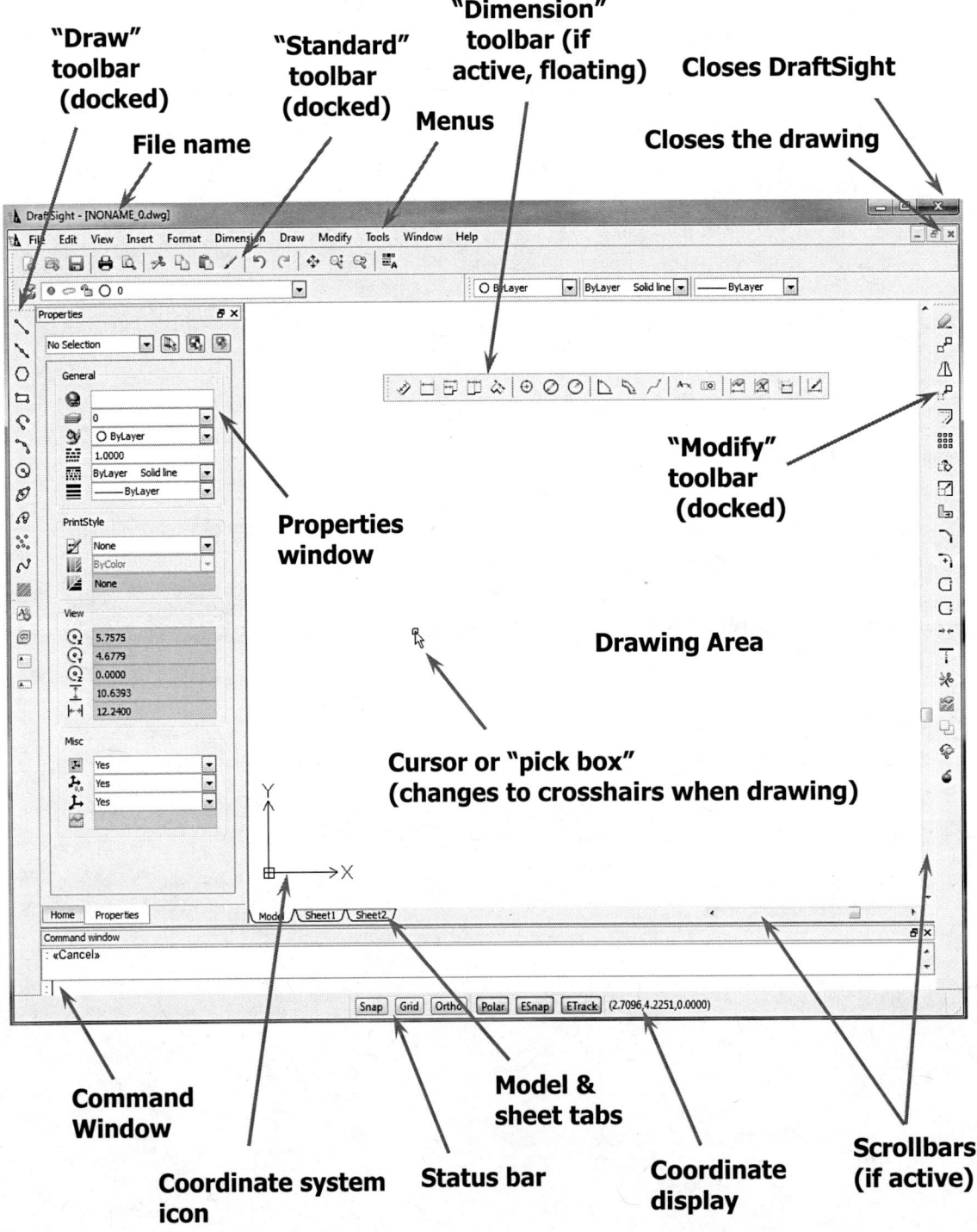

**"Draw" toolbar (docked)**

**"Standard" toolbar (docked)**

**"Dimension" toolbar (if active, floating)**

**Closes DraftSight**

**File name**

**Menus**

**Closes the drawing**

**"Modify" toolbar (docked)**

**Properties window**

**Drawing Area**

**Cursor or "pick box" (changes to crosshairs when drawing)**

**Command Window**

**Coordinate system icon**

**Status bar**

**Model & sheet tabs**

**Coordinate display**

**Scrollbars (if active)**

An explanation of the terms presented in the graphic on the previous page:

- **File name-** This is the name of the file that you are currently working on. The file extension for DraftSight drawings is "**.dwg**".

- **Toolbars-** These contain icons which when clicked will initiate a DraftSight command. Toolbars can be "docked" or "floating" by clicking on them with the left mouse button, dragging them into the desired position, and releasing the mouse button. Try it!

- **Menus-** Try clicking on one of the many DraftSight menus. You'll notice they expand to show a number of related commands in written format. If you see an arrow next to a particular command, that means a "cascading" or sub-menu will appear when selected.

- **Command Window-** Here commands are issued to DraftSight by typing them (as opposed to menus and icons). This is also where DraftSight interfaces with **you**, the user! DraftSight will ask you for inputs on the command line. **Its importance cannot be stressed enough!**

- **Model and Sheet Tabs-** Used to switch between model mode and sheet mode. We'll be in model mode most of the time; this is where most drawing is done. Sheet mode is a "paste-up" area of sorts, normally used shortly before plotting.

- **Status Bar-** Contains tooltips (if active), drafting option buttons which activate various drawing aids, and the pointer's X, Y & Z coordinates.

- **Coordinate system icon-** This indicates the X and Y axes as well as the drawing's **Origin**, or intersection of the X and Y axis (location 0,0).

- **Scrollbars-** These are used to **pan**, or move across the drawing area.

- **Properties window-** When an entity is selected, this window is used to determine an entity's properties and change them if needed.

- **Cursor-** used to select entities, changes to crosshairs when creating entities.

**Note:** Many of these features and toolbars can be turned off and on from the pop-up menu that appears by right-clicking on any docked toolbar and with a left-click, selecting the desired feature from the list.  Try turning on the toolbars shown in the graphic below:

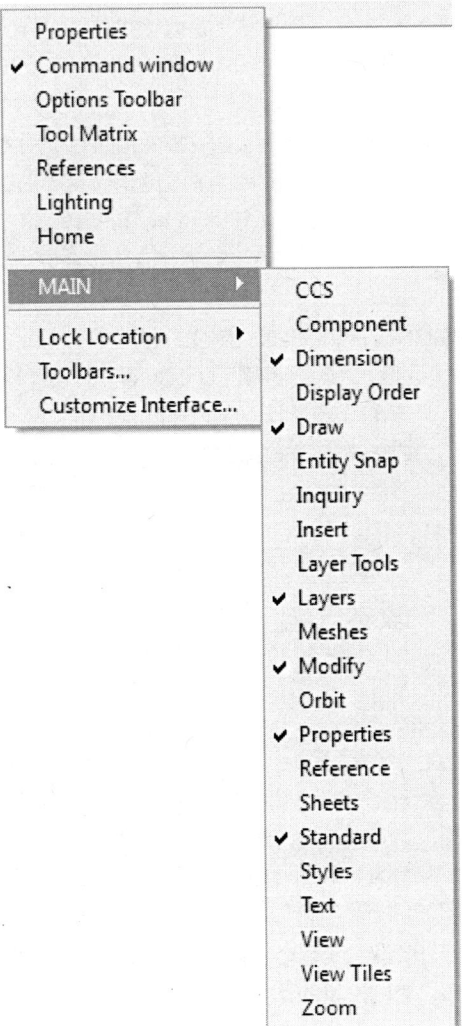

## Using the Icons

By far the most used method of entering DraftSight commands in this text will be selecting on icons.  These buttons are designed to look somewhat like the command they initiate. Can you find the **Delete** icon in the **Modify** toolbar?  That one is easy (it looks like an eraser), but others aren't so obvious at first.

If you want to know which command is related to a particular icon, simply point at it with your cursor. After a moment a small box will appear containing the name of the command. The **Modify** toolbar is shown below, "undocked".

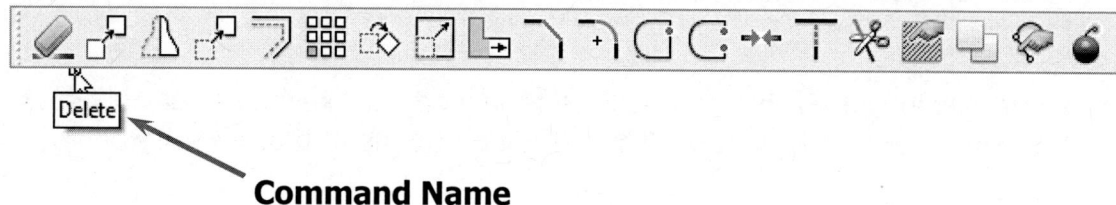

**Command Name**

## Opening a Drawing

1. Locate and left-click on the **Open** icon on the **Standard** toolbar. DraftSight will launch a window showing all the available files and prompt you to open one.

2. Select the local disk from the list of available drives (usually labeled **C:**). Find the **Examples** drawing folder. It's normally found under the following path: **C:\Program Data\DassaultSystemes\DraftSight\Examples**

3. Select the **pump housing** file, or another one your facilitator recommends. Depending on how DraftSight was installed, this file may or may not exist on your computer.

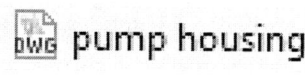

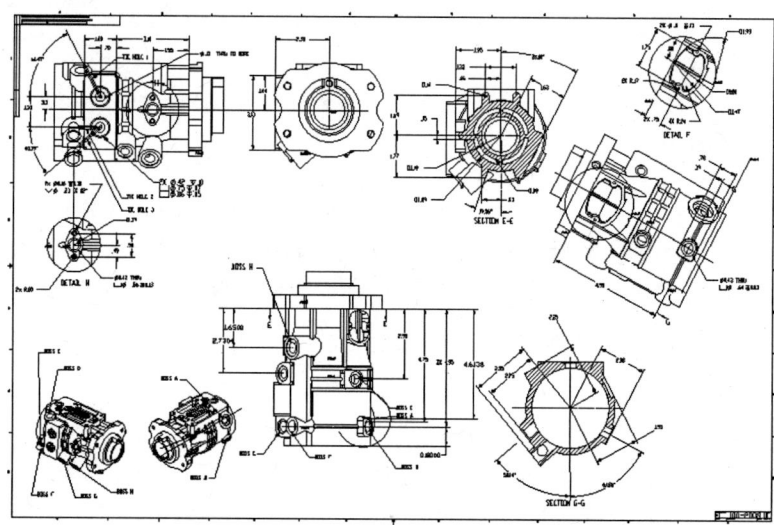

## Zooming and Panning

1. With an open drawing, left-click on the **Dynamic Zoom** icon located in the **Standard** toolbar. Left-click and hold near the middle of the drawing area, then move the mouse. What happens?

2. Exit the command by hitting the **Escape** key on your keyboard, or right-click with the mouse and select **Exit** from the pop-up menu that appears.

3. If the mouse has scrolling wheel for the middle button, left-click in the drawing area and try rolling it in both directions. What happens? It should have the same effect as **Dynamic Zoom** (if not, type "**ENBLMMBPAN**" in the command window and ensure that it is set to a value of "**1**").

4. If your mouse has a scrolling wheel, click and hold it while moving the mouse around. This will pan across the drawing.

5. Left click on the **Dynamic Pan** icon located in the **Standard** toolbar. Left-click and hold near the middle of the drawing area and move the mouse. A small hand appears and you should be panning (or moving) across the drawing.

6. **Right-click** in the drawing area and observe the pop-up menu that appears (shown at right). What else can you do besides Exit? Try switching between **Pan** and **Zoom** this way.

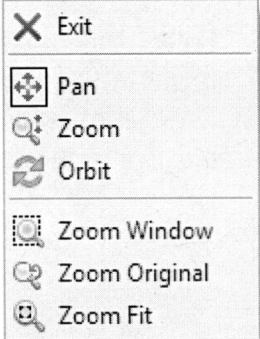

7. On your own: Try each of the other options available on the pop-up menu mentioned in the previous step. Note that **Orbit** is only used with 3D drawings. Be sure and use the **Undo** command found in the **Standard** toolbar after trying **Orbit**.

Some of the most useful Zoom functions are discussed below:

**Zoom Window-** Zooms in on a specified area indicated by drawing a box around the area by using the mouse.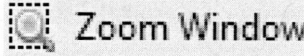

**Zoom Original-** Returns to a previous zoomed view.

**Zoom Fit-** Zooms out to the fit the entire drawing area.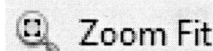

8. After experimenting with the various Zoom commands, **Close** the current drawing by left clicking on the small "**X**" in the upper right-hand in the corner of the drawing window (**NOT** the large red one, or DraftSight will close). When prompted to save the drawing, select **No**.

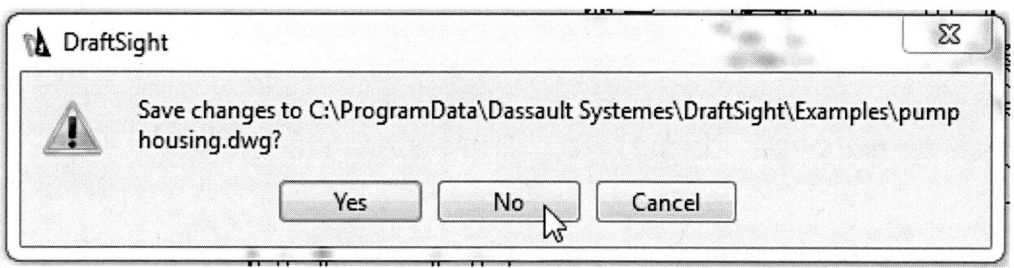

## Start a new drawing

1. Locate and left-click on the **New** icon in the **Standard** toolbar.

2. A new window should appear, prompting you to specify a "template". DraftSight has many uses. Templates are simply a way to start a new drawing the way you want it started, for your specific needs.

3. Select **standard** near the top of the list and left-click on the button labeled **Open** (or simply double-click on the file name).

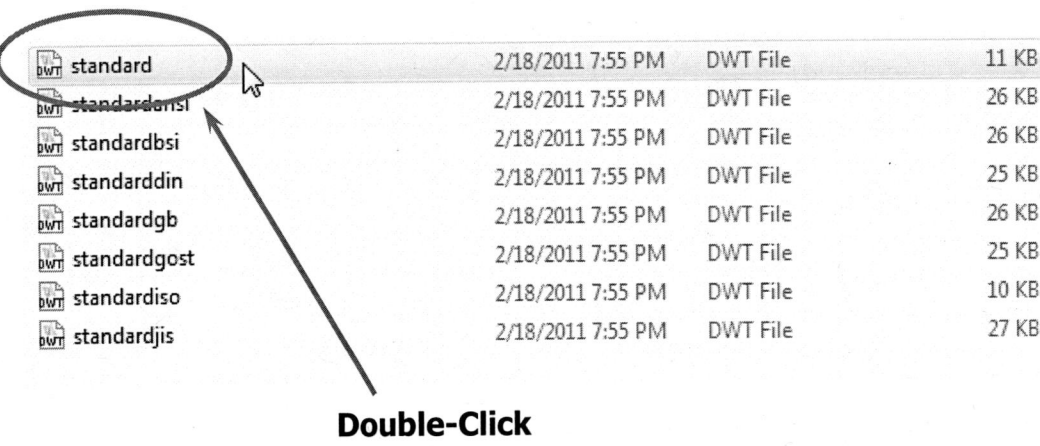

| standard | 2/18/2011 7:55 PM | DWT File | 11 KB |
| standardansi | 2/18/2011 7:55 PM | DWT File | 26 KB |
| standardbsi | 2/18/2011 7:55 PM | DWT File | 26 KB |
| standarddin | 2/18/2011 7:55 PM | DWT File | 25 KB |
| standardgb | 2/18/2011 7:55 PM | DWT File | 26 KB |
| standardgost | 2/18/2011 7:55 PM | DWT File | 25 KB |
| standardiso | 2/18/2011 7:55 PM | DWT File | 10 KB |
| standardjis | 2/18/2011 7:55 PM | DWT File | 27 KB |

**Double-Click**

4. Turn on the grid by left clicking on the **Grid** button in the **Status Bar**.

5. **Zoom** outward until you see the extent of the dots (grid) filling the drawing area. This represents approximately an "A" size, or 8 ½ x 11 piece of paper.

6. Normally we would now start to draw, but for now just **Close** DraftSight, as we are at the end of this chapter.

# Chapter 1  Suggested Learning Exercises

1. Open at least three other drawings that your facilitator recommends.  These may already be located on your computer or network, or downloaded from the internet.  Practice panning and zooming in each drawing to explore some of DraftSight's viewing options.  Also change between the Model and Sheet tabs.

2. Complete the crossword puzzle using the clues found at the bottom of this page and terms discussed in this chapter.

**Across**

2  Contains commands in written format.
3  Environment normally used just prior to plotting.
7  DraftSight file extension.
9  Contains a group of related icons.
11 Commands are entered here by typing them.

**Down**

1  Type of Zoom command used to instantly show the entire drawing.
2  Environment where most drawing is done.
3  Can be used to pan across the drawing.
4  Condition of a toolbar lying in the drawing area.
5  Condition of a toolbar attached to the edge of the drawing area.
6  View command not normally used in 2D drafting.
8  Type of Zoom used to designate a specific area for viewing.
10 A button containing a graphical representation of a command.

3. In the blanks provided, name the main features of the DraftSight window:

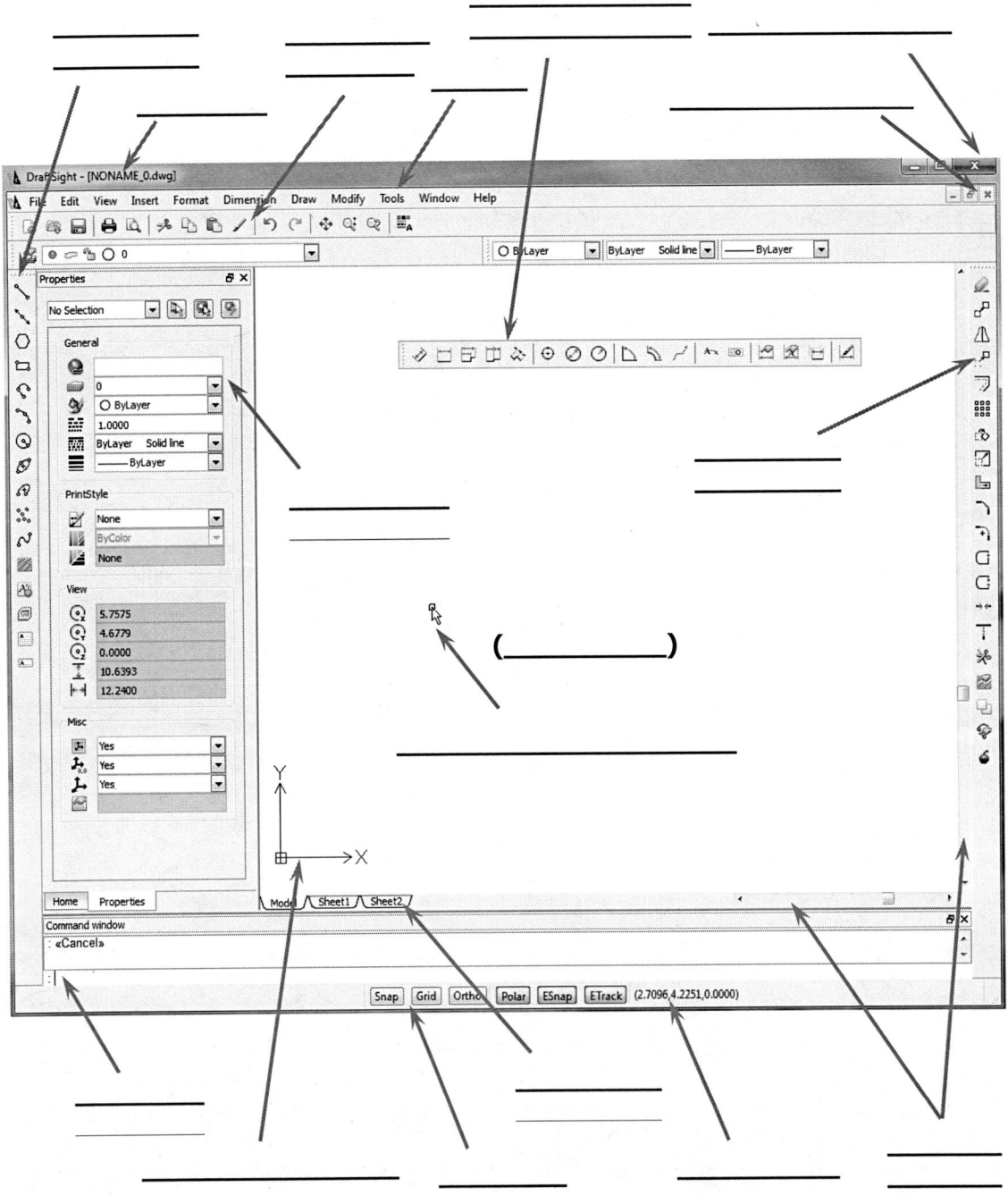

# Chapter 2- Command Entry

## Objectives:
1. Introduction to command entry
2. Draw a series of lines
3. Use the Ortho mode
4. Use the Undo command
5. Utilize DraftSight's Help feature
6. Save and Exit a drawing

## What is Command Entry?

While DraftSight is an advanced computer program, it cannot read your mind yet. Somehow we need to communicate with the program, telling it what we want it to do. This is called command entry. In the previous chapter you already did some command entry, like when you opened a drawing, or while panning and zooming.

Many methods of CAD command entry have come and gone over the years. The two most enduring forms are the menus, sometimes called "pull-down" or "drop-down" menus, and the command window. Also, icons and toolbars were added in the early 1990's as common operating systems adopted them. The icons have proven to be a very effective approach to command entry and will be the method most used in this text. In any case, nearly every available command can be issued from the pull-downs, the command window, or the icons.

## Drawing Lines

Let's start with probably the most used DraftSight command: **Line**.

1. If you haven't already, start a **New** drawing in DraftSight. If prompted, pick the **standard** template.

2. Locate and left-click on the **Line** icon found in the **Draw** toolbar.

3. A line is defined by two points. What does DraftSight ask for in the command window? Specify the **start point** by positioning your crosshairs in the lower left-hand corner of the drawing and left-clicking.

4. Again, look to the command window for the next step. DraftSight now wants the **next point**. Position the crosshairs to the right, about ½ way across the drawing area, and left-click again.

5.  DraftSight now asks for yet another point. Position the crosshairs straight above the second point about the same distance as the first line you created and left click.

6.  Note you have a few options presented to you at this time in the command window: Segments, Undo, Close, *Enter to exit* or... By typing the **underlined letter** you can exercise the related option. Try typing "**C**", and press the enter key. What happens? Your drawing should look like the one below:

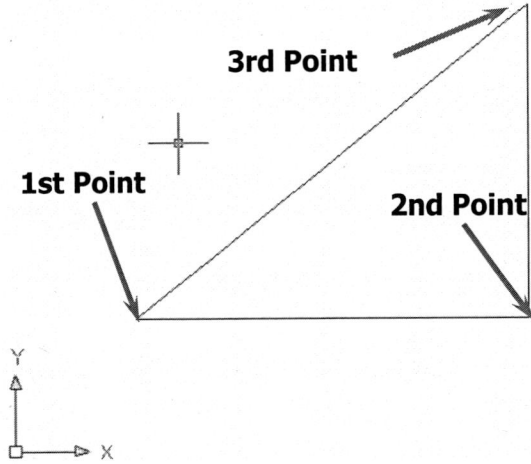

7.  On your own: Using the **Line** command, sketch your computer monitor. (Don't worry about things lining up exactly, just do your best.) Your sketch may look like the one below:

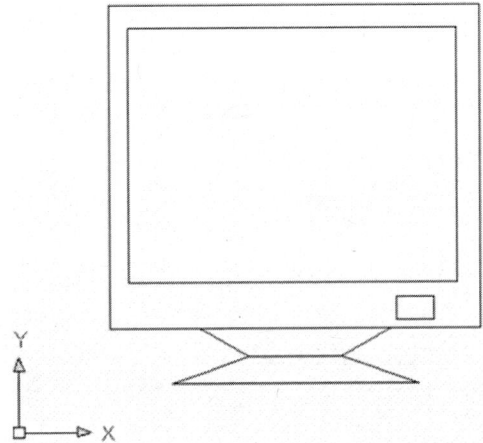

8.  Try the **Undo** option while in the line command (by typing "**U**"), what happens?

## Using ORTHO Mode

You may have found in the previous exercise that drawing perfectly straight lines is difficult. For this reason, DraftSight has **Ortho** mode in which only straight (horizontal or vertical) lines can be drawn. Think of **Ortho** as if you were drafting on a drafting board while using a t-square.

1.  Locate the **Ortho** button in the **Status Bar** and toggle it on by left-clicking on the button. The **F8** key on your keyboard has the same effect.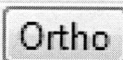

2.  Try re-drawing the computer monitor from the previous exercise. For non-orthogonal (diagonal) lines, **Ortho** will have to be turned off. There is no need to exit the **Line** command to toggle **Ortho** on or off.

3.  While sketching with the **Line** command, try this: After picking the first point of a line, position your crosshairs in the direction you want to go and type in a number like "**8**" (instead of clicking in the drawing area to specify the second point). What happens? This can be used for creating lines of a specific length. This is most useful in **Ortho** mode. We'll learn more about precision drawing in Unit 2.

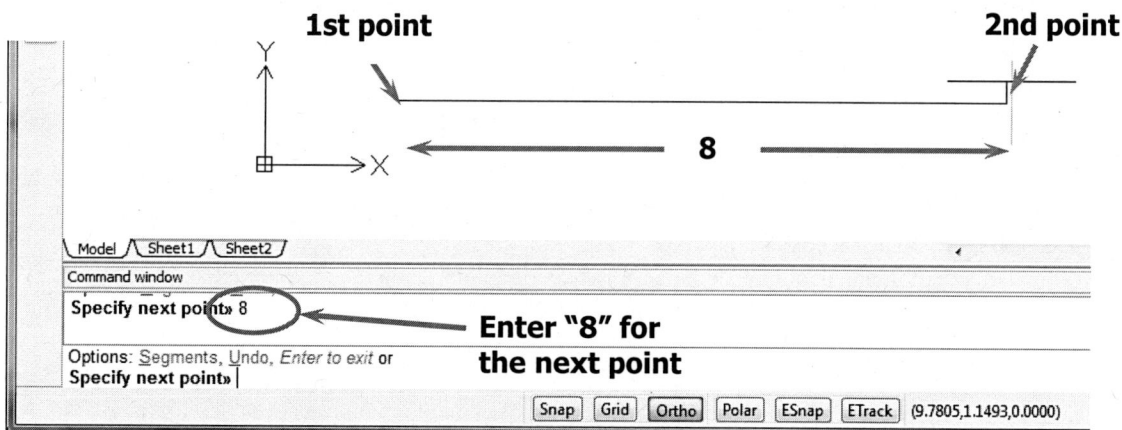

## Using the Undo Command

You've already tried the **Undo** option while inside of the **Line** command. It takes you back to the last point that you specified. There is another **Undo** that you can initiate by left clicking on the **Undo** icon in the **Standard** toolbar. This undoes everything accomplished by the last command. You can undo several times; it's like going back in time. If you go back too far, you can always **Redo**, by clicking on the **Redo** icon next to **Undo**. These commands are only available when there is something to undo or redo.

1. Sketch a series of lines in the center of the computer monitor you created in the previous section. Press the escape key after creating each line.

2. Delete each line one at a time by left clicking on the **Und**o icon, then re-create the last line by left clicking on the **Redo** icon.

## Getting Help

DraftSight comes with a **Help** utility. To access it, left-click on the **Help** menu, then choose "Help" from the options, or press the F1 key on your keyboard. You can search the contents for a specific topic or try some of the tutorials. Don't hesitate to use it! It is a valuable tool.

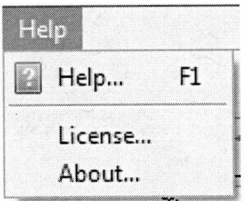

1. On your own: Start the DraftSight **Help** command. The *Help* window should appear like the one below:

2. Left-click on the **Index** tab and enter "lines" in the keyword field.

3. Left-click on the **lines** link that appears in the list below your question. Read through the instructions on constructing lines.

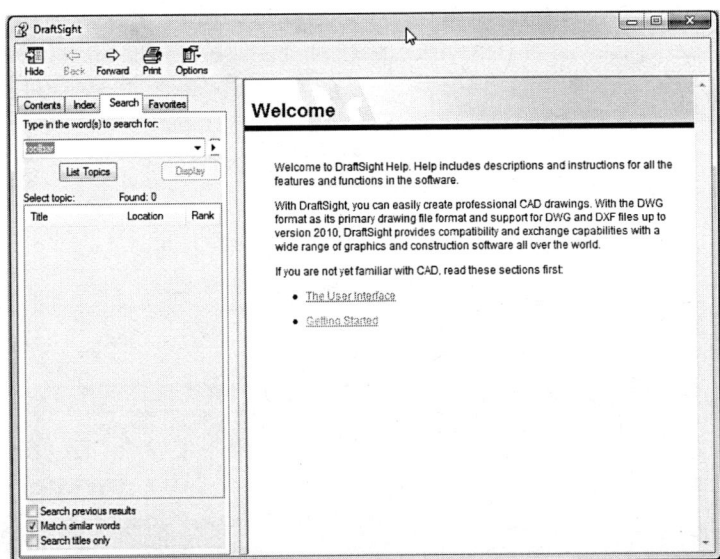

20

## Saving Drawings

1. Save the computer monitor you drew earlier. Left-click on the **Save** icon located in the **Standard** toolbar. A window will appear like the one below:

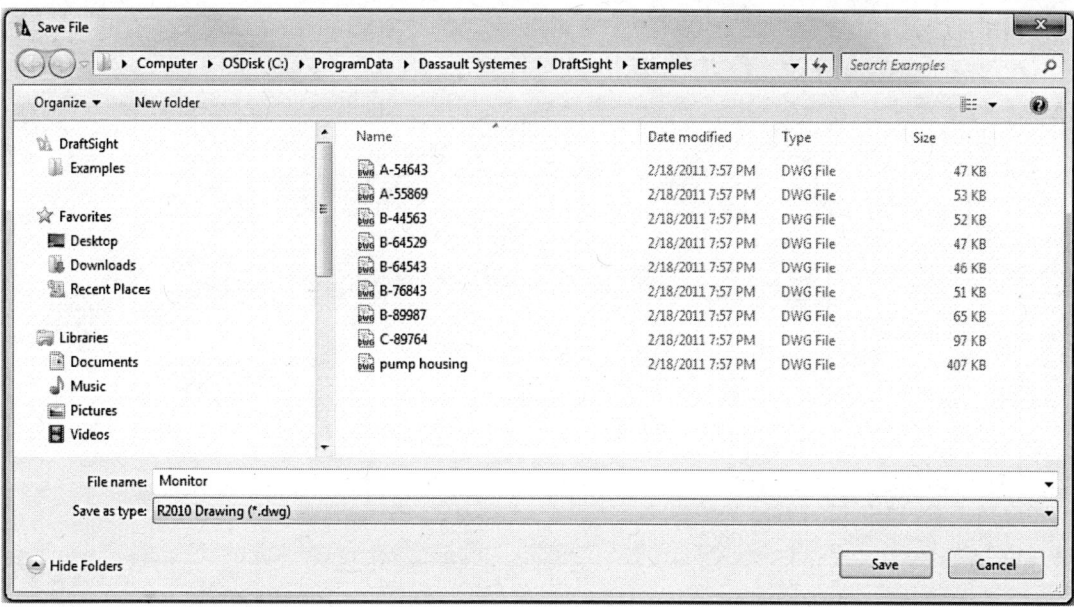

2. Search for the location you wish to save your drawing. Your facilitator may have created a folder for you already on a network drive.

3. In the *File name* field, enter "**Monitor**". You don't have to type the ".dwg" file extension; DraftSight will automatically assume it is a ".dwg".

4. Note that you can also change the file type, saving it down to an older version of .dwg, or even as a ".dxf" for transfer to other CAD or CAM (Computer-Aided Manufacturing) software.

5. Left-click on the **Save** button.

> ***Note:*** It's a good idea to save your drawings in at least one other place, like a USB memory "drive".

6. **Exit** DraftSight.

## Chapter 2 Suggested Learning Exercises

Based on your chosen drafting emphasis, pick from the following exercises:

### Mechanical-

1.  Start a **New** drawing and sketch the dumbbell shown below.  Use the **Line** command, **Ortho** mode for straight lines, and **Undo** if you make a mistake. Save your drawing as "**Dumbbell.dwg**".

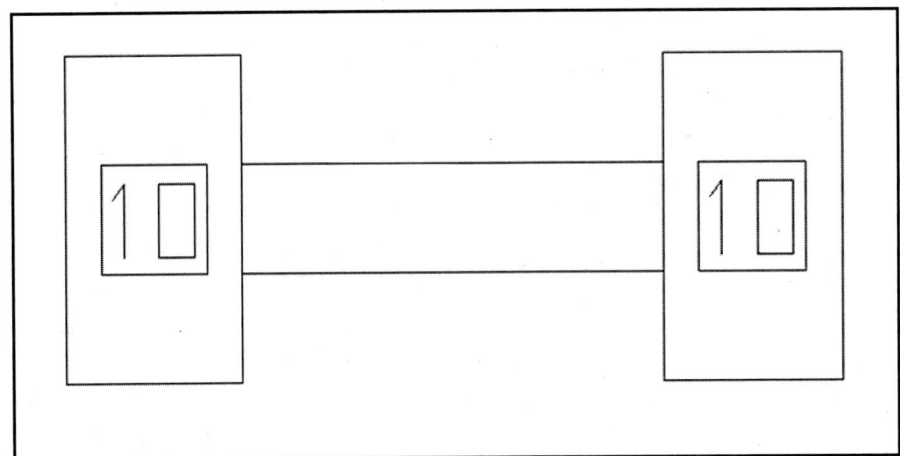

2.  Start a **New** drawing and sketch the alarm clock shown below.  Use the **Line** command, **Ortho** mode for straight lines, and **Undo** if you make a mistake. **Save** your drawing as "**Alarm Clock.dwg**".

3. Start a **New** drawing and sketch the screwdriver shown below. Use the **Line** command, **Ortho** mode for straight lines, and **Undo** if you make a mistake. **Save** your drawing as "**Screwdriver.dwg**".

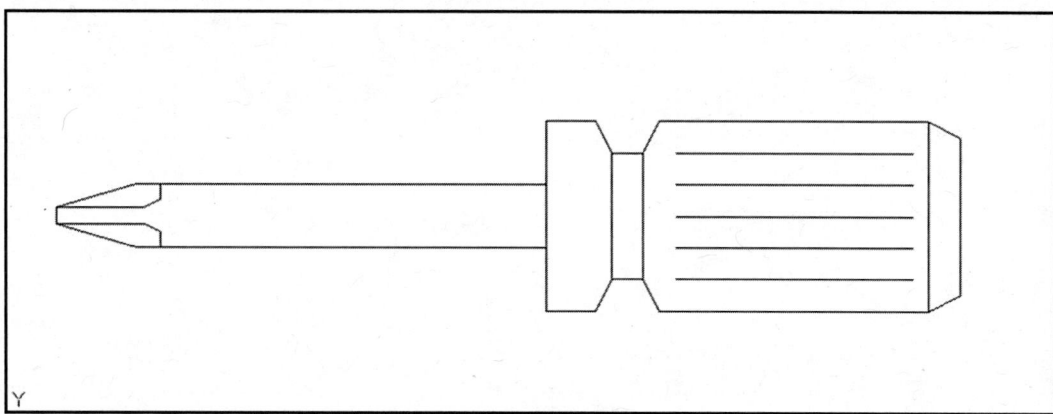

## *Architectural-*

Start a **New** drawing. Using the **Line** command and **Undo** (for mistakes), sketch the main floor of the home or apartment where you now live. Include walls, doors and stairs (if applicable). If time permits, sketch the major plumbing fixtures windows, furniture, and as well. You may want to use **Ortho** mode for creating straight lines, and don't forget you can **Pan** and **Zoom**!

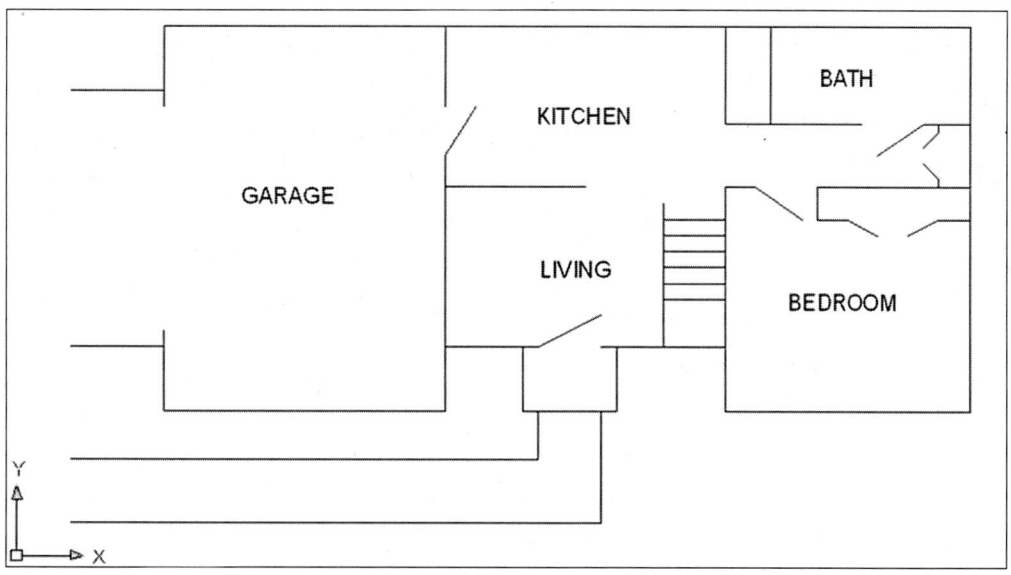

**NOTES:**

## Chapter 3- Creating Entities

Objectives:
1. Explore the Draw Toolbar
2. Draw circles, arcs and ellipses
3. Draw rectangles, polygons and points

## What are "Entities"?

You already created a few entities in Chapter 2. A line is an entity. So are circles, arcs, polygons, rectangles (when created using the rectangle command) and so on. There will be more on this subject later in Chapter 4, since you'll need to be able to pick entities in order to edit them.

## The Draw Toolbar

Start a new drawing using the **standard** template. Make sure the **Draw** toolbar is active (if you don't see it, right-click on an existing toolbar, left-click on **MAIN** pick it from the list). Here's what it looks like, together with the commands we'll be using in this chapter:

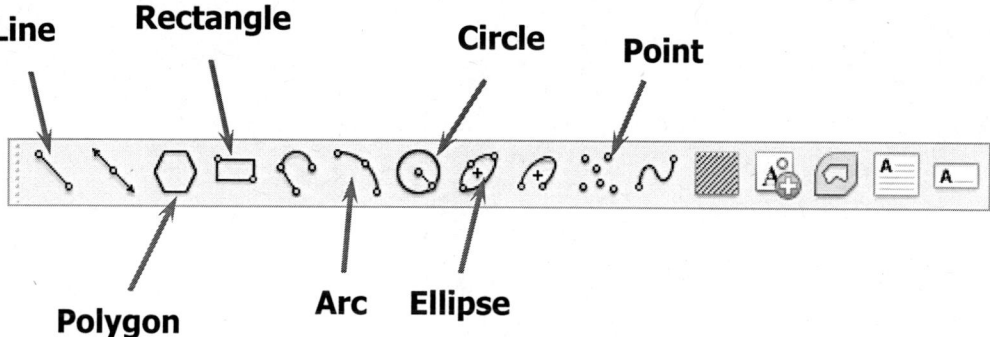

## Drawing Circles

1. Select the **Circle** command. What does the command window ask for?

2. Notice you have many options, but for now left-click near the center of the screen to specify the center point of the circle.

3. Move the mouse around. What happens? Notice the size of the circle grows and shrinks depending on the position of the mouse on the screen.

4. At this point, you may either enter a number for the **radius** of the circle (or you can enter the **diameter** by typing "**d**" first), or simply left-click when the circle is looks about the right size.

5. On your own, create at least two more circles using the **3P** and **2P** options. What does **3P** and **2P** mean?

6. There is one more very useful option called **TTR**, or tangent-tangent radius. Let's try it.  Draw two circles of 4 units in diameter, one on each side of the center of the drawing area as shown below:

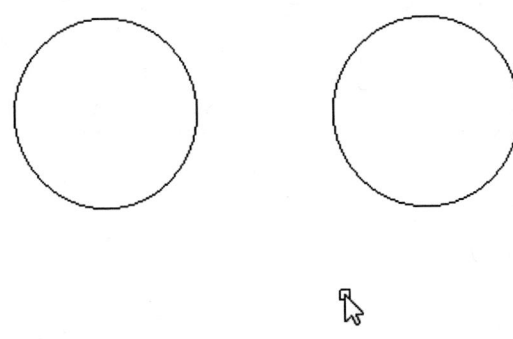

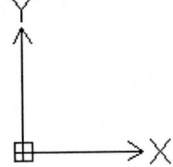

7. Next, start the **Circle** command again by selecting the **Circle** icon.  Type "**t**" in the command window.  What does DraftSight ask for?

8. Position the crosshairs near the upper-right area of the circle on the left and left-click to define the first tangency:

**Crosshairs**

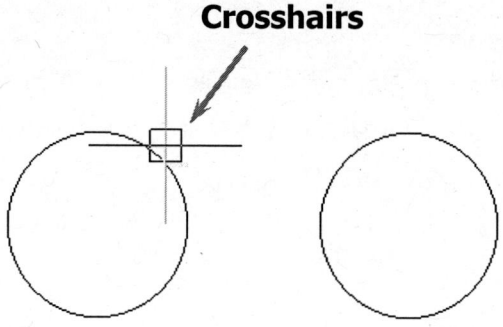

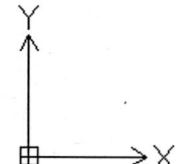

9. For the second tangency, left-click on the upper-left portion of the right circle.

10. When prompted, enter a value for the radius of "**1**" in the command window. Note that the last value that you entered is the "Default". If the default number happens to be the value you want, just press enter to accept it.

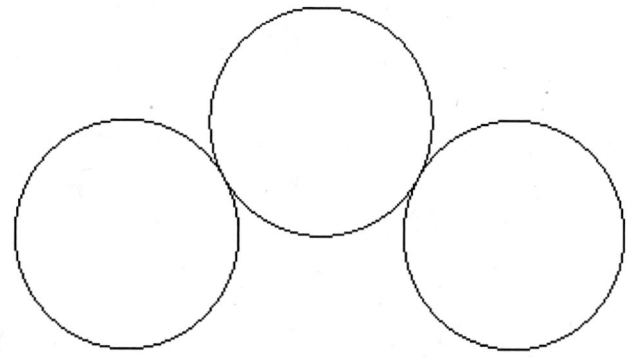

11. You should get a third circle that just touches (tangent) the other two (if you get an error that reads "circle does not exist" your circles are too far apart. Try it again with a larger value for the radius).

12. On your own, place a 4ᵗʰ circle opposite of the last one and tangent to the first two, so your drawing looks something like this:

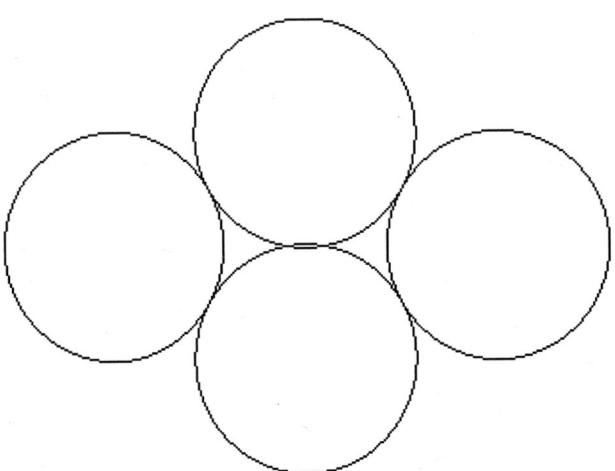

## Creating Arcs

Arcs are just portions of circles. In most cases you'll find it more helpful to draw a circle and change it into an arc using the modify commands discussed later. However, we will try a few ways to create arcs here:

1. Start with a clean drawing area either by starting a **New** drawing or deleting the circles done previously in this chapter. A quick way to do this is to type "**e**" in the command window (for "erase" or "delete") and press **Enter**. This invokes the **Delete** command. Now type "**all**" in the command window and press the **Enter** key. Everything should be deleted now.

2. Locate and left-click on the **Arc** icon in the **Draw** toolbar. What does DraftSight ask you to do next?

3. Specify a start point near the center of the drawing area. Then click two more places on the drawing area and observe how the arc is created. This is a 3-point method, similar to the **3P** option in the **Circle** command.

4. Now, let's try the **arc center** method. The important thing to consider here is that DraftSight creates arcs counter-clockwise. Left-click on the **Arc** icon and enter "**c**" in the command window followed by the **Enter** key.

5. Once more, position the crosshairs in the center of the screen and left-click.

6. For the start point of the arc, left-click to the right of the center point you just defined in step 4. For the end point move the crosshairs to the left of the center point and left-click. Note how the arc "sweeps" counterclockwise, over the top of the center point.

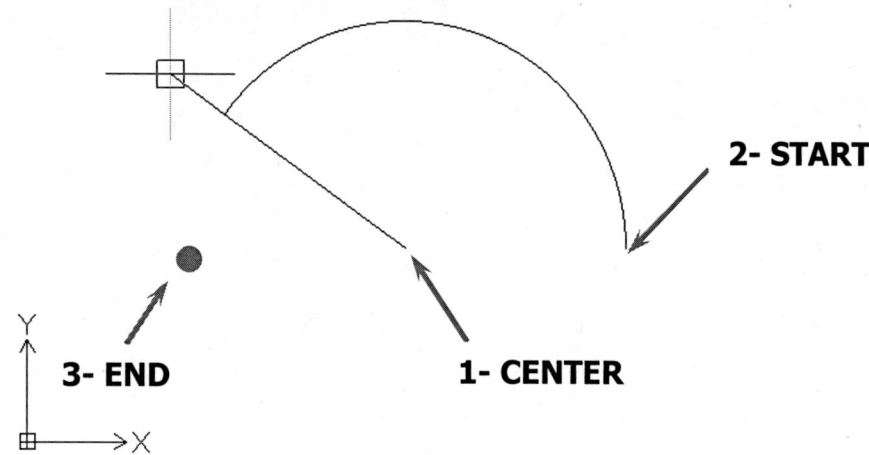

7. On your own, create another arc opposite of the first one using the center option, so your drawing area looks like this:

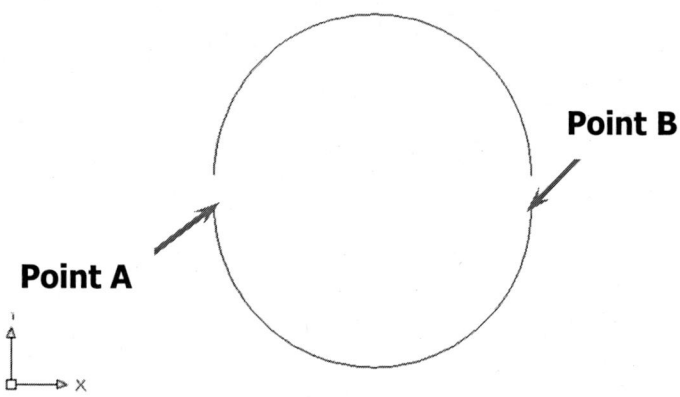

8. Which point did you have to specify first? Point A or B?

9. Last, try the **continue from last point** option. Create a small, somewhat open arc in the lower left-hand corner of the screen using the three point (default) option.

10. After specifying the last point, press the **space-bar** on your computer keyboard twice. What happens?

11. The **Arc** command should start again and pick up where you left off from the last arc.

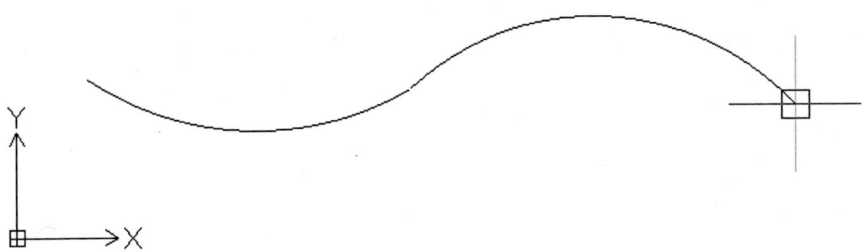

12. Continue this method until you create a sketch of a cloud similar to the one below:

> *Tip:* Pressing the **space-bar** is just like using the **Enter** key. In the example above, DraftSight initiated the previous command. Pressing either key again will specify the last point picked. This works with many of the draw commands, not just Arc.

## Creating Ellipses

An ellipse is an ob-round circle.  There are three major features to an ellipse:  The **center**, **minor axis** and **major axis**.  Ellipses are useful for many things, as will be shown in the learning activities at the end of this chapter. To create an ellipse:

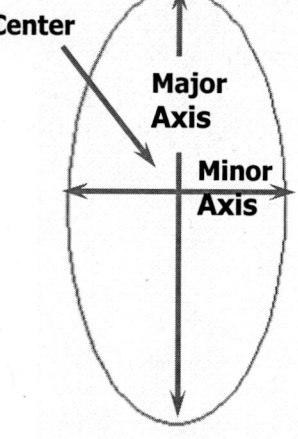

1.  Locate and left-click on the **Ellipse** icon in the **Draw** toolbar. DraftSight requests an **axis start point**. This is the default three-point method for creating an ellipse.  Position the crosshairs on the left side of the drawing area and left-click.

2.  Next, DraftSight asks for the **axis end point**.  Go ahead and pick any point.

3.  Finally, DraftSight asks for the **other axis end point**.  Pick yet another point and left-click. Note that the major and minor axes are up to you to decide, depending on which three points you select.

4.  Try drawing other ellipses with the **Ortho** option in the **status bar** turned off or on. What is the difference using or not using **Ortho**?

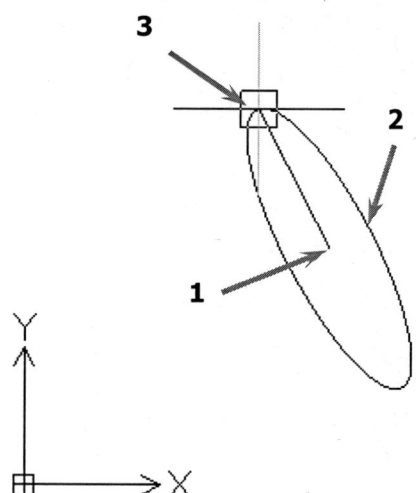

5.  Now try drawing ellipses using the other two options available.  After initiating the **Ellipse** command, entering "**e**" in the command window will draw an **elliptical arc**.  An "**r**" for rotation allows you to enter a number (in degrees) that it will appear the ellipse has been rotate from its circular form.

## Drawing Rectangles

The Rectangle command allows the user to quickly create a rectangle (or square) by specifying the opposite corners of the rectangle.

1. Locate and left-click on the **Rectangle** icon in the **Draw** toolbar. Pick two points on the screen for the opposing corners.

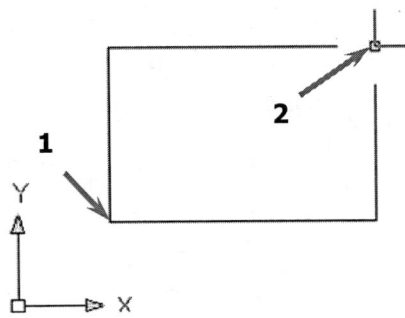

2. Click on the **Rectangle** icon again. Note that before you pick the second point that there are other options: "**A**" for area, "**D**" for dimensions, and "**R**" for rotation. Try each of these.

3. Once again, initiate the **Rectangle** command. Before you select the first point, note the options available. The most useful ones are **Chamfer, Fillet** and **Width**. A chamfer "breaks" the corners, fillets (pronounced "fill-its") rounds corners, and the width will thicken the lines of the rectangle. On your own try to duplicate the two rectangles shown below (one inside the other). Use the **Chamfer, Fillet** and **Width** options.

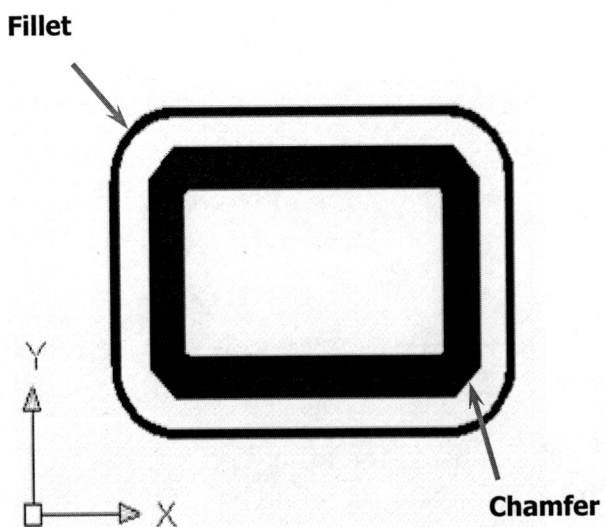

Fillet

Chamfer

## Creating Polygons

Polygons are many-sided objects such as triangles, squares, pentagons, hexagons, etc. DraftSight will either create them inscribed within a circle (circle through the points), or circumscribed about a circle (circle tangent to the sides). The method you chose depends on what you need at the time.

1. For this exercise, create a large **Circle** near the center of the drawing area.

2. Locate and left-click on the **Polygon** icon in the **Draw** toolbar. The first parameter is the number of sides. Enter "**6**".

3. Left-click near the center of the circle you drew in step one to specify the center of the polygon (Tip: Turn on the **Esnap** option in the status bar to get the exact center- more on this later). Now type "**s**" for "side" (creates a circumscribed polygon).

4. Click on the edge of the circle. The polygon should exist more or less outside of the circle. Try creating another hexagon in the same place, but this time using "**co**" for "corner" (creates an inscribed polygon). Try to make the resulting hexagons and circle look like the ones below:

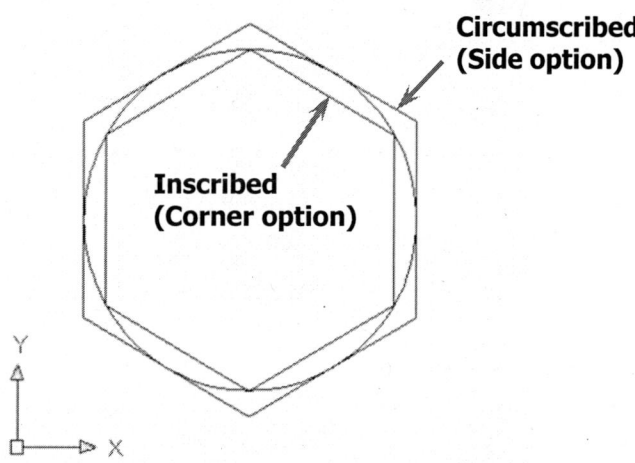

Circumscribed
(Side option)

Inscribed
(Corner option)

5. On your own, try the **Side length** (rather than center) option. Type "**S**" and press enter after entering the **Polygon** command. What is the difference between **Side length** and **Center**?

## Creating Points

DraftSight has the capability of creating points at locations specified by the user in the drawing area. This command is used by drafters of various CAD disciplines. The type and size of the points are specified in the **Options** window.

1.  Select the **Tools** menu, and choose **Options** and **Drawing Settings**. Click on the plus sign next to **Points** to expand the point options.

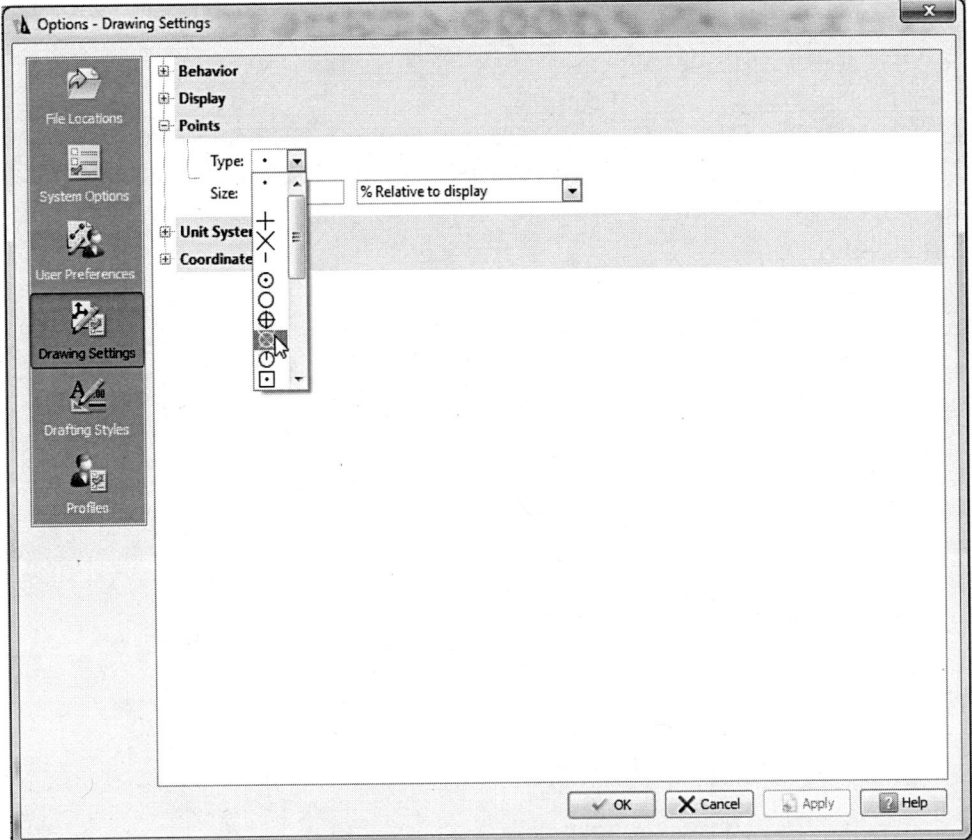

2.  Note you can set the point type and size. Additionally, the point size can be relative to the drawing area, or an absolute value.

3. On your own, using the **Point** command create the representation of the Big Dipper shown below:

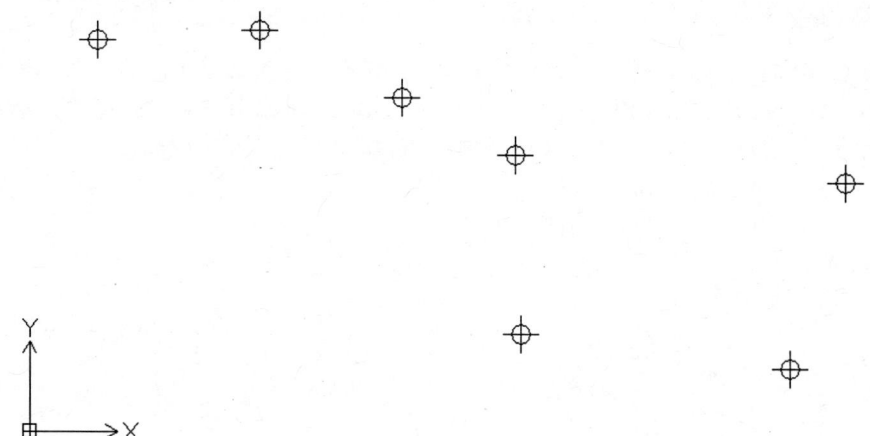

Note: Changing the point style and size variables effects **all** the points the drawing, even the ones you've drawn previously!

4. Finally from the **Draw** menu, locate the **Point** cascading menu. Notice that you can use the **Point** command to divide-up another entity equally by segments and lengths.

5. O your own, draw a random line and divide it into six segments like the one below:

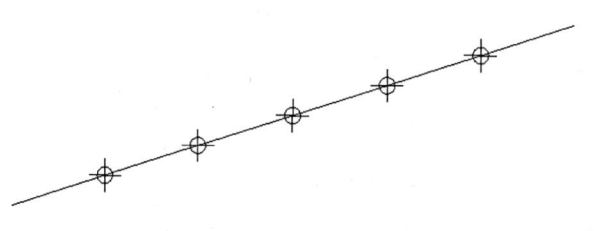

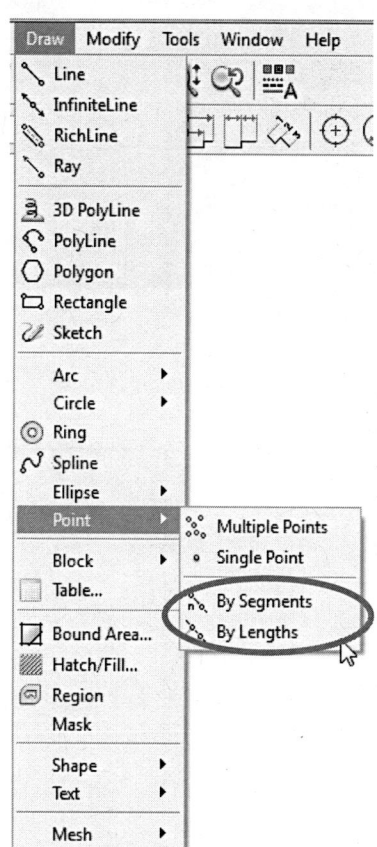

## Chapter 3 Suggested Learning Exercises

Based on your chosen drafting emphasis (mechanical or architectural), choose from the following exercises:

### *Mechanical-*

Start new drawings for each of the sketches that follow. Use the commands and command options discussed in this chapter along with the **Line** command and **Ortho** mode. **Save** your drawings with the drawing name (e.g., "lamp.dwg"). Don't worry about things lining up perfectly; we'll cover that in a later chapter.

1. Schematic:

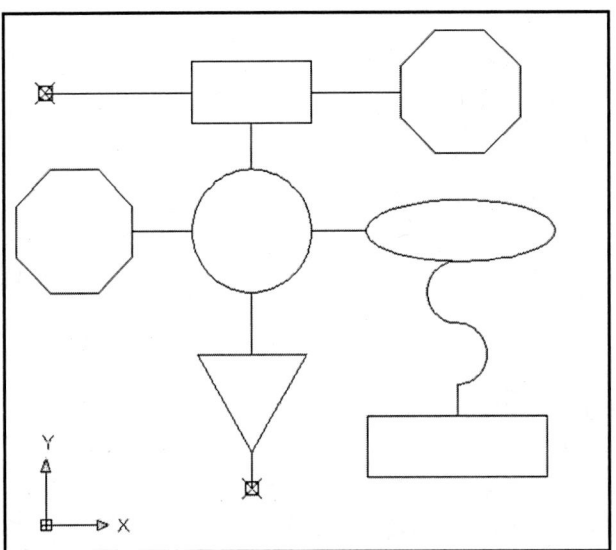

2. End Block (use a series of short lines to make the hidden & center lines):

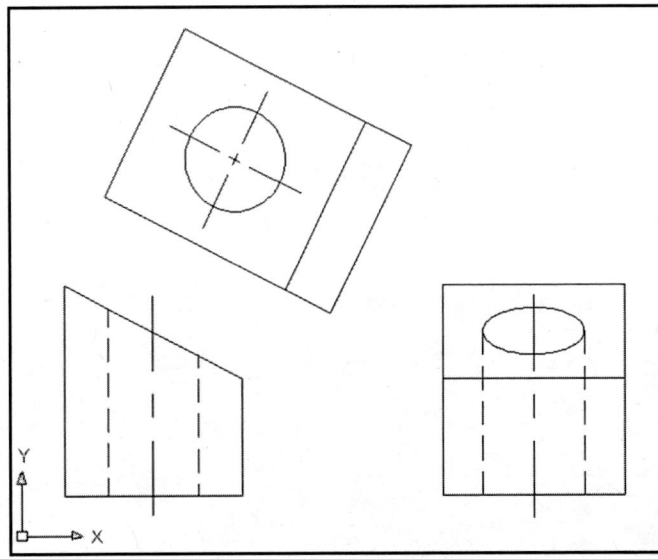

3.  Lamp:

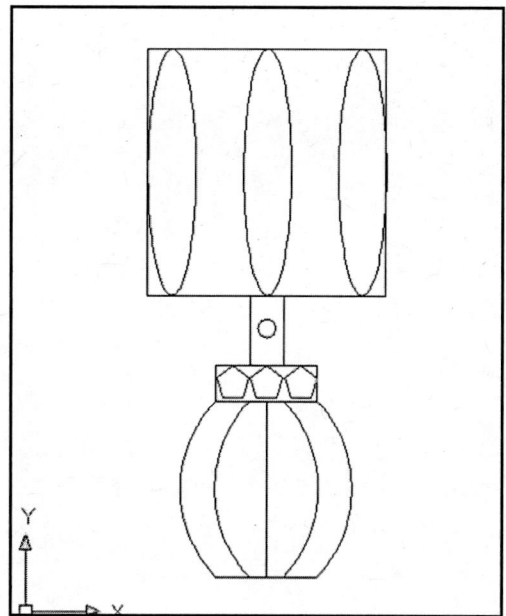

## *Architectural-*

Using the commands discussed in this chapter along with **Line** and **Ortho** mode, sketch a landscape plan like the one shown in the drawing below.  Save it as **"landscape.dwg"**.

**NOTES:**

## Chapter 4- Selecting Entities

Objectives:

1. Activate and use EntityGrips
2. Use the Delete command
3. Use both Noun-Verb and Verb-Noun command manipulation.
4. Select entities using a pick-box
5. Select entities using a window
6. Select entities using a crossing-window
7. Select entities using "All", "Remove", "Add" & "Previous"

In this chapter we learn how to select entities. DraftSight has powerful editing capabilities which will be discussed in the next chapter. But first, you have to be able to select entities in order to use these editing capabilities.

## Activating EntityGrips

EntityGrips, similar to "handles" in other software programs (and just called "grips" for the purposes of this text) are a useful means in selecting entities and even editing them. To activate an entity's grips, simply click on the entity without any command active.

1. Start a **New** drawing. Create a square shape using the **Line** command.

2. Create another square next to the first one using the **Rectangle** command.

3. Without any command active (press the **Escape** key if necessary), left-click on the top-most line of the first square, and the corresponding line from the second. What is the difference?

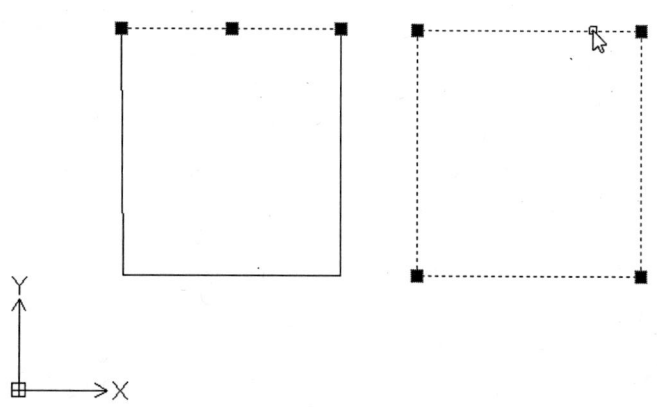

4. The blue boxes are **entity grips**. Note that with the first square, only the line you selected is highlighted. In the case of the second square, the entire object is highlighted. The first square is made of four entities, or four lines. The second is one entity, a rectangle.

5. Locate and select the **Delete** icon in the **Modify** toolbar. What happens?

---

***Tip:*** This is called Noun-Verb selection. You picked the entity first (the noun) and the command second (the verb). DraftSight supports both Noun-Verb and Verb-Noun selection. The method you choose is up to you.

---

6. Both the selected entities (the line as well as the second square) should have been deleted. Use the **Undo** command to bring back the deleted entities.

7. Turn on the **Grips** of the left most line by left-clicking on it. Activate a **Grip** by left-clicking on one of the grips located at each of endpoints of the line. Note that the Grip turns red. Move your mouse around, what happens? Using this method you can stretch lines in any direction by moving its endpoints (for the full effect, turn **Ortho** mode off).

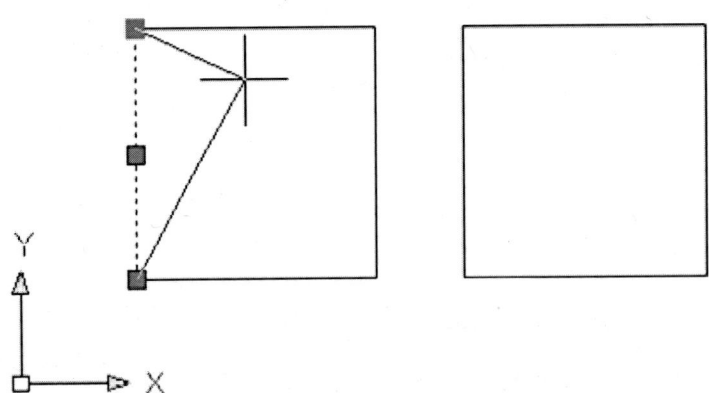

8. Press the **Escape** key to turn the grips off. **Undo** if you changed the location of the line endpoints. Select the line again, this time left-click on the grip in the center (or midpoint) of the line. Move the mouse. What happens this time? The line should be moving.

9. Now select any entity to turn its grips on, select a grip to activate it. Right-click in the drawing area. A pop-up menu should appear containing several modify commands. You can try a few, but we'll be covering their counterparts in the **Modify** toolbar in the next chapter.

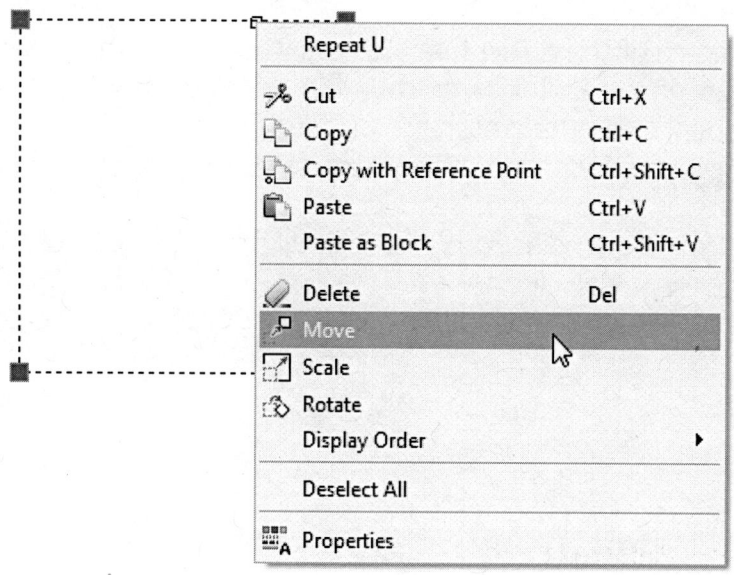

10. Using grips, modify the squares to look like the arrow below (there is no need to use the pop-up discussed in the previous step), save the drawing:

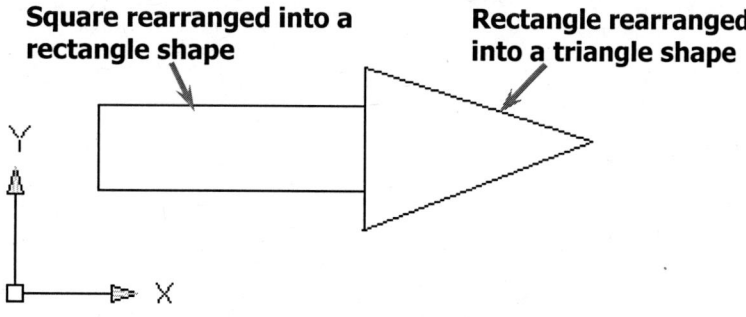

**Square rearranged into a rectangle shape**

**Rectangle rearranged into a triangle shape**

## Entity Selection with a Pick Box

Previously in this chapter we discussed Noun-Verb selection (selecting the object to modify and then selecting a modify command, like delete). This time we'll do it backwards, using Verb-Noun selection.

1. With the sketch of the arrow that was created in the previous section, locate and left-click on the **Delete** icon found in the **Modify** toolbar. Note that two things happen: First, the crosshairs turn into a small square called a **Pick Box**. Second, the command window asks you to specify an entity to delete.

2. Using the **Pick Box**, select one of the lines from the body of the arrow. Position the **Pick Box** directly over the line and left-click. The line should "highlight" or take on a dashed look indicating that it is selected.

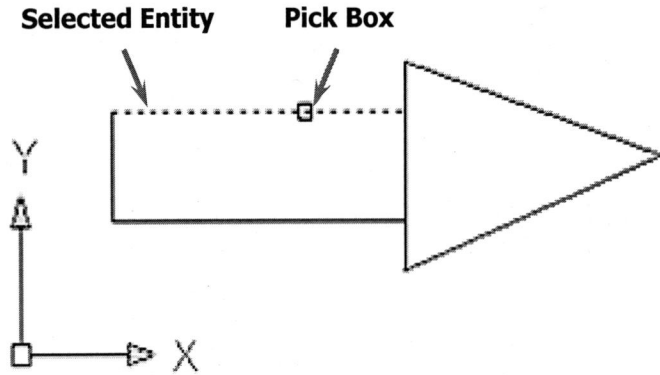

Press the **Enter** key, or the space bar, or right click. All of these methods have the same result: the line should disappear.

3. One by one, delete all of the entities of your drawing by using the **Pick Box**. When you are finished, use the **Undo** command so the sketch of the arrow reappears. What happens if you "missed your target"? Notice that the **Pick Box** became a window instead. We'll cover that next....

## Entity Selection Using a Window and Crossing window

As you may have noticed, what the **Pick Box** has to offer in accuracy, it lacks in speed. Sometimes you want to delete more than one entity without having to pick each of them individually. DraftSight offers the **Window** and **Crossing** window options to accomplish this.

1. Using the sketch of the arrow created earlier in this chapter, select the **Delete** command from the **Modify** toolbar.

2. This time, click towards the upper-right of the sketch of the arrow, intentionally missing any of the geometry with the **Pick Box**.

3. "Sweep" the mouse down and to the right, creating a **Window** around the geometry. Left-click when the entire sketch is contained inside the **Window**.

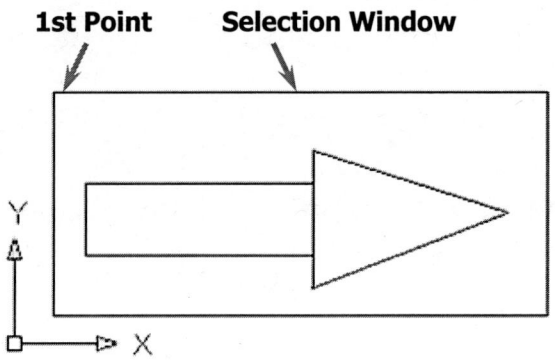

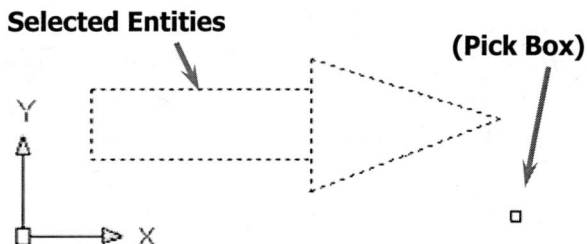

4. Press **Enter**, the entire sketch should disappear. Now **Undo** the **Delete** command so the sketch comes back.

5. On your own, try erasing each the entities within the sketch using a **Window**. Notice that **the entire entity must be with in the window**. Otherwise, the entity will not be selected. Bring the sketch back by undoing.

Next, we'll try the **Crossing** window option of selecting entities. There is a major difference between **Window** and **Crossing**. Essentially, **Window** will select all entities contained inside the window. **Crossing** window not only selects those, but also the entities *crossing* the selection window. This method is used by clicking to the right of the entities and sweeping to the left (or typing "**c**" in the command window while selecting entities). Let's try it:

6.  With the sketch of the arrow in the drawing area, select the **Delete** icon in the **Modify** toolbar.

7.  Position the **Pick Box** above and to the right of the geometry and left-click. Sweep the mouse to the left and down, what form does the selection window take? (Note the dashed lines and green color). This is a **Crossing** window.

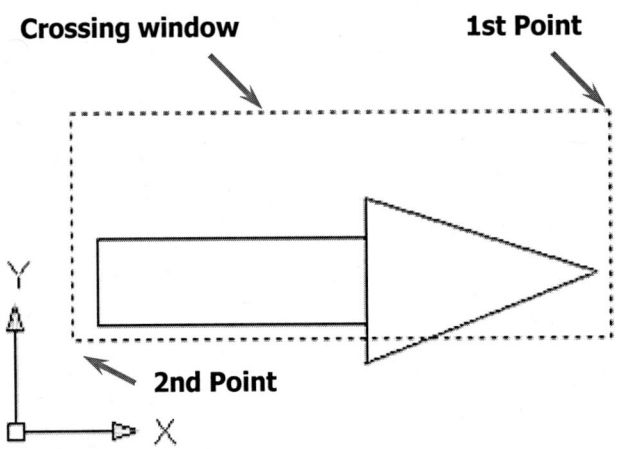

8.  Position the **Crossing** window as shown in the figure above and left-click. How much of the sketch is now selected to be deleted? It should be all of it. A Crossing-Window selects every entity inside the window **and** crossing it.

## Other Options for Entity Selection

DraftSight has a few other tricks when it comes to entity selection besides **Window** and **Crossing**.  For example:

1. **All:** If you want to delete (or modify) all entities in the drawing area, select the **Delete** command and type "**all**" in the command window.  Press **Enter** twice.  Everything should go away.  This can be much faster than using a **Window** or **Crossing** window when you want to delete everything.

2. **Remove:** If, when using a **Window** or **Crossing** you accidentally select something you don't want to delete or modify, simply type "**r**" in the command window.  Now your Pick Box *de-selects* entities as you pick them. Those entities are no longer highlighted and won't be deleted or modified.

3. **Add:** The opposite of **Remove**, this option can be used to select entities after you have removed them from the selection set.  Just type "**a**" at the command window during entity selection.  Now as you select objects they will be added back into to the selection set in case you change your mind.

4. **Previous:**  This option selects everything that you selected last time.  Not used in conjunction with the **Delete** command (since your previous selection doesn't exist anymore), **Previous** is useful for quickly modifying an object multiple times in succession.  For example, to copy an object and then rotate it.  We'll address this option again in a future chapter.

5. **Fence:**  A **Fence** is similar to a **Crossing** window, except that it resembles a line, not a window. Every entity that crosses the **Fence** will be selected.  To use the **Fence** option while selecting entities, type "**f**" and press **Enter** in the command window.

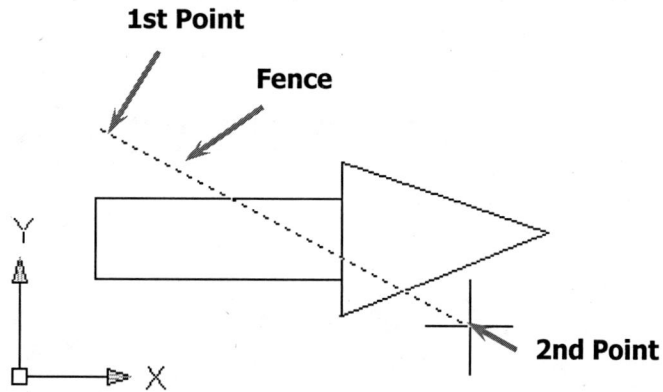

6. For practice, try selecting each of the objects in the arrow sketch using a **Pick Box**, **Window**, **Crossing** window, and **Fence**. Deselect the objects using "**r**" for **Remove**, then re-select them using "**a**" for **Add**.

**Objects Removed From the Selection Set**

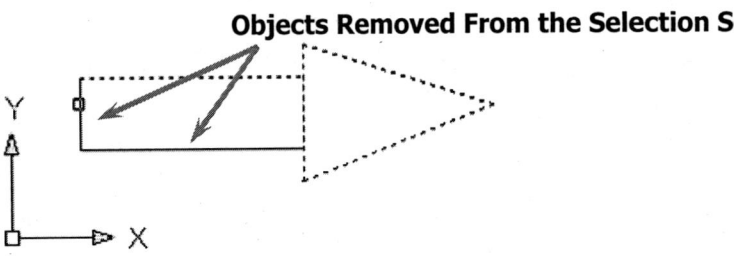

7. On your own, go to DraftSight's **Help** utility and do search on "entity selection". Select "Applying Entity Selection Methods" from the list and explore the many options of entity selection which are available to the DraftSight user.

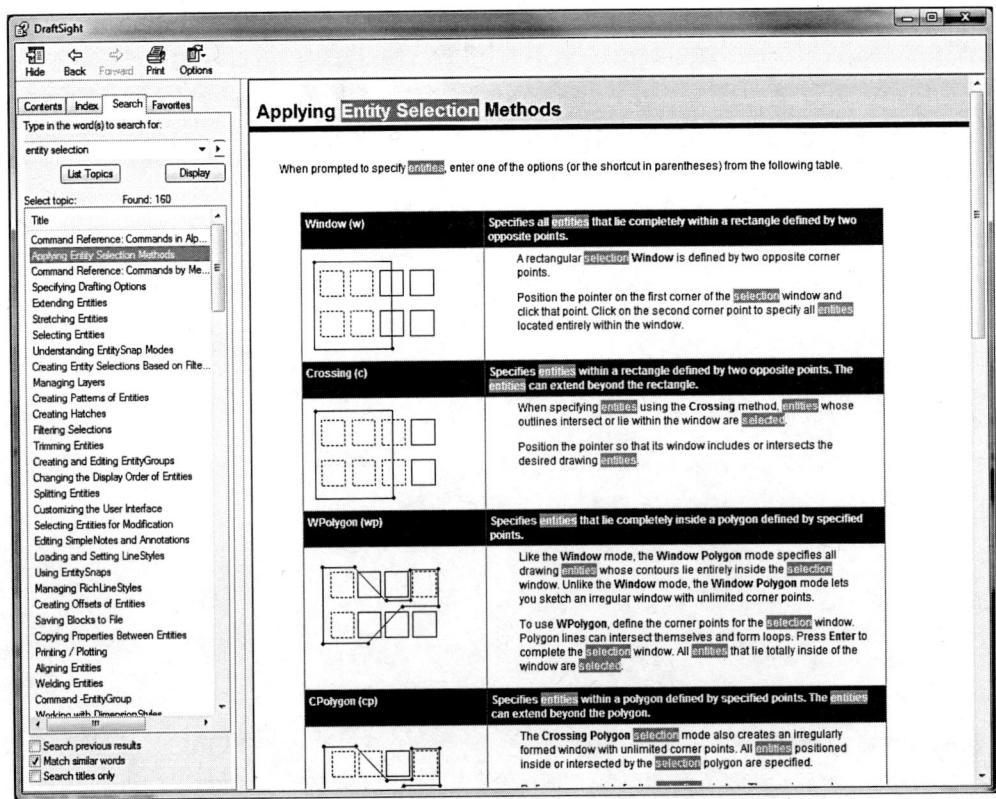

## Chapter 4 Suggested Learning Exercise

Start a **New** drawing using the **standard** template. Using the commands learned in Chapter 3, sketch the office symbols shown below near the top of the drawing area. The commands used to draw them are given for each. **Save** your drawing as "**Office Symbols.dwg**".

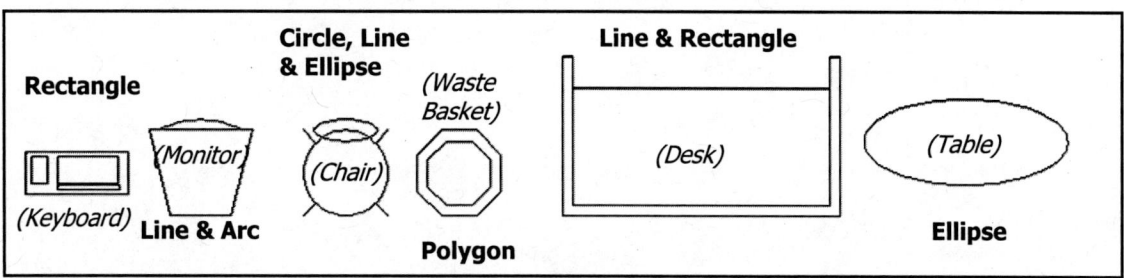

Next, draw two large rectangles along the edges of the drawing area to represent walls. Sketch the window and door symbols as shown in the sketch below. Using grips, reposition the office symbols as shown. Finally, use grips to resize the ellipse to represent a large conference room table.

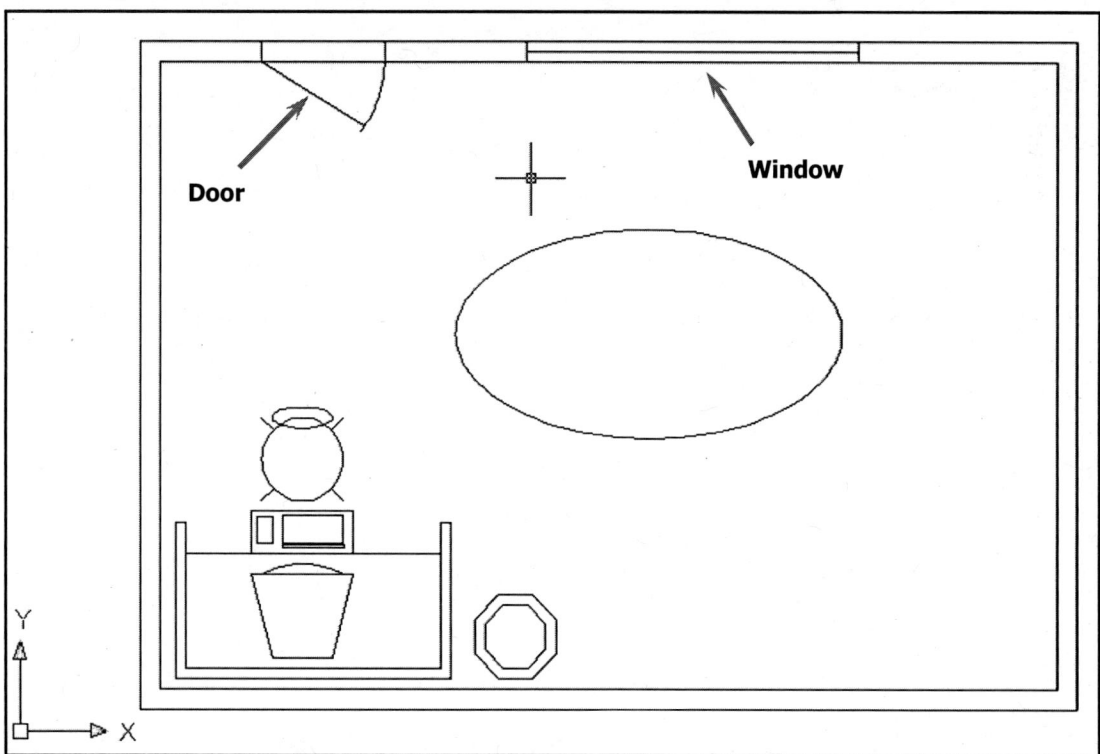

Save the drawing again as "Office Layout.dwg" before exiting. **This drawing will be used extensively in the next chapter!**

**NOTES:**

## Chapter 5- Modifying Entities

Objectives:

1. Explore the Modify Toolbar
2. Move and copy, and rotate entities
3. Mirror, offset and pattern entities
4. Scale and stretch entities
5. Split, weld, trim and extend entities
6. Fillet and Chamfer the corners of objects

One of the major benefits of using CAD software is its powerful editing capabilities. Things that are nearly impossible or time consuming to accomplish on a drafting board take just a few clicks of the mouse in DraftSight. Many of the commands used to edit entities are found in the **Modify** toolbar. Start a new drawing and activate the **Modify** toolbar if isn't already active. Here's what it looks like, along with the commands we'll discuss in this chapter:

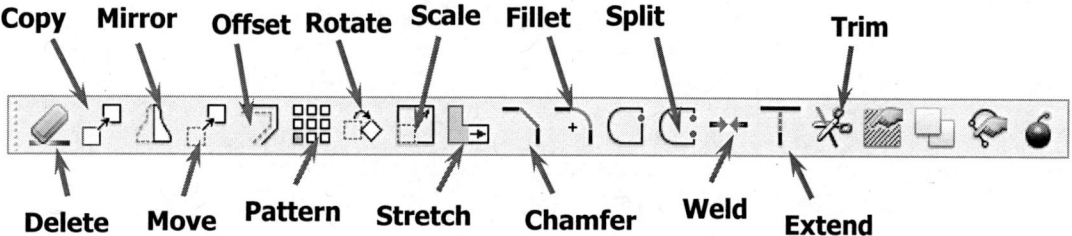

## The Move, Copy and Rotate Commands

These commands are related in that they change an entity's position, orientation, or quantity of an object. Let's try the **Move** command first.

1. **Open** "Office Layout.dwg" that was created in the previous chapter (if you haven't drawn it yet, take a few minutes now to do so).

2. Left-click on the **Move** icon in the **Modify** toolbar. Just like the **Delete** command covered previously, DraftSight prompts you to "**Specify entities**".

3. Using a **Window** or **Crossing** window, select the waste basket. Press **Enter** when you're finished selecting it.

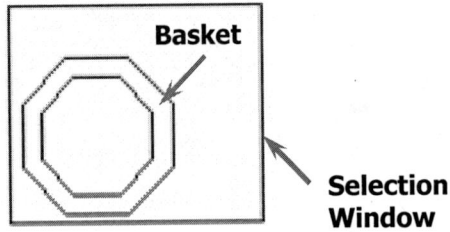

4. Next, DraftSight asks you to "**Specify from point**".  This is the point you will be moving the wastebasket *from*.  Left-click near the center of the basket.

5. Note that the crosshairs now guide the object to its new location.  Position the wastebasket to the left of the chair and left-click to "**Specify destination**."

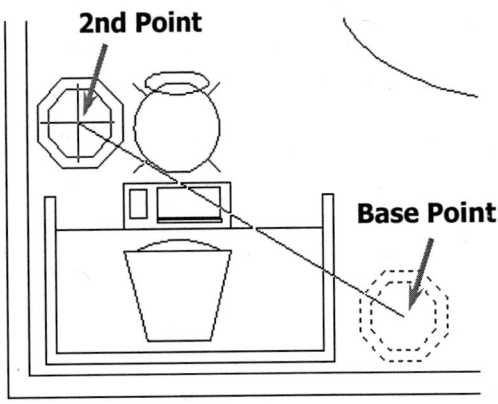

6. On your own, use the **Move** command rearrange the furniture in the office to look like the figure below:

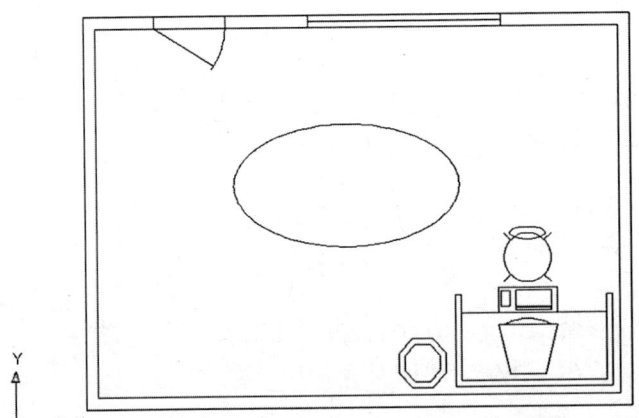

*Tip:* The **Move** command (as well as **Copy**) can be used to go a specified distance.  When prompted for the destination, simply type in a value like "**3**" and point the crosshairs in the general direction you want to move. Try it!

7. Next, we'll duplicate an object using the **Copy** command.  You'll find that copying is very similar to moving. Locate the **Copy** icon and select it to initiate the command.

8. Just like before, DraftSight expects the user to "**Specify entities**" to copy. Select the chair using a **Window** or **Crossing** window. Press **Enter** when finished selecting the objects.

9. Now DraftSight wants a **from point**, just like the **Move** command. Specify the **from point** by left-clicking in near the center of the chair's seat. For the **second point**, position the copy of the chair near the upper-center of the conference table.

10. Note that you can still copy the chair to yet another location. Left-click to place another chair at the left of the table. Press **Enter** to end the command.

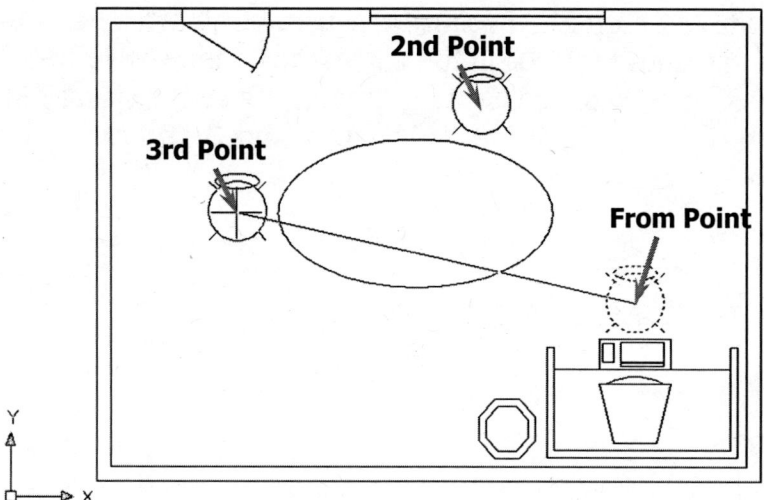

11. On your own, use the **Copy** command to make your drawing look like the figure below. Note that using **Ortho** mode while copying will keep the copied objects aligned with the originals.

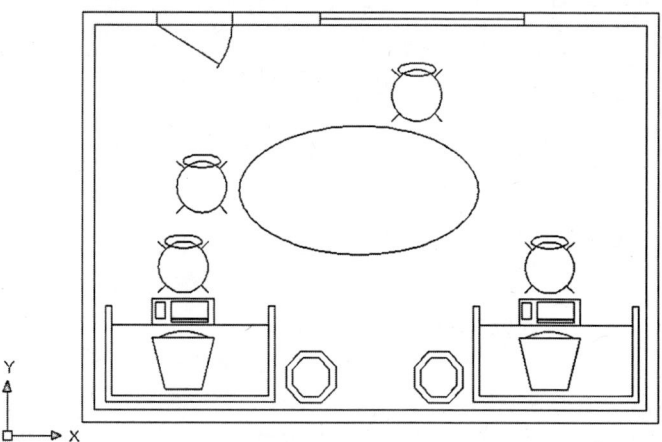

12. Finally, we'll use the **Rotate** command to clean things up a bit. Left-click on the **Rotate** icon and select the chair we placed to the left of the table.

13. DraftSight asks for a **pivot point**. This is the center of rotation. Position the crosshairs near the center of the seat of the chair and left-click.

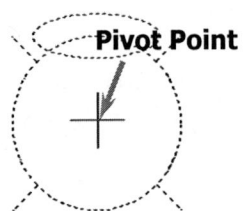

14. Next DraftSight requests a **rotation angle**. The software works counter-clockwise, so entering "**90**" in the command window will rotate the chair 90 degrees counter-clockwise. You may rotate the chair visually instead just by moving the mouse around. Note that by using **Ortho** mode the chair rotates in 90 degree increments.

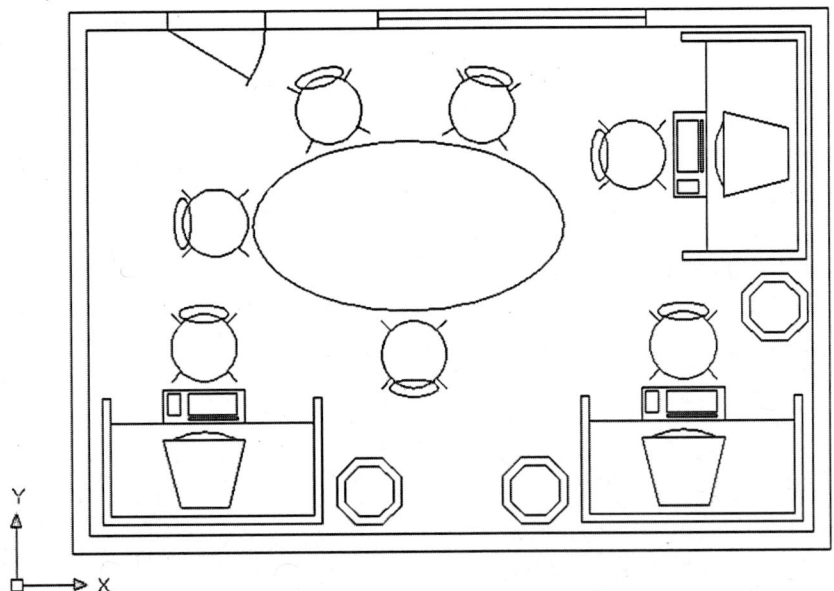

15. On your own: **Copy, Rotate** and **Move** one of the workstations into the upper right-hand corner of the room. Also **Copy** and **Rotate** two more chairs around the table so they look like the ones in the figure above. Use **Window, Crossing** window, **Add, Remove**, and **Previous** as needed.

## The Mirror, Offset and Pattern Commands

Closely related to **Copy**, **Move** and **Rotate** are **Mirror**, **Offset**, and **Pattern**. These commands copy objects *and* displace them.

The **Mirror** command is a real time saver and can be used to copy half of any symmetrical object to create the other half. There is much symmetry in drafting. Recognize it, use the **Mirror** command, and your productivity will increase.

1. Start a **New** drawing using the **standard** template. Using **Ortho** mode, create a horizontal line along the line of symmetry (mirror line) as a guide, and then sketch half of the top view of the aircraft shown below.

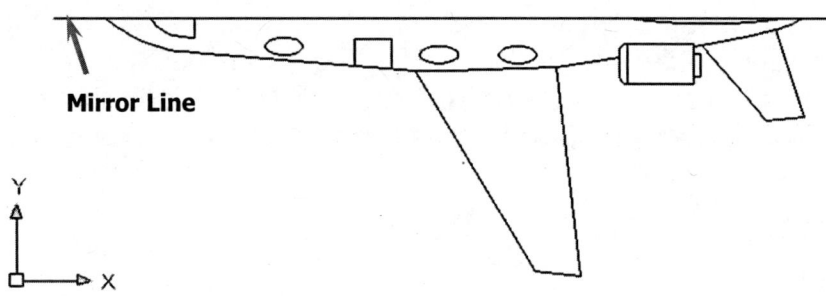

Mirror Line

Y

X

2. Select the **Mirror** icon from the **Modify** toolbar. As always, DraftSight prompts you to "**Specify entities**". Select everything but the mirror line and right-click to accept.

3. Next, DraftSight asks for the **start point of the mirror line**. Since you already have one, use your crosshairs to left-click near the left end of the mirror line for the start point. For accuracy, you may want to activate **Esnap** mode in the **Status Bar** first. **Esnap** will be discussed in a later chapter.

4. For the **end point of the mirror line**, position the crosshairs and select the far right end of the mirror line you drew. Note that the mirror line doesn't have to run down the center of the part being mirrored, it could be at any angle in relationship to the object.

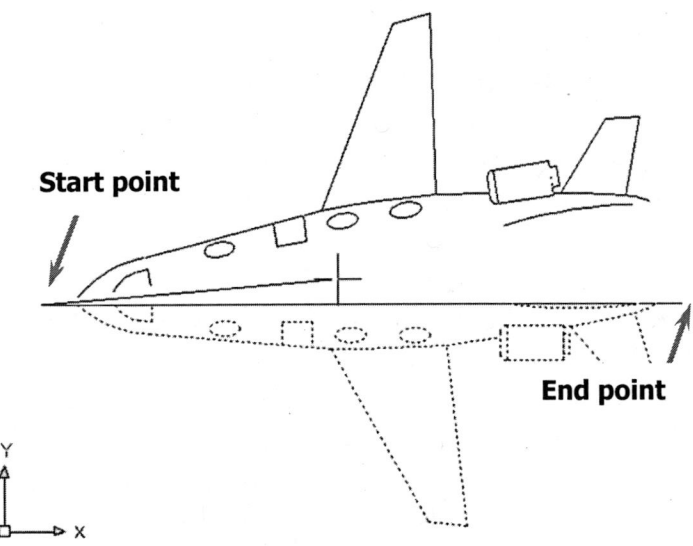

5. Finally, DraftSight asks if you want to delete the **source entities**. These are the entities you just mirrored. In this case the answer is "**no**", so press **Enter** to accept the default (or enter "n" in the command window). **Delete** the mirror line and the extra door. Your drawing should look somewhat like the one below. **Save** your drawing as "**Plane.dwg**". We'll use it in the next several steps.

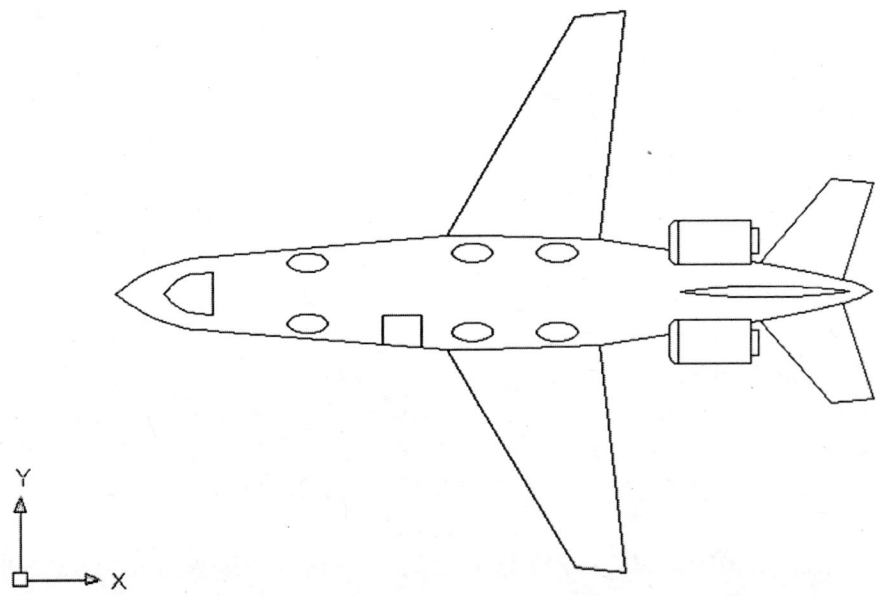

6. Next we will **Offset** an object (or copy and move it to the side a specified distance). Using **Zoom** and **Pan**, get a closer look at the aircraft's left wing.

7. Select the **Offset** command from the **Modify** toolbar. DraftSight asks for an offset **distance**. Normally, you would enter a number here. Since this is a sketch with no known scale, we can instead specify an **offset distance** by picking two points. Select the trailing wingtip, then another point about 1/4 the way along the outboard edge of the wing.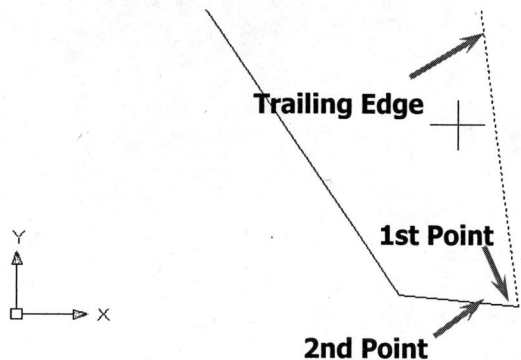

8. DraftSight prompts you to select the object to offset, or **source entity**. With the pick box, select the trailing edge of the wing.

9. Next pick a point on the **side for destination**. Left-click near the center of the wing. You have now created a copy of the trailing edge and placed it next to the original to form an aileron.

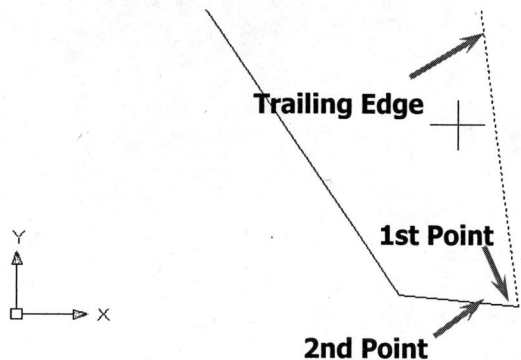

10. On your own, use **Entity grips** to clean-up the endpoints of the offset line so your sketch looks similar to the one below. Using the **Offset** command, create another line to represent an elevator on the horizontal stabilizer. **Mirror** the aileron and the stabilizer to the opposite side of the aircraft (use the nose and tail of the aircraft to specify the mirror line). **Save** the drawing.

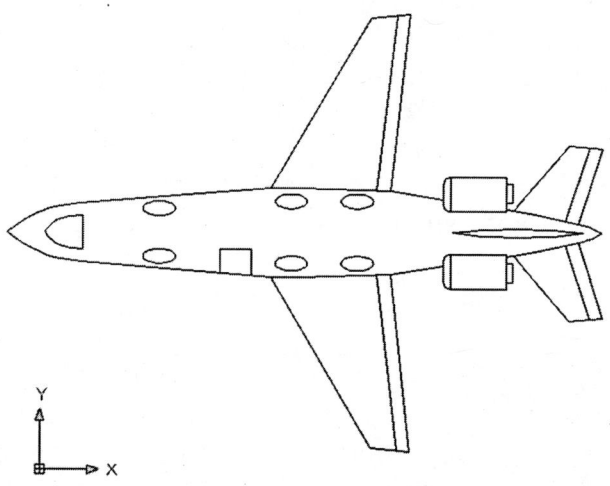

11. The **Pattern** command is used to copy objects in a pattern. There are two kinds of patterns: **Circular** and **Linear**. These can be helpful for everything from drawing bolt circles on a mechanical drawing, to creating parking lot stalls for an architectural plan.

12. **Zoom** out so you can see the entire plane in the drawing area. Pick the **Pattern** command from the **Modify** toolbar. The following window should appear:

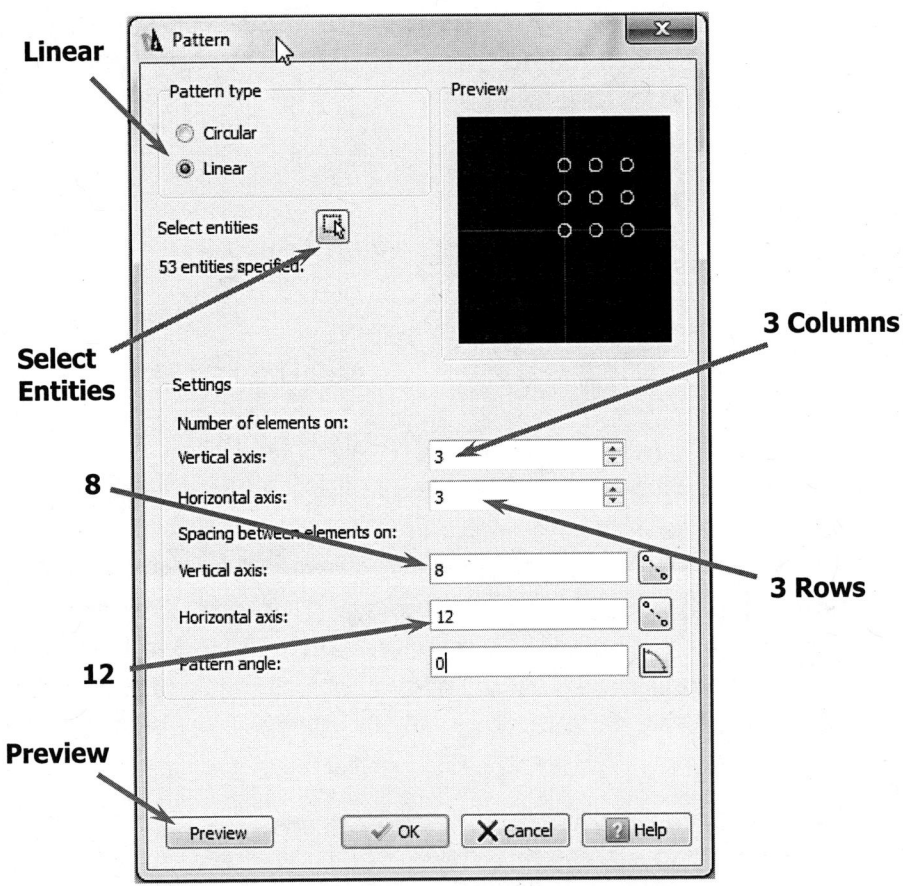

13. We'll first try a **Linear Pattern**, so make sure that one is selected. Left-click on the icon next to **Select entities**. The dialog box disappears temporarily; now select the entire airplane in order to pattern it.

14. Next, specify is the number of elements on the vertical and horizontal axis. For the purposes of this exercise, enter "**3**" for each. The spacing between elements is the distance between the new elements. Note that you can either enter a value or graphically pick these distances. For now enter "**8**" for

the vertical axis and "**12**" for the horizontal.  Left-click on the **Preview** button to see what the result is.  Your drawing should look similar to the one below (you will need to zoom out to see the entire pattern).

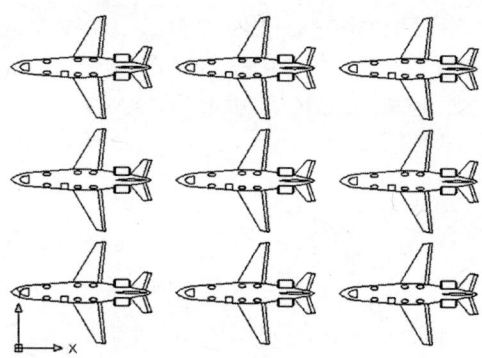

15. On your own, try different numbers of rows and columns.  Also try various offset distances and angles.

16. Let's try the **CircularPattern** option.  Start the **Pattern** command and select the **Circular** button.  Note how the pattern window changes.

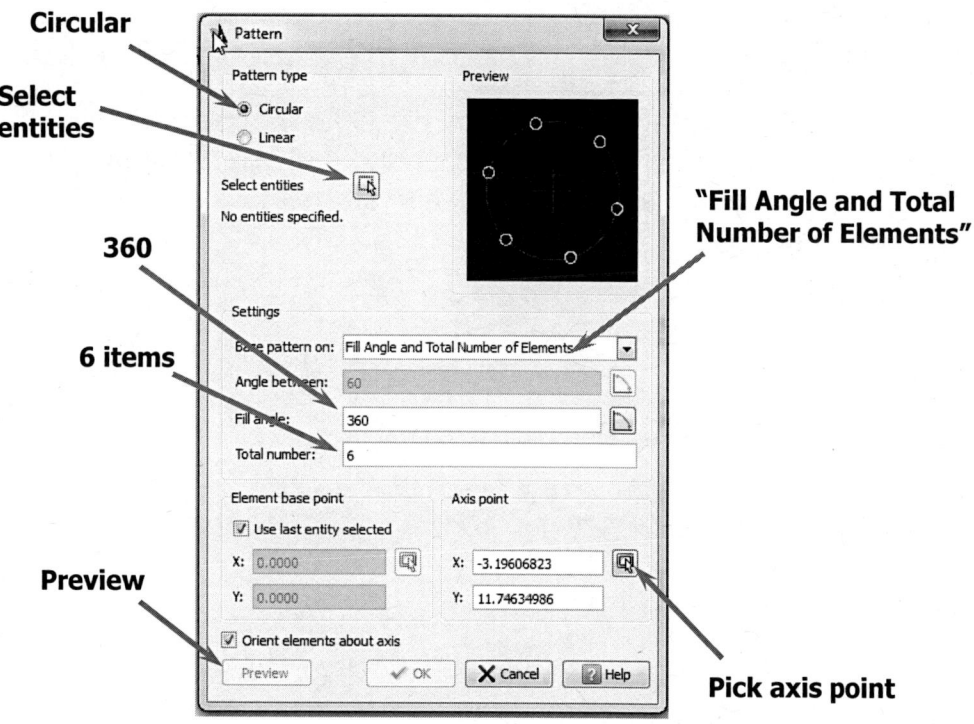

17. Left-click on the **Select entities** icon and select one of the previously patterned aircraft. Left-click on the **Axis point** icon. The dialog box temporarily disappears so you can pick an axis point. Position the crosshairs above and to the right of the selected aircraft some distance and left-click.

18. Select "Fill Angle and Total Number of Elements" from the "Base Pattern on:" drop-down. Enter "**6**" for the total number of items and leave the fill angle at "**360**" degrees. Do a preview and check your results.

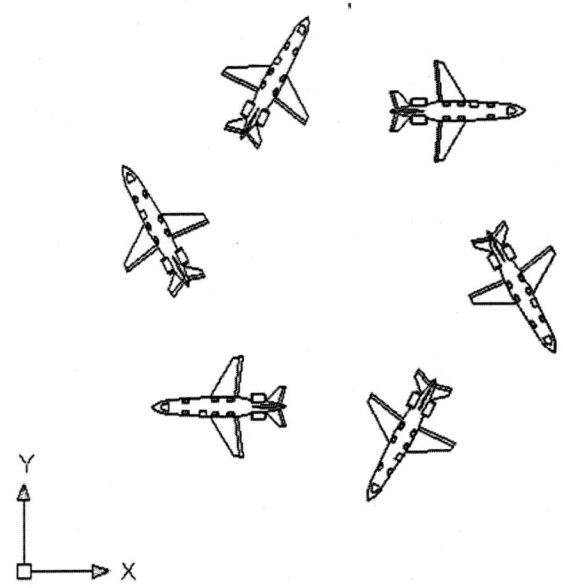

19. On your own, **Undo** the pattern and try the different options related to a circular pattern. What effect does un-checking the **Orient elements about axis** box have? Try to make an array of aircraft that looks like the one below. **Save** your drawing.

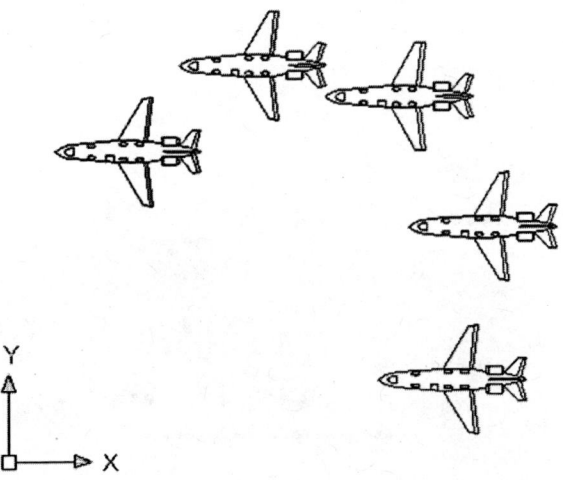

## The Scale and Stretch Commands

These commands are used to change an object's proportions. **Scale** changes the size of an object, while **Stretch** is used to change its shape in any one direction.

1.  Using the plane which was created in the previous section, select the **Scale** command. When prompted, select one of the aircraft copies to modify by using a **Window** or **Crossing** window. Then press the **Enter** key.

2.  Note that DraftSight now asks for a **base point**. This is the point about which the object will scale, or grow/shrink. Select the nose of the aircraft.

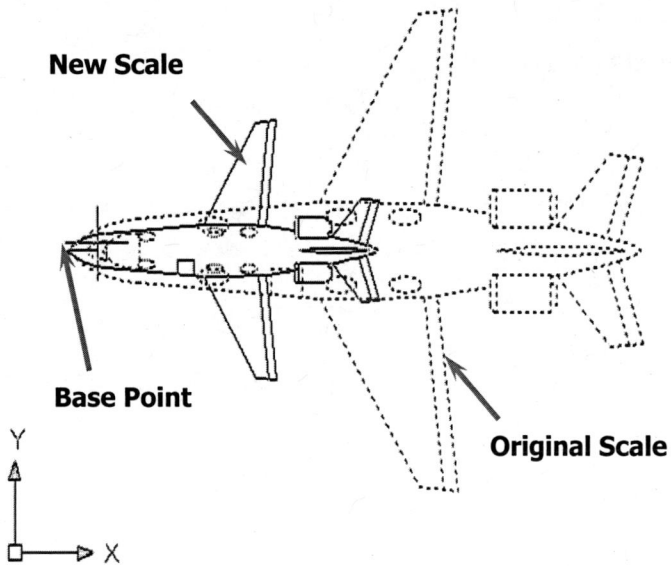

New Scale

Base Point

Original Scale

Y

X

3.  Note the choices: You can enter a **scale factor**, or type "**r**" for reference. First though, try dragging the aircraft with the crosshairs so it is about ½ its original size, like in the figure above. As you move the crosshairs towards the **base point**, the plane gets smaller and When you think the plane is about ½ scale, left-click to lock in the scale.

4.  Try it again, this time specifying a **scale factor** by entering a value. Start the **Scale** command again and pick the plane again (remember, you can type "**P**" and enter to select the previous entities). Once again, for the base point select the nose of the aircraft.

5.  When prompted for the scale factor, type "**2**" and press **Enter**. What is the result? Your plane should have doubled in size.

6. Repeat the last step several times using different values. Note that if you want to make the aircraft smaller, you enter a value less than 1 (e.g., .5 would make the aircraft half as big). What would you enter to make the aircraft 50% larger? (1.5)

7. Now we will stretch the aircraft's fuselage. Select the **Stretch** command from the **Modify** toolbar. Note that with **Stretch**, the only way to select objects is with a **Crossing** window (or polygon). You'll recall the easiest way to do this is to click to the right of the objects and sweep to the left. Pick a point just forward and above where the leading edge of the wings intersects the fuselage.

8. Sweep the **Crossing** window down and to the left, such that the forward half of the aircraft is included in the **Crossing-Window** and left-click. Press **Enter** when you're finished selecting objects.

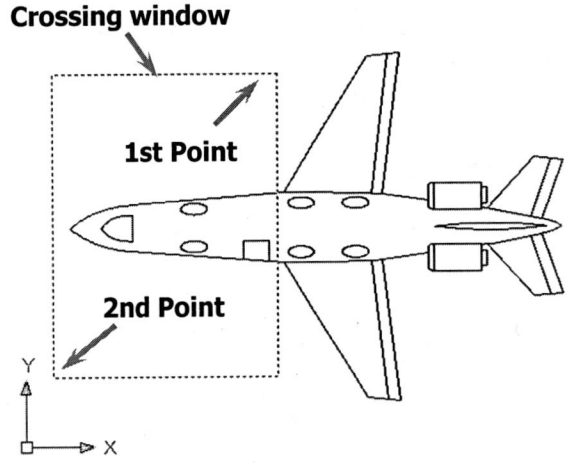

9. DraftSight now requires a **base point**. Select the nose of the aircraft and slide to the left about the distance of the length of the cockpit. Left-click.

10. On your own, **Stretch** the wings and horizontal stabilizer (tail) outward to accommodate the extra payload. **Copy** a set of windows to fill in the empty row forward of the wing. Your aircraft should look like the one at right. **Save** the drawing.

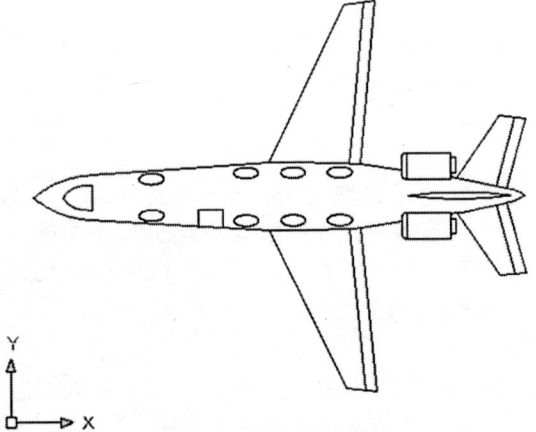

## The Split, Trim, Extend and Weld Commands

The **Split** command removes portions of entities (like lines and circles). **Trim** has much the same effect, except it slices off one entity using another entity as a cutter. **Extend** does just the opposite of **Trim**, and **Weld** is the opposite of **Split**. We'll work with these commands by creating what will look like a pie chart.

1.  Start a **New** drawing using the standard template. In the center of the drawing area, draw a **Circle** with a radius of **3** units.

2.  Select the **Split** command in the **Modify** toolbar, then position the pick box at the 3 o'clock position of the circle and left click. This both specifies the entitiy and selects the first split point.

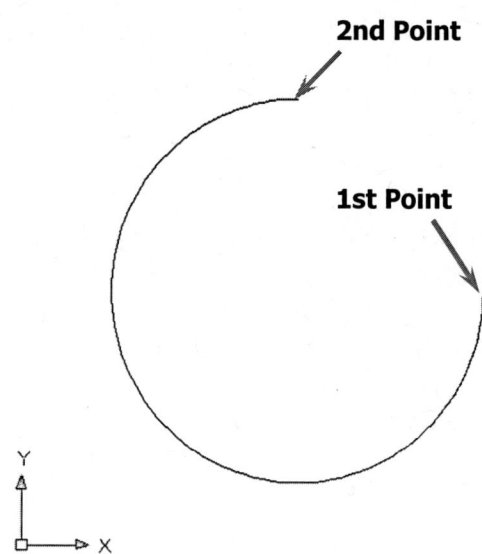

**2nd Point**

**1st Point**

3.  DraftSight now asks for a **second split point** (or you may backup and specify a first point by typing "**F**"). Select a point near the circle's 12 o'clock position for the second point. Press **Enter**. Does your circle look like the one above?

4.  Use the **Weld** command to repair the **Split**. Select the **Weld** icon in the **Modify** toolbar. When prompted for the base entity, select the circle. Now enter "**L**" for the **cLose** option. The circle should now be whole again.

5. **Undo** two times and try splitting the circle again on your own. This time pick the 12 o'clock position first, and the 3 o'clock position as the second point. Was there a difference? Notice that DraftSight breaks objects in a **counter-clockwise** direction.

6. Next, create two lines originating from the center of the circle, now an arc. Terminate one just short of the edge of the arc, but as if it would intersect the arc. Draw the other line so it goes just beyond the arc *and* intersects it. Note: You may use **Esnap** if desired to locate the center of the arc, but turn it off to specify the other line endpoints.

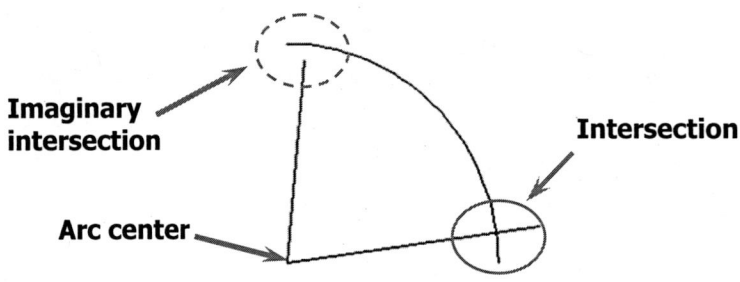

7. Now we'll trim the second line to the arc. Select the **Trim** command on the **Modify** toolbar.

8. DraftSight prompts you first for the **cutting edges**. These edges are the entities you are trimming to. In this case, use the **Pick Box** to select the arc as the cutting edge. Press **Enter**.

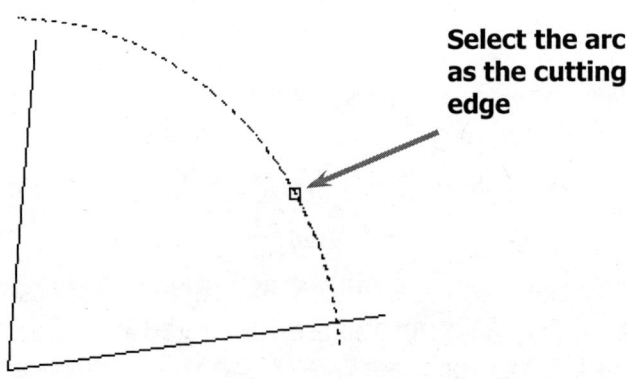

Select the arc as the cutting edge

9. Next, just as the command window says, select the **segment to remove**. This would be the line, but you must click on the portion of the line that lies outside of the arc. *Pick the portion of the entity that you want to go away.*

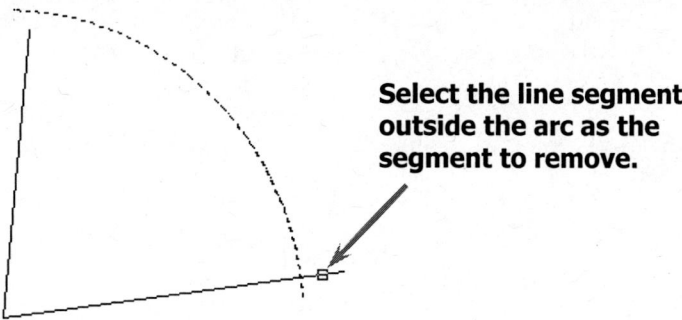

**Select the line segment outside the arc as the segment to remove.**

10. On your own, trim the arc to the line so it looks like the drawing below:

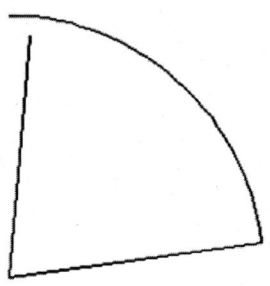

*Tip:* For faster results, you may pick multiple items for the cutting edges, and then trim those items to each other. In this case you could have selected both the arc and the line as cutting edges then selected both portions of each to trim in the final step. Undo and try it!

11. Now we'll try extending an entity. As mentioned previously, the **Extend** command is the opposite of **Trim**. Select the **Extend** icon on the **Modify** toolbar.

12. DraftSight requires that **boundary edges** be selected. This is the entity you want to extend to. Select the arc and then press **Enter**.

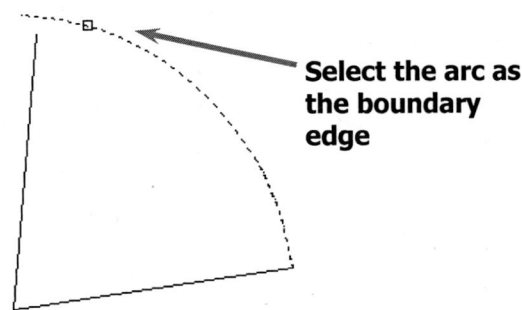

**Select the arc as the boundary edge**

13. Next, DraftSight asks for the **segments to extend**. Select the end of the line that is nearest the arc. The two should now meet. Press **Enter** to exit the command. <u>Note:</u> For this command to work, the boundary edge and segment to extend must share some imaginary intersection point.

**Select this end of the line as the segment to extend**

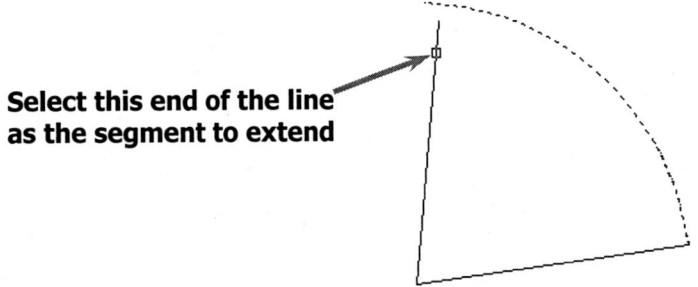

14. On your own, **Trim** the remainder of the arc that extends past the line. Create the rest of the pie chart as shown in the figure below. **Zoom** to verify all entities meet at their corners and don't overlap or have gaps between them. **Save** the drawing as "**Pie Chart.dwg**"; we'll use it later.

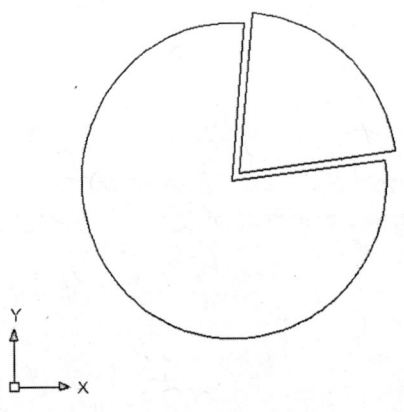

## The Fillet and Chamfer Commands

**Fillet** (pronounced "fill-it") and **Chamfer** are used to break the corners of an object. Fillet uses a radius, and Chamfer a line set at an angle. Nearly all consumer products have filleted or chamfered edges. It gives the object a softer, more inviting look. Fillets and chamfers also reduce safety hazards related to sharp edges.

1. Start a **New** DraftSight using the standard template. Using the **Line** command and **Ortho** mode as needed, sketch the rough outline of the meat cleaver shown in the figure below:

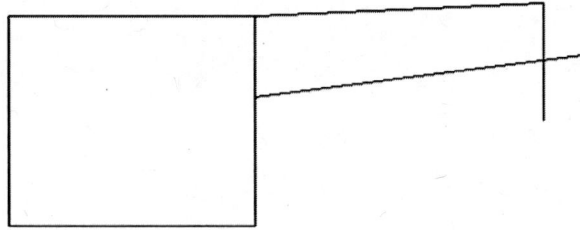

2. Select the **Fillet** icon on the **Modify** toolbar. Notice the current settings, probably indicating you are in **trim** mode with a radius of **0**. Set the radius by typing "**R**" for radius, then pressing **Enter**. Now type "**.25**" and press **Enter** when it asks you to specify the radius.

3. Select the upper line of the handle (1) and the line making the right side of the handle (2). Press the **spacebar** to repeat the **Fillet** command. Select the lower line of the handle (3) and the right side again (2). Your drawing should look close to the one below (you may need to adjust the radius size as needed, since we didn't create the drawing to scale).

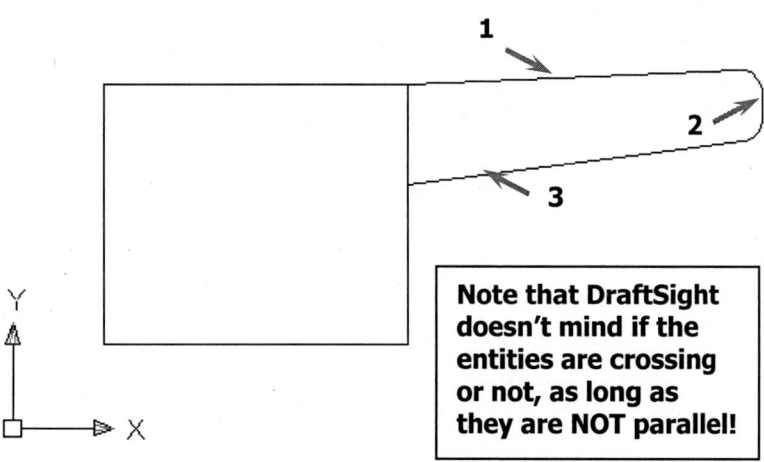

**Note that DraftSight doesn't mind if the entities are crossing or not, as long as they are NOT parallel!**

4. The trim option allows you to decide if anything gets trimmed when filleting. You'll note in the previous step both lines were trimmed to the fillet. Select the **Fillet** command and type "**t**" and **Enter**.

5. You may now decide whether to **trim** ("**t**") or not to trim ("**n**"). Type "**n**" and **Enter**. Set a fillet radius of **.38** and select the two lines that make up the bottom of the handle (1) and the right side of the blade (2). Notice the difference in trimming. The cleaver should now look like the one below:

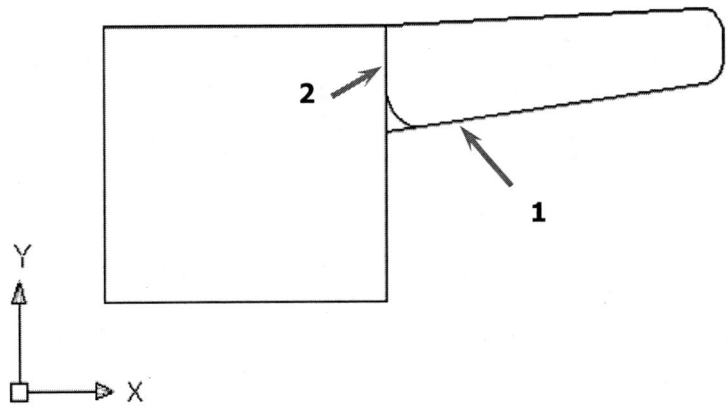

6. On your own, **fillet** the upper left-hand corner of the handle at **.25** radius.

7. The **Chamfer** command works much the same way as **Fillet**, but has a couple of more options. Select the **Chamfer** command from the **Modify** toolbar. The first thing to notice is that you can chamfer using **distances**, or a **distance and an angle**. The method depends on the information you're given.

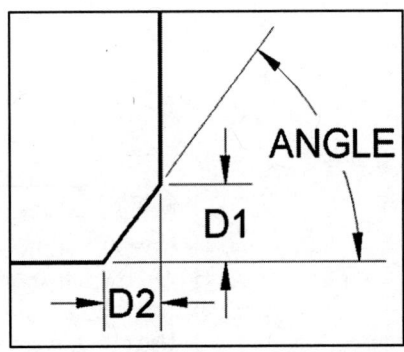

8. Type "**D**" and press **Enter**. When prompted, enter **.5** units for the first distance and **.38** for the second. Now set the trim mode to "trim". Select the right side of the blade for the first line, and the bottom of the blade for the second (note the order of selection will determine which chamfer distances are applied).

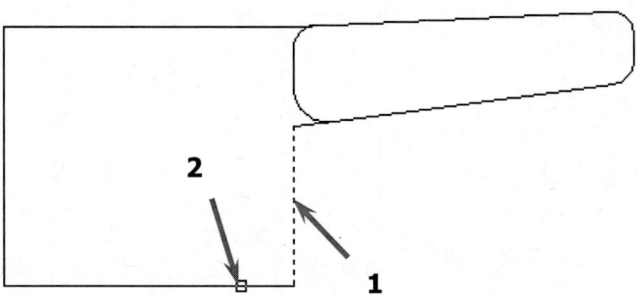

9. On your own, **chamfer** the upper left corner **.25** units equally. Experiment with the **angle** method while chamfering the inside corner where the handle and blade meet. Complete the drawing as shown in the figure below and **Save** it as "**Cleaver.dwg**".

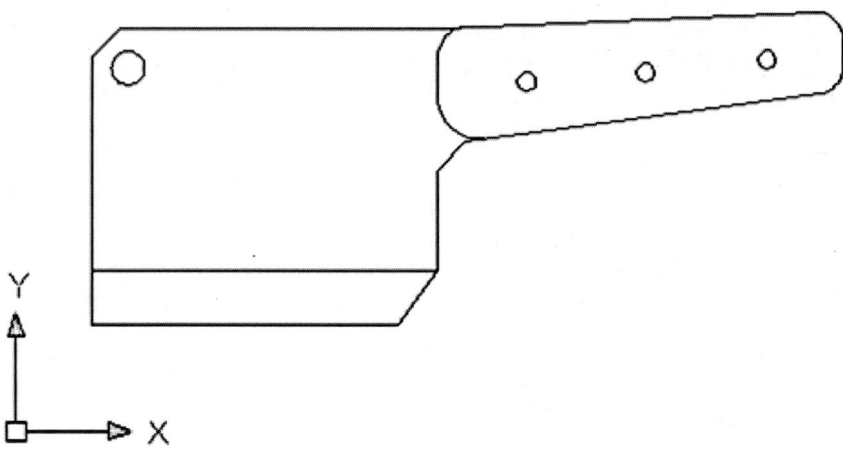

## Chapter 5 Suggested Learning Exercises

Based on your chosen drafting emphasis, pick from the following exercises:

### *Mechanical-*

1.  a) Sketch the left cell phone shown in the figure on the right. Round all corners using the **Fillet** command. Also use **Mirror, Fillet, Offset** and **Pattern**.

    b) **Copy** the cell phone, then scale the copy to 75% of its original size. **Stretch** to make your cell phone resemble the one on the far right. **Save** the drawing as "**Cellphone.dwg**"; we'll use it in a later chapter.

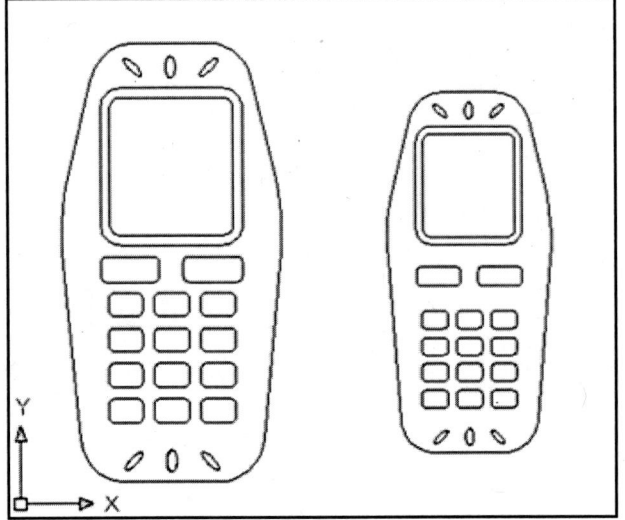

2.  Sketch the watch shown in the figure at right. Use **Pattern** to distribute the minute and hour markings. **Save** your drawing as "**Watch.dwg**".

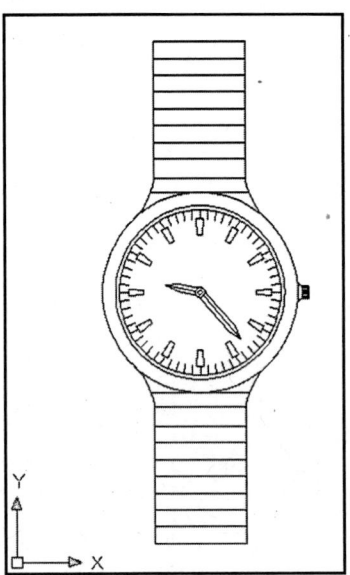

3.  Sketch the front view of the vehicle shown below. Note the **symmetry** between the left and right halves (hint). Save the drawing as "**truck.dwg**".

## Architectural-

Sketch a concept for a parking lot like the one in the figure below. Try to find uses for many of the commands discussed in this chapter (**Move**, **Copy**, **Rotate**, **Mirror**, **Offset**, **Pattern**, **Scale**, **Stretch**, **Split**, **Trim**, **Extend**, **Fillet** and **Chamfer**). **Save** the drawing as "**Parkinglot.dwg**". It will be used in a future exercise.

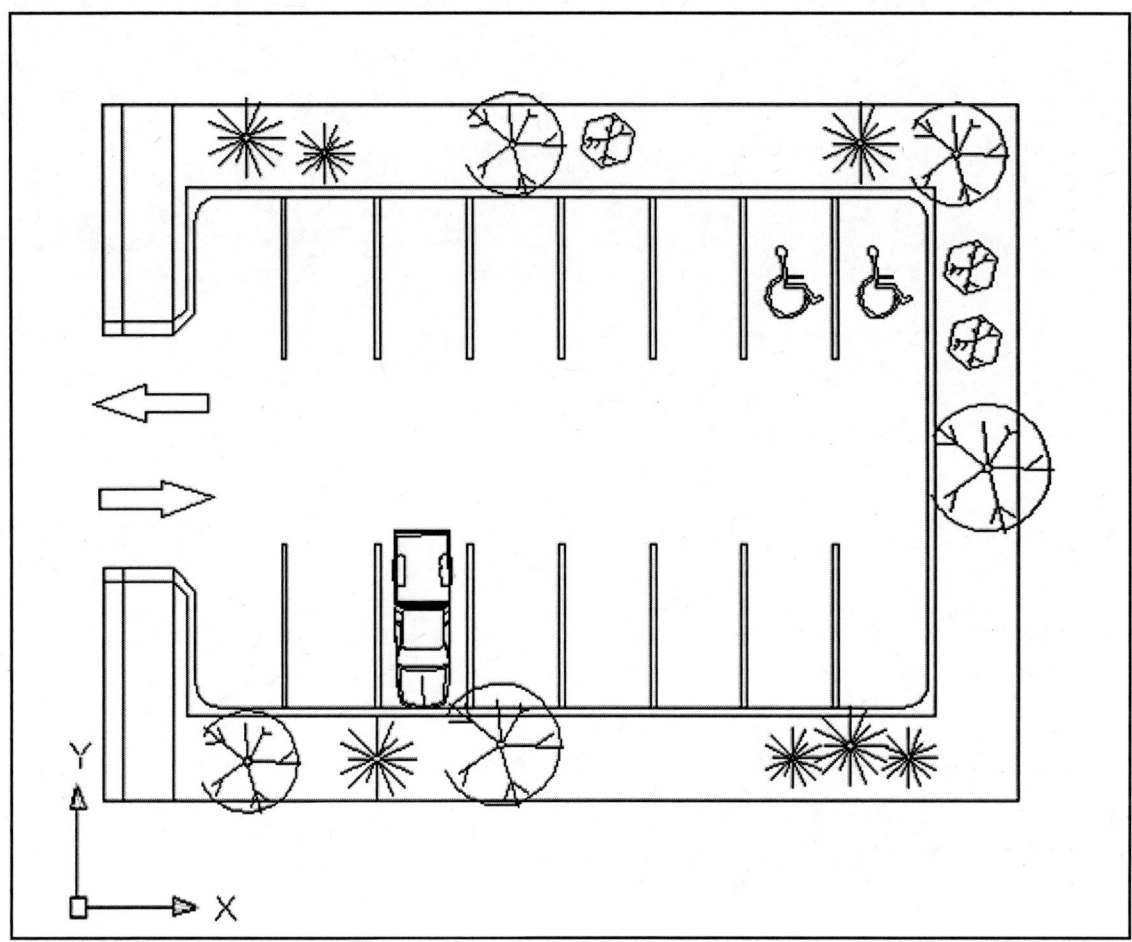

**NOTES:**

## Unit 1 Review- Test Your Knowledge

1. Match the commands and modes listed below with each of their respective actions. Write the letter of the action in the blank provided in front of the appropriate command.

| | | |
|---|---|---|
| __ **Undo** | a. Copies objects into an array. | |
| __ **Pan** | b. Creates objects with multiple sides. | |
| __ **Mirror** | c. Used to repair broken entities. | |
| __ **Point** | d. Duplicates an entity. | |
| __ **Pattern** | e. Removes a portion of an entity. | |
| __ **Polygon** | f. Creates a round entity with no beginning or end. | |
| __ **Trim** | g. Reflects an object about a line to make it symmetric. | |
| __ **Open** | h. Creates a straight entity using two points. | |
| __ **Ortho** | i. Copies an object and sets it to one side at a distance. | |
| __ **Chamfer** | j. Changes an object's proportions. | |
| __ **Weld** | k. Used to mark a specific location on a drawing. | |
| __ **Zoom** | l. Rounds off a corner with a radius. | |
| __ **Copy** | m. Used to join two entities at an intersection. | |
| __ **Ellipse** | n. Creates or edits entities in a straight (horiz./vert.) fashion. | |
| __ **Stretch** | o. Changes the orientation of an entity. | |
| __ **Rectangle** | p. Changes the relative size of an entity. | |
| __ **Extend** | q. Cuts-off one entity with another. | |
| __ **Line** | r. Command used to access an existing drawing. | |
| __ **Fillet** | s. Changes the detail and area shown in the drawing area. | |
| __ **Offset** | t. Creates an ob-round circle. | |
| __ **Arc** | u. Creates a four-sided object by specifying two points. | |
| __ **Move** | v. Creates a portion of a circle. | |
| __ **Split** | w. Used to back-up a step. | |
| __ **Scale** | x. Changes an object's location. | |
| __ **Rotate** | y. Breaks a corner with an angled line. | |
| __ **Circle** | z. Used to move across the drawing view. | |

2. From memory, provide the names of the commands associated with the indicated icons found in the standard toolbar:

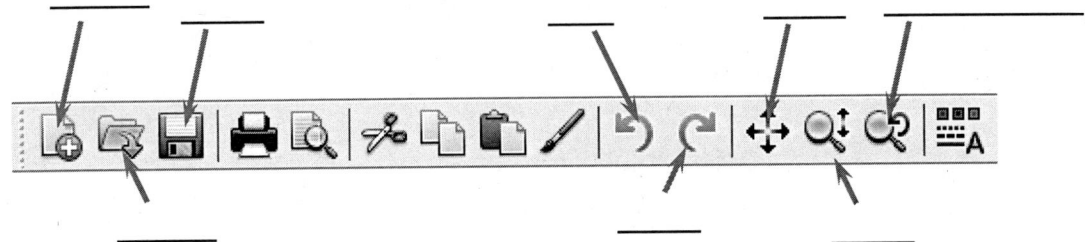

3. From memory, provide the names of the commands associated with the indicated icons found in the draw toolbar:

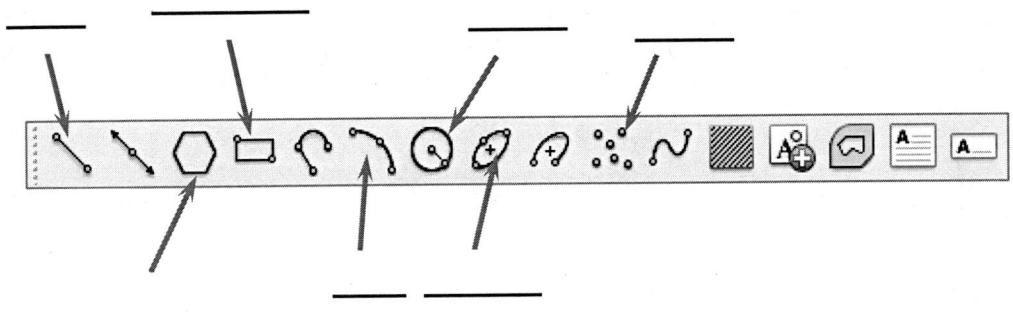

4. From memory, provide the names of the commands associated with the indicated icons found in the modify toolbar:

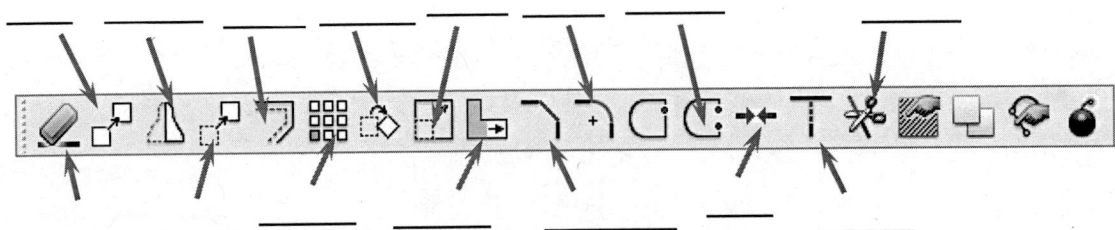

# Unit 2- Drawing and Detailing

## Chapter 6- Coordinate Entry

Objectives:

1. Introduction to the Cartesian Coordinate System
2. Create objects using absolute, relative and polar coordinate entry methods
3. Explore an object's geometric properties
4. Modify objects using coordinate entry methods

In Unit 1, we created sketches without any concern for exact dimensions. While sketches are fine for conceptualization, they have very little other use in the real world of CAD. We need to now learn to draw with precision, that is, to exact size. In order to do this DraftSight uses the Cartesian Coordinate System.

## The Cartesian Coordinate System

Developed centuries ago by mathematicians, you may recognize the Cartesian Coordinate System from your junior-high math classes. In short, it's a method to specify a location in three-dimensional (3D) space. These locations are based on three intersecting number lines, labeled the X, Y and Z axes. The intersection point is labeled 0,0,0. While DraftSight has some marginal 3D capabilities, it is best at 2D drafting. This means we'll only concern ourselves with two of the axes: the X and Y.

Let's review two features of the DraftSight workspace, the **coordinate display** and the **coordinate system icon**. Start a **New** drawing using the standard template. Take note of the following features:

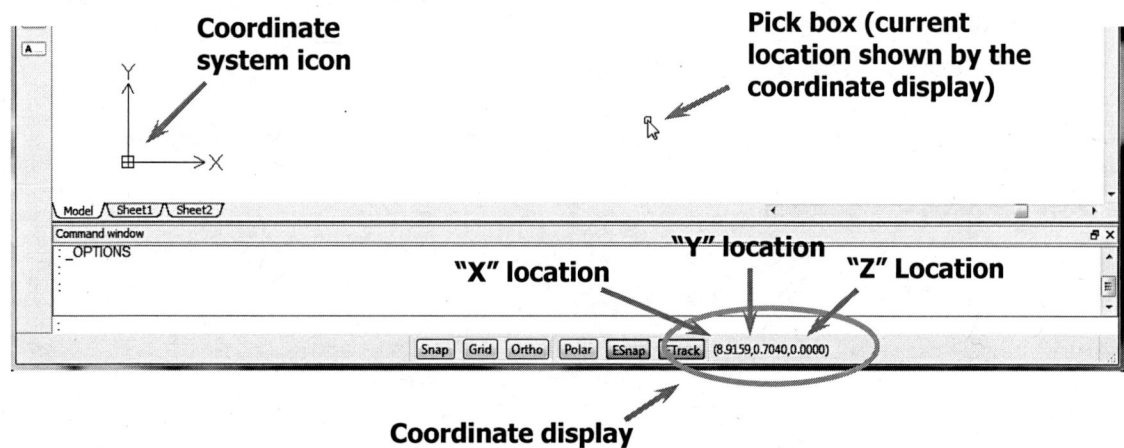

**Note:** If the coordinate system icon is missing, turn it on by going to Tools>Options, Drawing Settings, Display, **Coordinate System Icon**. Check the "Display Icon" box. The coordinate display can be turned on by right-clicking in the space to the right of the **ETrack** button in the status bar and selecting **Absolute** from the pop-up menu.

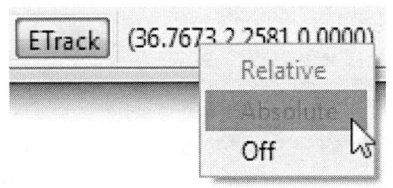

Move the mouse around the screen. Notice that the **coordinate display** reports the location of the pick-box in X, Y, Z space.

The purpose of the **coordinate system icon** is to indicate the positive **X** and **Y** axes. It also lies at the **origin**, or intersection of all axes.

Note that when indicating a location with the Cartesian Coordinate System, the **X** axis is listed first, the **Y** second and finally the **Z**. These are separated by comas: **X,Y,Z** just like in the coordinate display. Note in the drawing to the right that there are four areas, or quadrants, in the Cartesian Coordinate System. We'll be working in the upper-right one, called the positive-positive quadrant since both the **X** and **Y** axes are positive numbers in that quadrant.

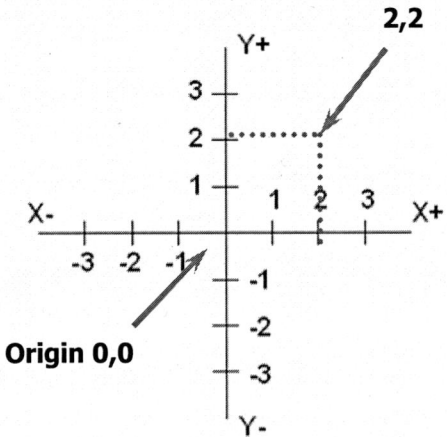

## Coordinate Entry Methods

DraftSight basically uses three methods for precision drawing relying on the coordinate system: **Absolute, Relative** and **Polar**. Of those, Relative and Polar are probably the most useful.

The **Absolute** method is exactly that: Using the coordinate system literally.

1. Start the **Line** command. Instead of clicking randomly in the drawing area for the first point, we'll enter an **Absolute location**. Enter **0,0** in the command window for the **start point**.

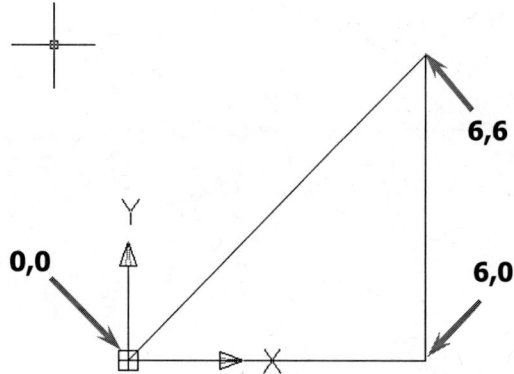

2. For the **next point** type **6,0** and press **Enter**. DraftSight should have now created a straight line 6 units long from location 0,0 to 6,0.  For the next point enter **6,6** and enter the final point of **0,0**. **Zoom** out if needed. Did you draw a triangle like the one below?

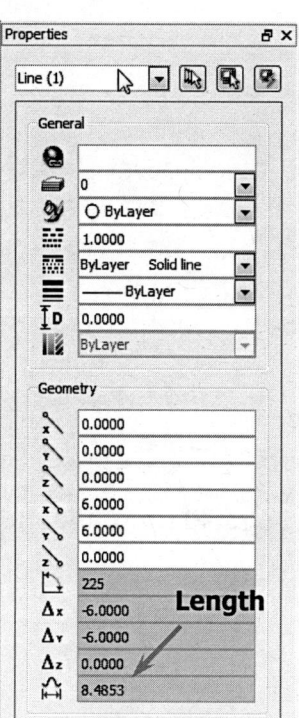

3. Double-click on the diagonal line of the triangle. The **Properties** window should appear (shown at right).  This window tells you everything you need to know about an object.  Note it gives the coordinates for the start and end of the line.  It lists the change in **X** and **Y** (or "Delta"- ΔX).  Also, it gives the length of the line.

4. **Undo** or **Delete** the triangle. On your own, start the **Line** command and enter the **Absolute coordinates** that follow in the chart below:

| Start Point | Next Point | Next Point | Next Point | Next Point | Next Point | Next Point | Next Point | Next Point | Next Point | Next Point |
|---|---|---|---|---|---|---|---|---|---|---|
| .63,0 | 3.13, 0 | 3.75, .25 | 3.75, 3.75 | 0, 3.75 | 0, .25 | .63, 0 | .75,0 | .75, .5 | 2.63, .5 | 2.63, 0 |

Made a mistake? You can always go back a step by typing "**u**" & **Enter** (**Undo**).

5. Does the resulting drawing look like the one below?  The absolute point 3.75,3.75 is labeled for your reference.

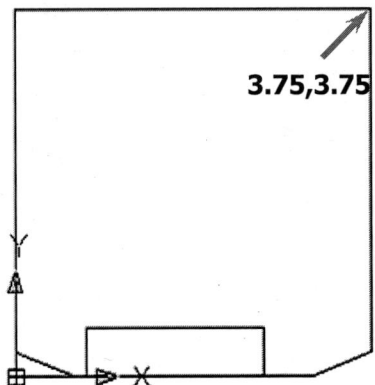

Next we'll cover **Relative** coordinate entry.  A relative coordinate is entered in a similar fashion as absolute, but is preceded by the "@" symbol, then **X,Y** (e.g., **@X,Y**).  This makes the next point *relative* to the last one.  Let's draw that triangle again:

6. **Delete** everything and initiate the **Line** command. For the **start point** enter an **Absolute coordinate** of **0,0**. For the next point enter a **Relative coordinate** of **@6,0**.  This makes a line ending 6 units to the right of the first point.  For the **next point** enter **@0,6** and then **@-6,-6**. The last line should go to the first point.

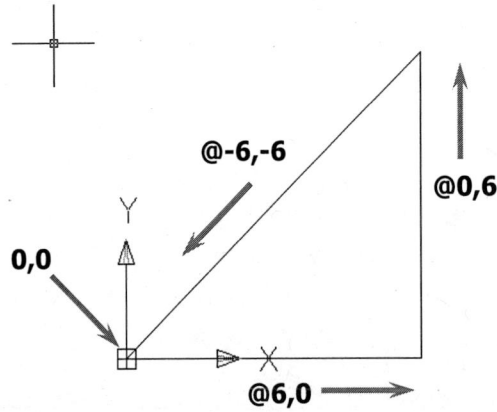

7. Notice what happened, each new point is an "address" related to the last point. What are the benefits of using Relative over Absolute?

8. **Delete** the triangle we drew in the previous step. On your own, start the **Line** command again and enter the following **Relative** coordinates (the start point is an Absolute coordinate to get things started):

| Start Point | Next Point | Next Point | Next Point | Next Point | Next Point | Next Point | Next Point | Next Point | Next Point | Next Point |
|---|---|---|---|---|---|---|---|---|---|---|
| .63,0 | @2.5, 0 | @.63, .25 | @0, 3.5 | @ -3.75, 0 | @0, -3.5 | @.63, -.25 | @.13, 0 | @0, .5 | @2,0 | @0, -.5 |

9. The resulting drawing should look like the last one we did. Note that using a negative number for an **X** coordinate will result in created a line to the left. A negative number for a **Y** coordinate results in a line going downward. A couple of the **Relative** coordinates you specified are given on the drawing below for your reference.

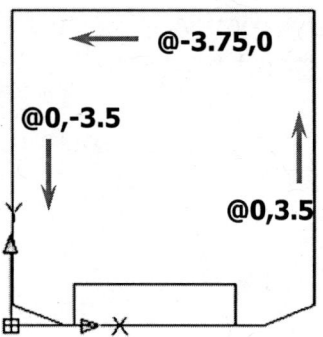

You'll notice that with **Relative**, it doesn't really matter where you are, just where you are going. Imagine the following scenario: You're visiting a major city for the first time and are hopelessly lost. You decide to stop and ask two people standing on the street for directions to your destination. Person one replies "Just go to the intersection of Monroe Ave. and Elm Street, you can't miss it." Person two replies "Go two blocks that way" (pointing) "then turn right at the stop sign, go four more blocks straight ahead from there, you can't miss it". Which set or directions are more helpful? You probably already had the information offered by person one: an **Absolute** coordinate. Person two gave directions based *relative* to where you were, which is way more helpful.

Finally, we'll try **Polar** Coordinate entry, which uses the polar coordinate system. It consists of entering any distance "**d**", and some angle "**a**", e.g. "**@d<a**". Note that Polar entry starts with an "**@**" symbol, just like Relative. A **Polar** entry is also relative to the last point, but uses a **distance and angle** to jump to the next point instead of horizontal and vertical units. Study the graphic below regarding polar angles. Note that angle "0" is to the right, and goes counterclockwise from there:

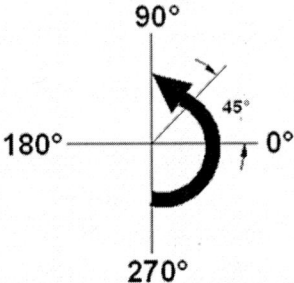

10. Start the **Line** command. For the **first point** type **0,0** and press **Enter**. For the **second point** type **@6<0**. A line should now run from the origin six units to the right. Next type **@6<90**, and finally **@8.485<225**. Did you draw a right triangle just as before?

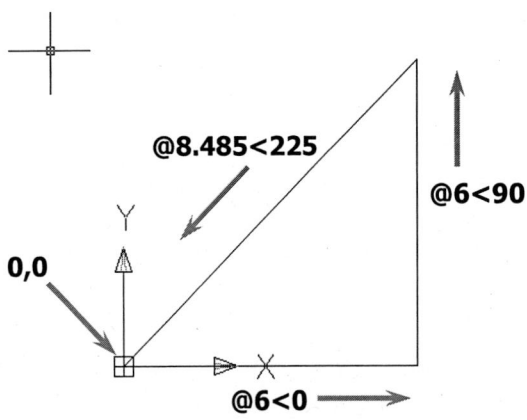

11. **Delete** the triangle you created in the previous step. On your own, start the **Line** command again and enter the following **Polar** coordinates (the first one is an Absolute coordinate to get things started):

| Start Point | Next Point | Next Point | Next Point | Next Point | Next Point | Next Point | Next Point | Next Point | Next Point | Next Point |
|---|---|---|---|---|---|---|---|---|---|---|
| .63,0 | @2.5 <0 | @.68 <22 | @3.5< 90 | @3.75 <180 | @3.5 <270 | @.68 <-22 | @.13 <0 | @.5<90 | @2<0 | @.5< 270 |

12. The resulting drawing should look familiar. A few of the **Polar** coordinates that were specified are shown below. **Save** the drawing as "**Disk.dwg**", we'll finish it in a minute.

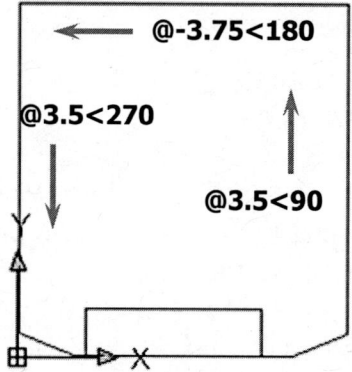

13. There is another way to use Polar coordinates. Right-Click on the **POLAR** button in the **Status bar**. A small pop-up window should appear, Left-Click on **Settings**. The **Options** window appears, set the increment angle to **15°**.

14. Turn the **Polar** button on in the **Status bar**. Go ahead and start drawing using the **Line** command. What are the effects of this drawing aid? Remember you can type in any number for the distance, and then use the displayed value for the angle. What are the limitations of this method?

---

*Tip:* To use feet and inches instead of decimal inches, go to the **Tools** menu and select **Options**. Left-click on the **+** next to **Unit System**. Choose **Architectural** from the **Length-Type:** pull-down menu. Select **OK** to close the Options window. When entering coordinates you'll have to use the foot marks to indicate feet (e.g., @8'6,0 = 8 ft., 6 in.), otherwise DraftSight assumes decimal inches are being used.

---

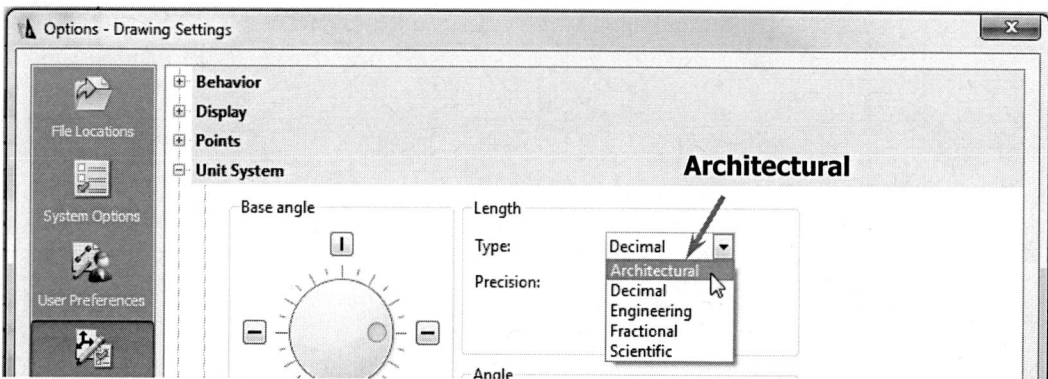

## Editing and Coordinate Entry

Coordinate entry methods are used for more than just creating entities, they can be used edit them as well. Let's finish the drawing of the "old-school" disk we started earlier:

1.  **Open** Disk.dwg (if it's not already). **Zoom** in so that just the disk and little else is visible in the drawing area.

2.  Select the **Copy** icon in the **Modify** toolbar. Pick the horizontal line running across the top of the object to copy and press **Enter**. Click anywhere in the drawing area for the **from point**. Enter **@0,.08** for the **second point**. There should now be a copy of the line at .08 units above it (the **Offset** command would've been easier in this case, but what if you wanted a copy 1 inch above and 1 inch to the right?).

3.  Using the **Move** command, move the entire object from the origin to point **1,1** on your own. Your disk should resemble the one to the right.

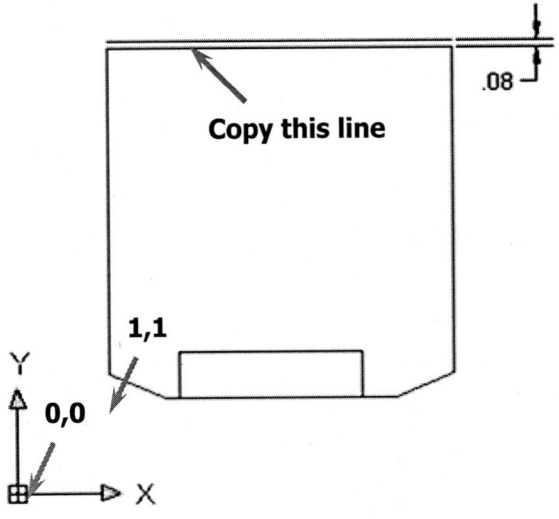

Copy this line

Using the modify commands learned from the previous chapter, complete your disk to look like the one below. Estimate any missing dimensions. Don't create the text for now. **Save** the drawing.

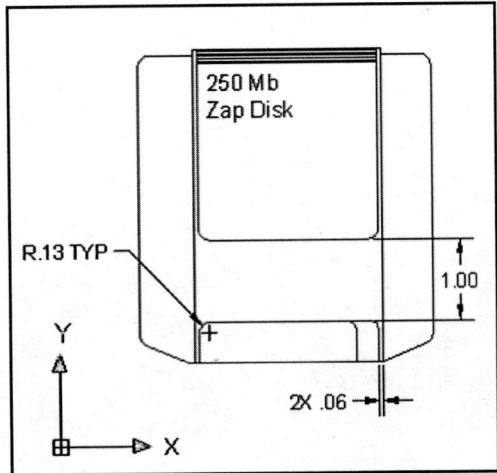

250 Mb
Zap Disk

R.13 TYP

1.00

2X .06

> **Tip:** Always draw objects full size in DraftSight, don't scale anything! Whether it's a 650' property line or a .12" X .12" microchip, **ALWAYS DRAW TRUE TO SIZE!** We'll learn later how to plot to a scale.

## Chapter 6 Suggested Learning Exercises

**Unit 2 Project:** Based on your chosen drafting emphasis, select either the Mechanical or Architectural project to follow. **The exercises at the end of each subsequent chapter will build on exercises from the previous one.**

### Mechanical- POCKET TOOL PROJECT

Start a **New** drawing. Create the objects to size with the given dimensions. **Save** the drawing containing all three objects as "**Pocket Tool.dwg**".

**1. Large Flat Screwdriver**

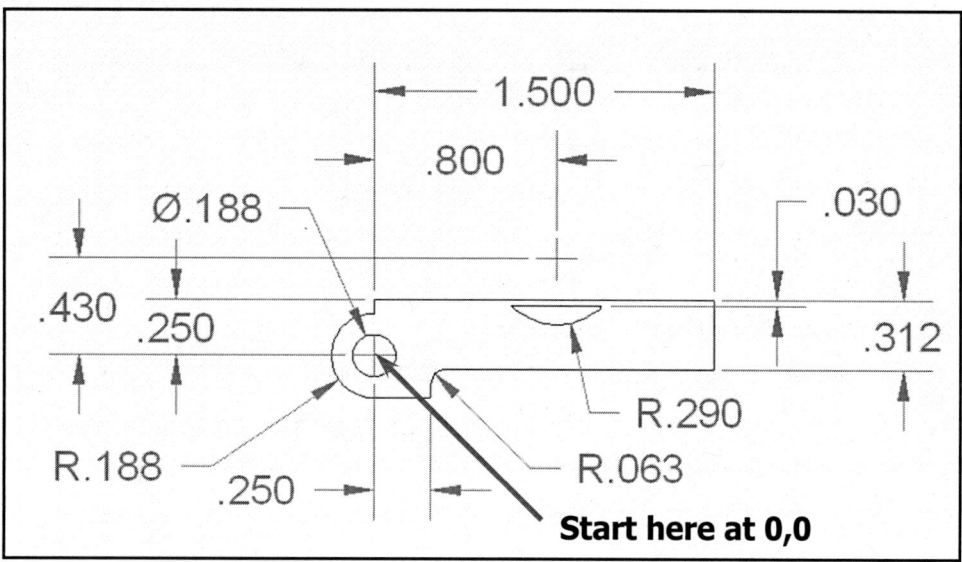

**2. Small Flat Screwdriver**

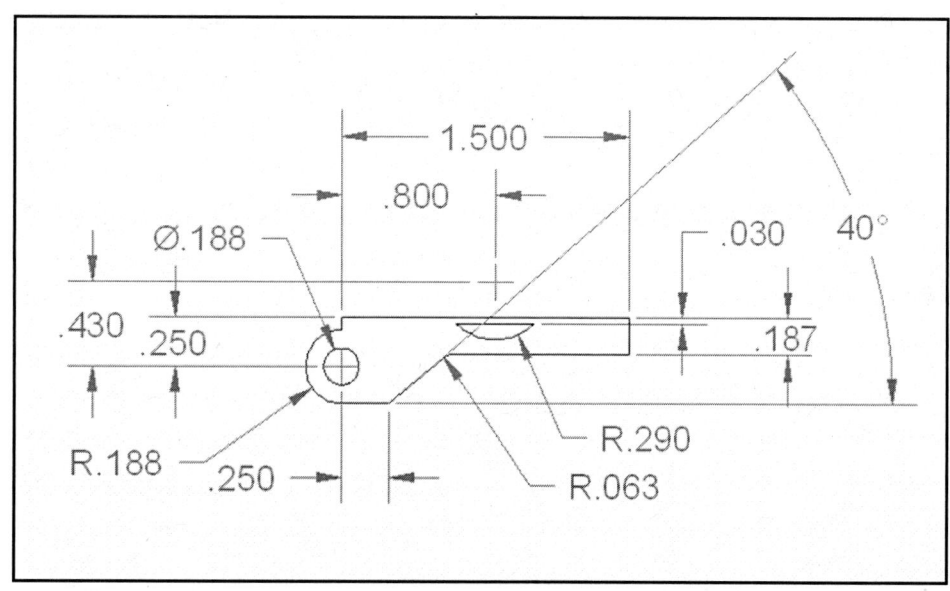

## 3. Blade

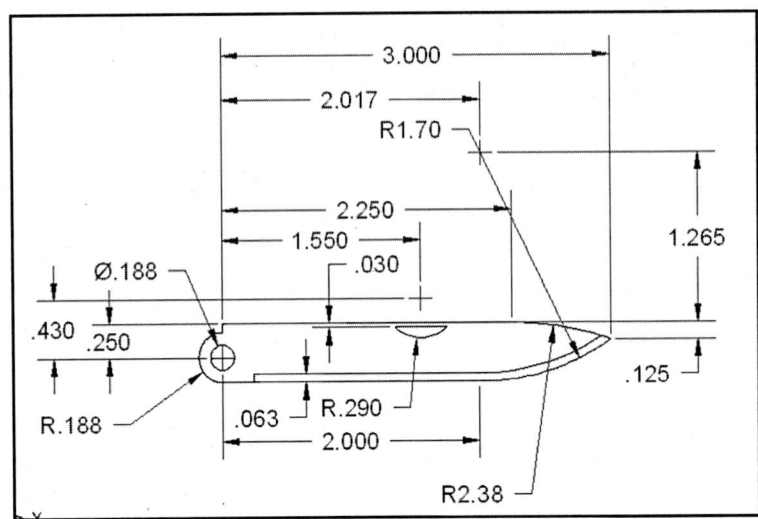

## *Architectural- GARAGE PROJECT*

Create a plan view drawing of the garage shown on the next page.

Tips:

- Start a **New** drawing using the standard template and do two things to set up the drawing for an architectural A-Size at a scale of ¼"=1':

  1. Change the units to architectural by entering "**units**" in the command window and selecting **Architectural** from the **Length-Type** drop-down.
  2. Enter "**limits**" in the command window. Set the upper right corner at **576,432**. Enter **Zoom** and then **Bounds** in the command window.

- Start the garage in the lower left hand corner at absolute coordinate **72,72**.

- **DRAW THE GARAGE FULL SCALE**. Estimate any missing dimensions.

- Draw one each of the door and window symbols. **Copy** them into place using coordinate entry. **Save** as "**Garage.dwg**"

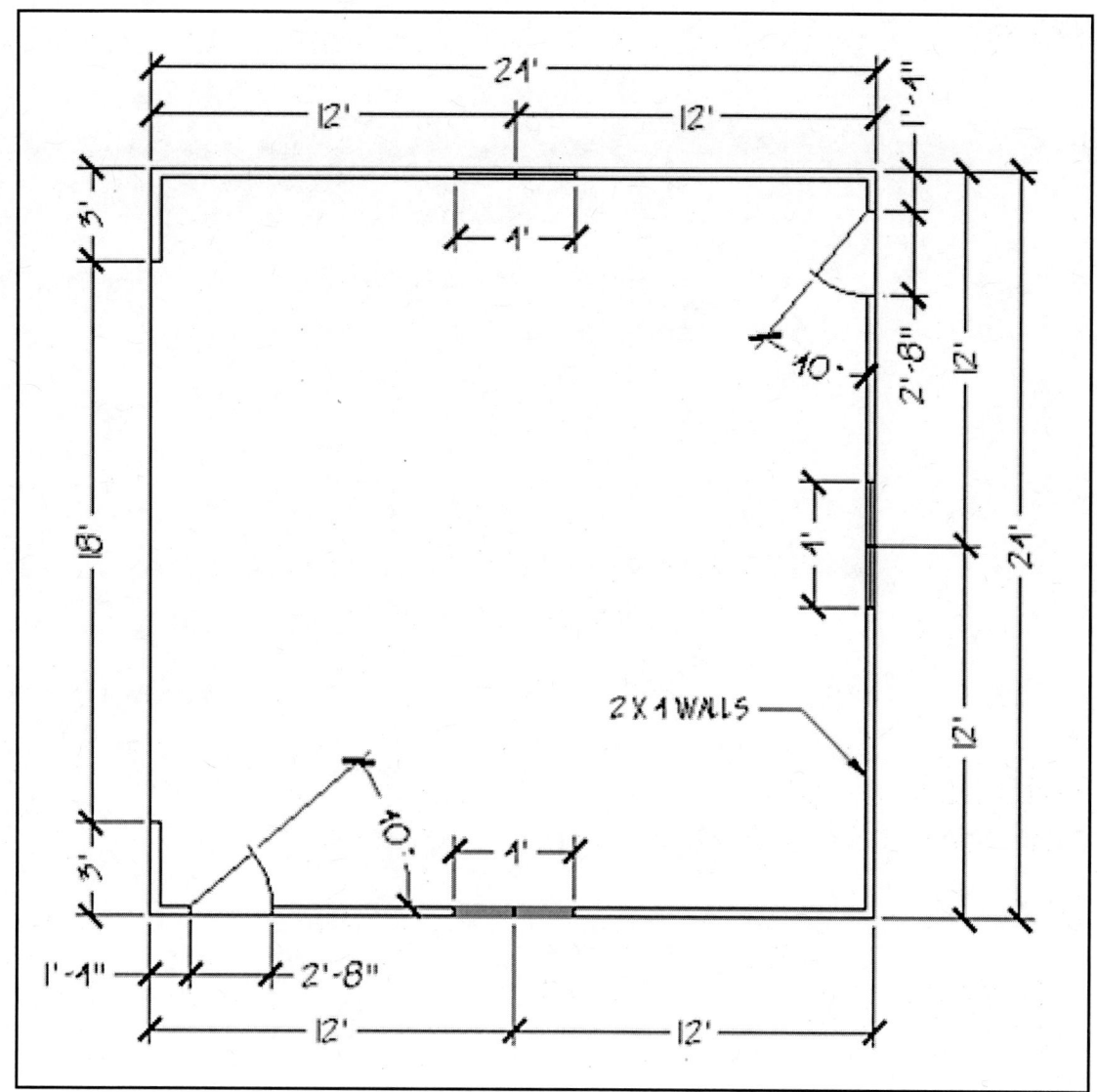

**NOTES:**

Chapter 7- Drawing Aids

Objectives:
1. Use the ESnap (Entity Snap) and ETrack (Entity Tracking) drawing aids
2. Specify Entity Snaps using the ESnap toolbar & pop-up menu
3. Use the ESnap "Snap-From"
4. Use Snap and Grid for creating drawings and isometric views

Besides coordinate entry, DraftSight has other tools to help us draw with precision. **ESnap** locates entities precisely using existing geometry. **Snap** and **Grid** are used in tandem to create geometry on a pre-defined grid pattern.

## Entity Snaps

ESnaps work like a magnet on the end of the crosshairs. They allow you to begin, end, or locate an entity based on features of another entity. These entity features are end-points, mid-points, center-points and tangent-points to name a few. First, let's take a look at the settings for ESnap:

1. Start a **New** drawing. Locate and activate the **Esnap** button in the **status bar** at the bottom of the DraftSight window. Place the cursor over it and right-click. A pop-up menu should appear, select **Settings**.

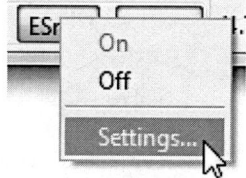

2. The *Options - User Preferences* window should appear, revealing the Entity Snap settings.

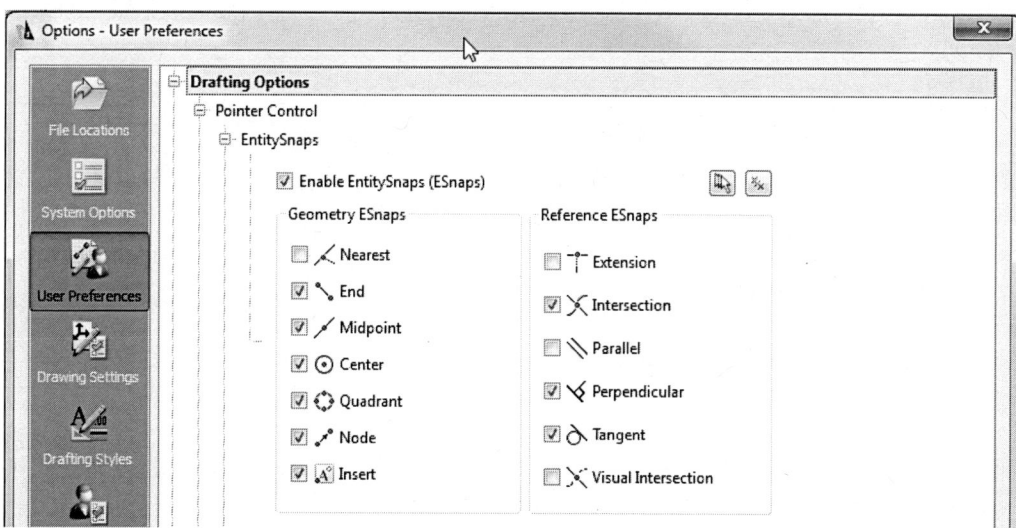

3. Note the many choices presented. These are geometric features that you can reference when creating or modifying entities. Select the options shown in the previous graphic. Select the **OK** button to close the window and return to the drawing.

4. We'll now draw a tape dispenser to demonstrate the functionality of Esnaps. Begin with a **Line** from coordinate **1,1** to **2.5,1**. Switch to **Arc**. For the arc's **start point**, put the crosshairs over the second point (2.5,1) of the line.

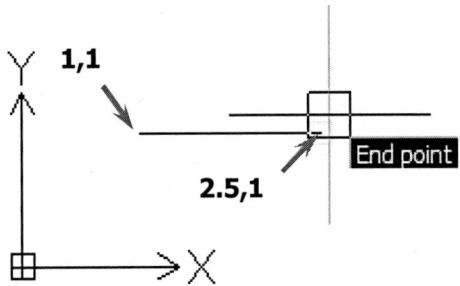

5. Pause long enough, and the words "**End point**" will appear. This indicates that the crosshairs have locked on to the endpoint. Left-click to select the endpoint of the line. For the next two points, enter **@.75<35** and **@.75<80**.

6. Switch to the **Line** command. For the **start point** select the upper endpoint of the arc you just created. For the next points enter **@-.25, 0** and **@.375<245**. Your drawing should now look like the one below:

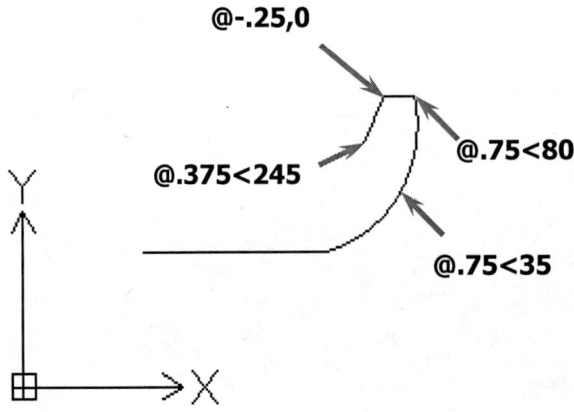

7. Turn on the **ETrack** button in the **status bar**. This option helps you track away from ESnaps. Select the **Circle** command, for the center-point place the crosshairs over the right-end of the first line you drew (at point **1,1**). Once the endpoint Esnap locks on, move the crosshairs slightly upward. An Entity Tracking, or **ETrack** icon should appear showing your position in relation to the endpoint (in this case perpendicular). Enter **.5** to establish the center point. For the radius of the circle, select the left endpoint of the first line again.

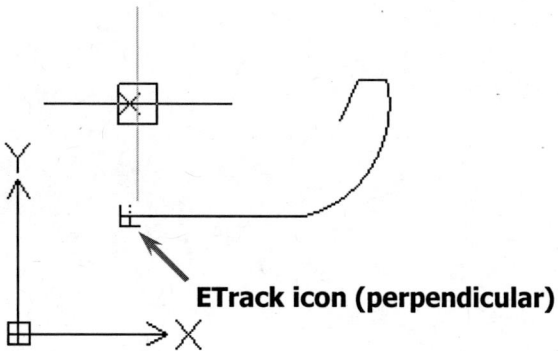

**ETrack icon (perpendicular)**

**Note:** If using a white drawing area background, the ETrack icon might be difficult to see, as its default color is yellow. Colors can be adjusted by going to the **Tools** menu, selecting **Options**, then **System Options** in the Options window. Click on **Display** and **Element Colors**. Blue is a good choice for the ESnap Cue.

8. Draw a vertical line from the left quadrant of the circle you just created at .5 units long.

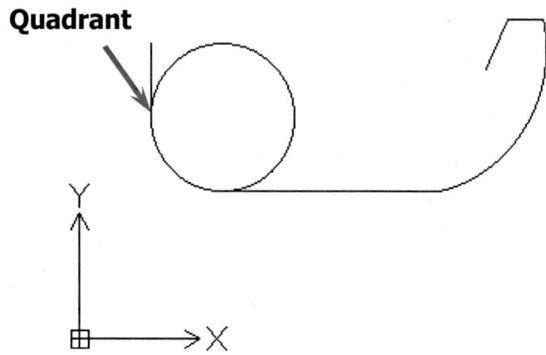

**Quadrant**

9. Create a **tangent-tangent-radius circle** tangent to the line just drawn and the first one created in this drawing. Enter **1** for the radius.

10. Next, draw a **.75"** diameter circle in the center of the circle you created in the previous step.

11. Select the **Line** command; select the upper-end of the diagonal line for the **start point**. Using **ETrack**, hover the crosshairs over the upper end of the diagonal line, then move away to the left and watch for the perpendicular icon to appear at that intersection (it may take a few tries). Enter "1" in the command window to draw a line 1 unit long, perpendicular to the diagonal one.

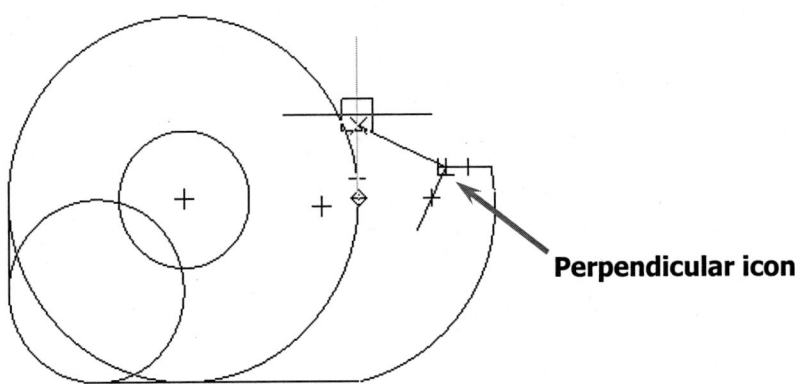

**Perpendicular icon**

12. **Copy** the diagonal line to the intersection of the last line drawn and the large circle. Draw a **2 Point circle** using the lower endpoints of the diagonal lines for the two points. Use **Trim** and **Delete** to finish the drawing so it resembles the one below. **Save** the drawing as "**TapeDispenser.dwg**". We'll use it again in Chapter 11.

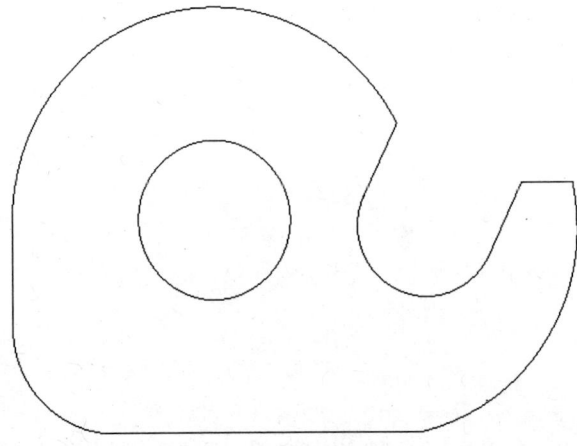

So far we've been using "running" **ESnaps**.  These are active as long as you have the **ESnap** button toggled on.  There are ways to specify a particular entity snap if the one you want isn't being located by the running ESnap.  There is an **ESnap toolbar**.  It is activated just like any other toolbar: Right-click over an existing docked toolbar, select **Main** from the list presented in the pop-up, then **Entity Snap**. The **Entity Snap** toolbar should appear.

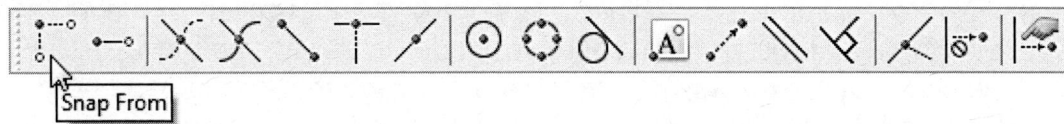

Snap From

13. Many of the icons are easy to identify. One that isn't, and can't be used as a running ESnap: **Snap From**. What if you wanted to create the two holes on the drawing of the plate below?  First, draw the 4 X 3 rectangle.  Next, start the **Circle** command.  For the **center point**, pick the **Snap From** icon from the **Entity Snap** toolbar and then the lower left-hand corner of the object (endpoint).  Now enter **@1,1.5**.  Enter **1** for the diameter of the circle. On your own, draw the other circle per the dimensions shown.

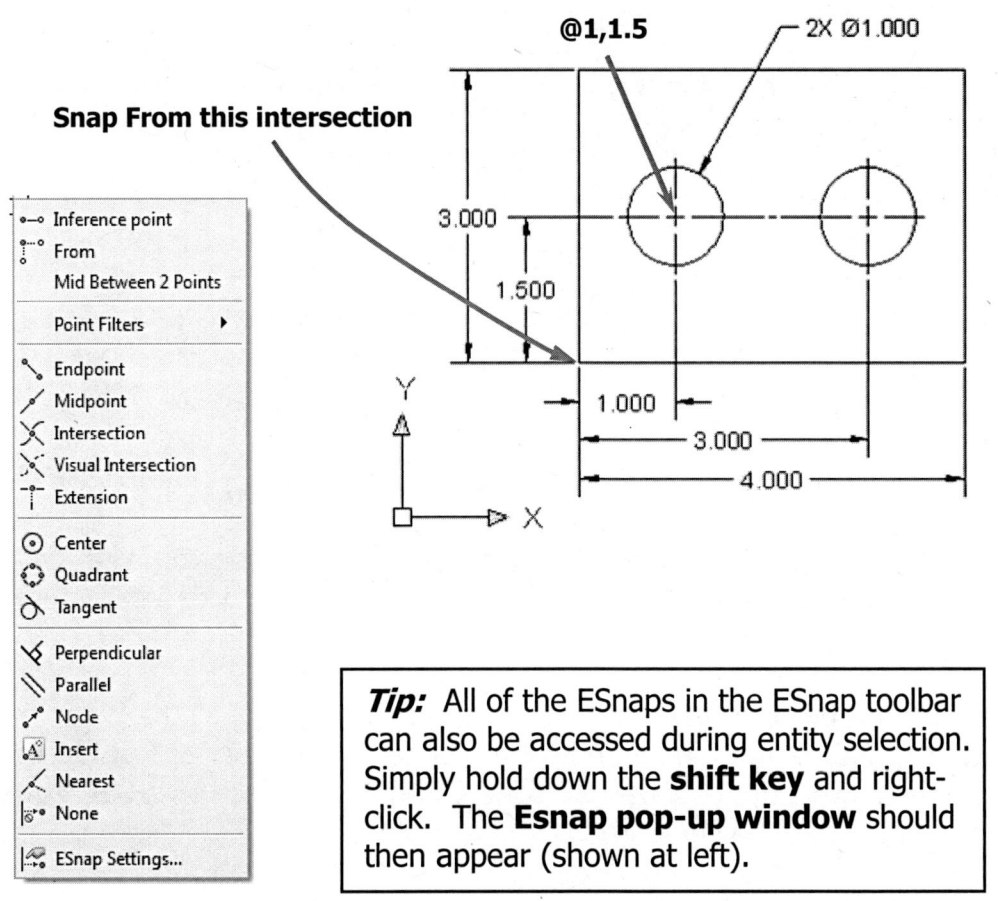

**Tip:** All of the ESnaps in the ESnap toolbar can also be accessed during entity selection. Simply hold down the **shift key** and right-click.  The **Esnap pop-up window** should then appear (shown at left).

## Snap and Grid

**Snap** and **Grid** are normally used together for precision drawing, but with some limitations. They are used for creating entities that require a set spacing between them, and for creating isometric views of objects.

1. Start a **New** drawing. In the **status bar** toggle the **Snap** and **Grid** buttons on. You should notice two things: The drawing area is filled with dots (this is the **grid**), and the crosshairs jump from dot to dot as you move around the drawing area (this is **snap**). If you get a message in the command window that reads "grid to dense to display" then **Zoom** in until it appears

2. Like we did with ESnap, right-click on either the **Snap** or **Grid** buttons and activate the **Settings**. The *Options* window should appear.

3. Set the spacing to **2"**. Check both the "Match Grid spacing" and "Match horizontal spacing" boxes. Select **OK** to exit the *Options* window.

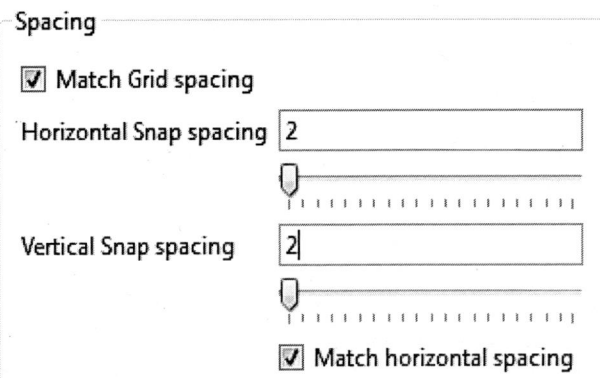

4. **Zoom** out until you see the end of the grid. This defines the drawing **boundary** (currently 12" x 9", or roughly an A-size paper). You can draw outside of the boundary but there won't be a grid to guide you. Let's change the drawing boundary so you can draw something large, like a bathroom vanity.

5. Select **Drawing Boundary** from the **Format** Menu. Leave the lower left corner at **0,0**. Press **Enter**, and set the upper right corner at **96,72**. This sets the drawing up to plot at 1/8 scale on an A-Size piece of paper. **Zoom** out until you see the entire grid.

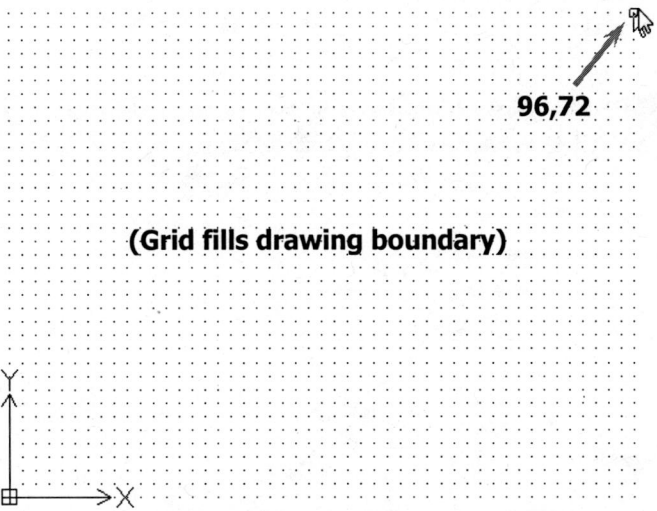

(Grid fills drawing boundary)

96,72

6. On your own, draw the vanity shown below. Use the **2" Grid** and **Snap** as your guide. The door and drawer bevels can be made with a ½" offset. **Save** the drawing as "**Vanity.dwg**" when you're done.

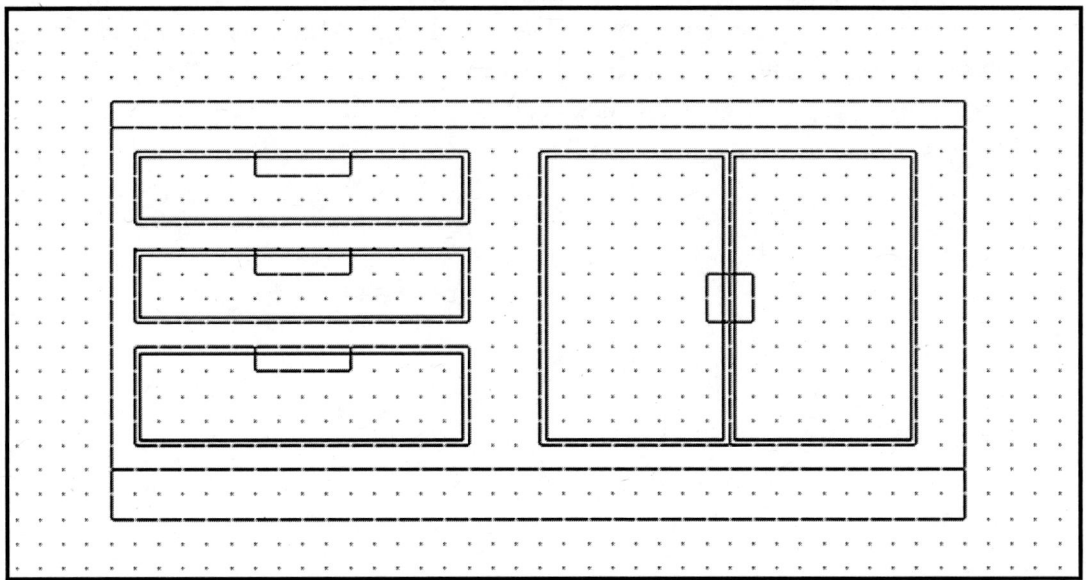

7. Finally, we'll briefly look at **isometric drawing** using **Grid** and **Snap**. Start a **New** drawing. Toggle-on **Snap** and **Grid** in the **status bar**. Right-click on the **Grid** button and select **Settings** from the pop-up menu. Change the *Orientation* to **Isometric**, check the "Match Snap spacing" box, and set the spacing to **.25**. Select the **OK** button to exit.

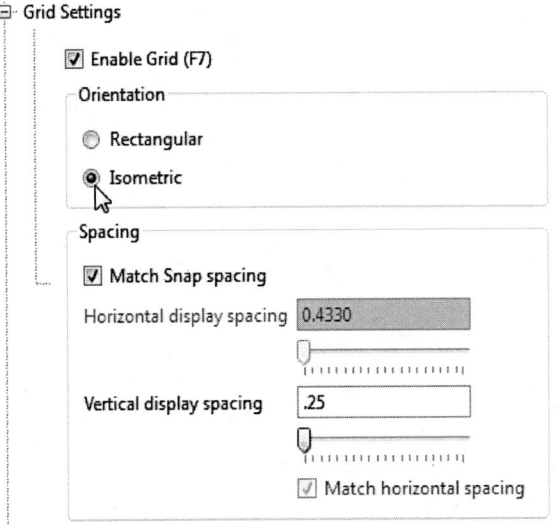

8. Initiate the **Line** command. Note the layout of the grid, and the shape of the crosshairs. Now toggle the **F5 key** repeatedly while observing the crosshairs and the command window. Note the crosshairs adjust to accommodate drawing in the three different isometric planes. On your own, create the isometric drawing shown below. Use the .25" grid as your guide. Switch between the **Top**, **Left** and **Right** planes as needed. **Save** the drawing as "**Clevis.dwg**" (Hint: Use **Ellipse** with the **Isocircle** option to draw the holes).

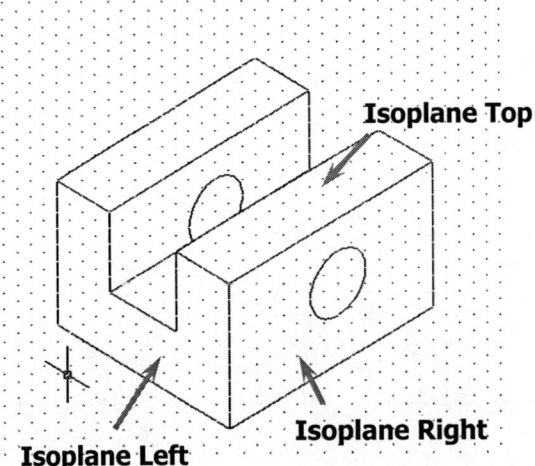

## Chapter 7 Suggested Learning Exercises

Continue the project started in Ch. 6.

### *Mechanical Project (Pocket Tool)-*

Open Pocket Tool.dwg and create the following objects to size using the provided dimensions.

**1. Phillips Screwdriver**

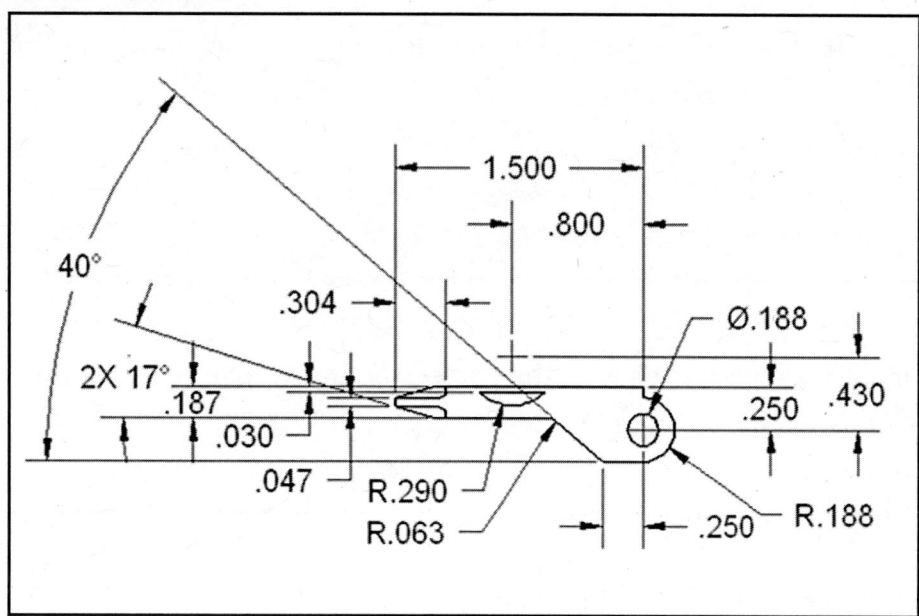

**2. Can Opener**

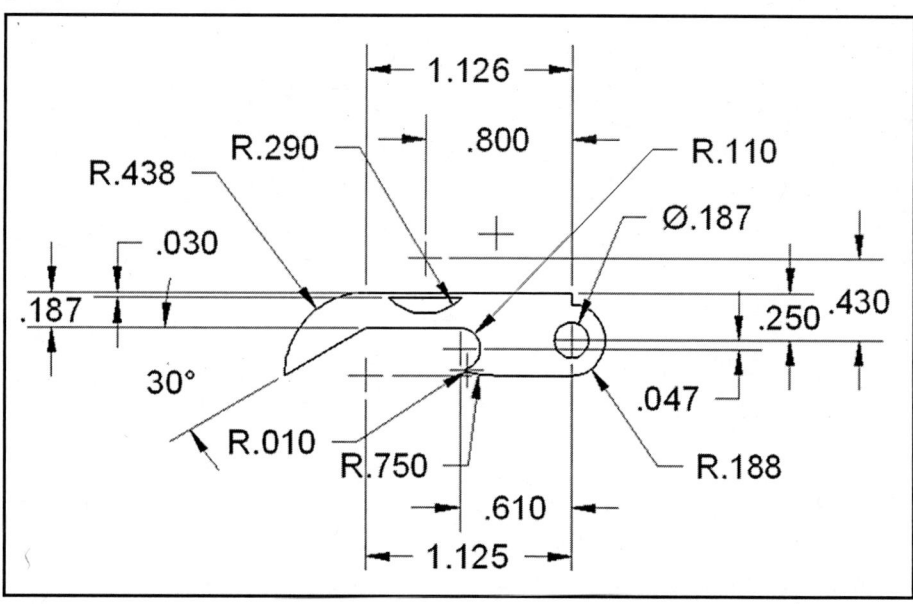

### 3. Plier Nose

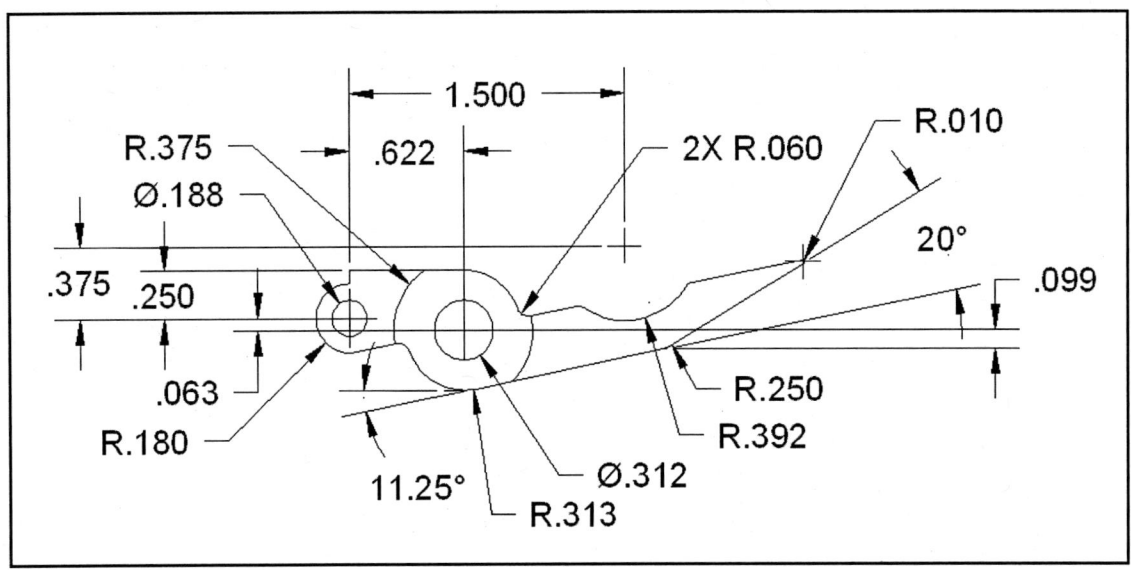

4. Create an isometric view of the Large Flat Screwdriver from Ch. 6. Use a **.063" Isometric Grid** as a guide.

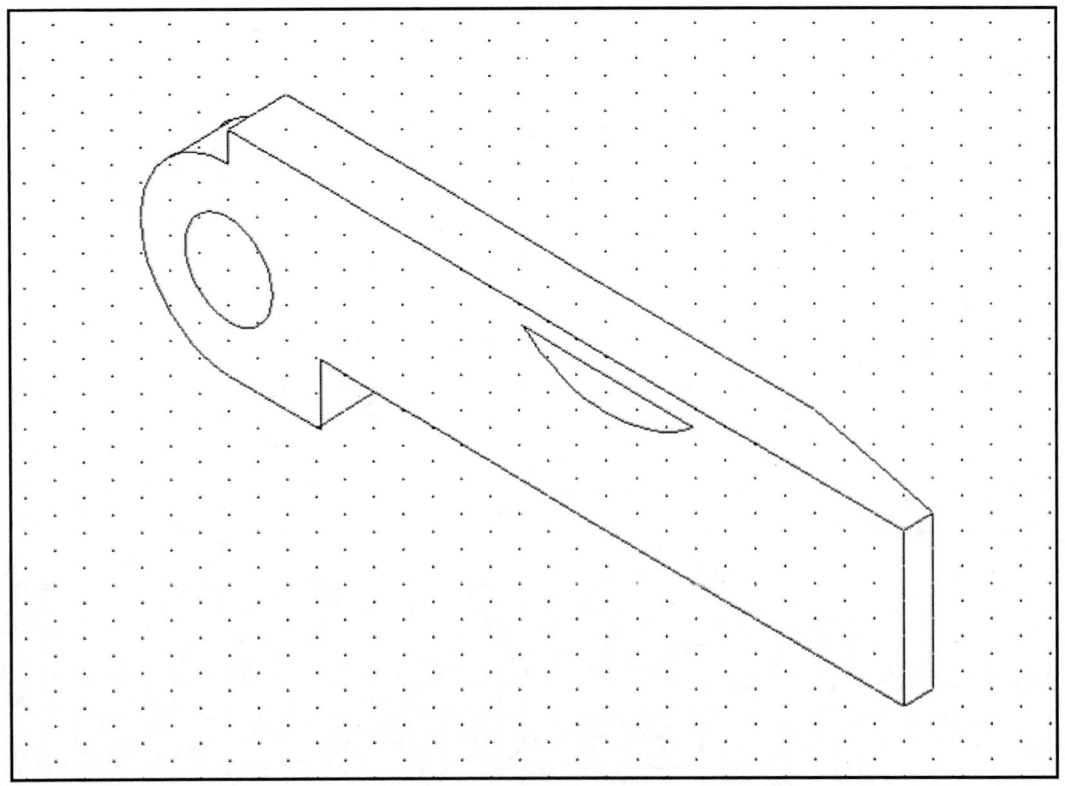

## *Architectural Project (Garage)-*

1. Open Garage.dwg. Draw the electrical symbols shown below using a **2' Grid** to help place them.

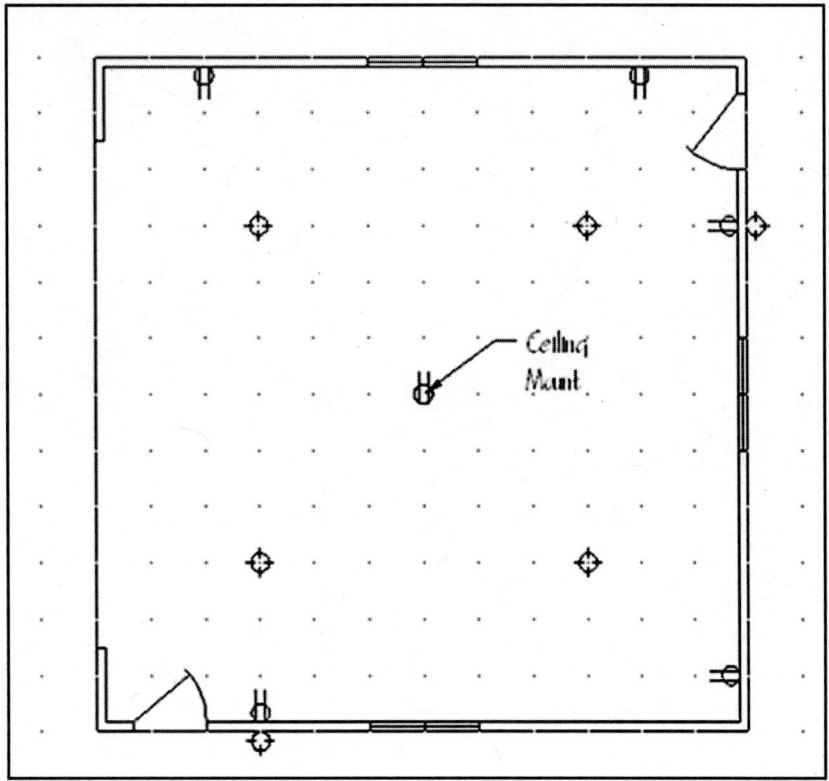

2. Using the dimensions given in Ch. 6 as a guide, create an isometric view of the garage on a **1' Isometric Grid**. Roof pitch is 5-12 with a 4" fascia.

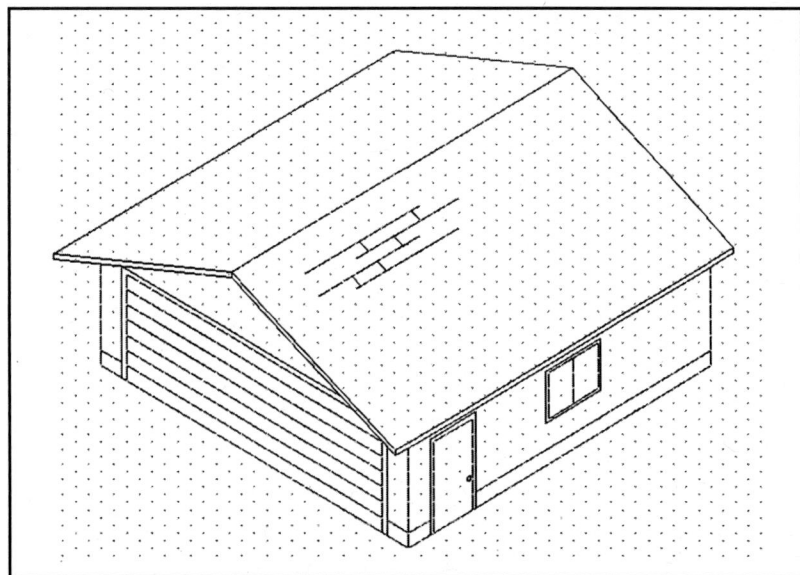

**NOTES:**

**NOTES:**

## Chapter 8- Drawing Management

Objectives:

1. Create layers by line type and color
2. Manage layer display and protection
3. Change the layer an entity resides on
4. Create multiple views using construction lines and layers

## Layers and LineStyles

DraftSight uses layers to manage objects and line types within your drawing. Think of layers as a stack of transparencies (as the **Layers Manager** icon suggests). They can be "added" or "removed" from the stack by turning them on and off. In mechanical drawing, layers are usually assigned by line type: object, hidden, center, phantom, etc. For architectural drawings, layers are more object-oriented: walls, footings, electrical, plumbing, cabinets, etc. Let's create some layers in the drawing of the Clevis.

1. **Open** Clevis.dwg from the previous chapter. Select the **Layers Manager** icon in the **Standard** toolbar. The *Layers Manager* window should appear. Reference the graphic on the next page.

2. Select the **New Layer** icon. DraftSight creates a new layer. Replace its default name ("Layer1") with the word "**Object**". Leave the color and LineStyle as is: **White** and **Continuous**.

3. Create another layer called "**Hidden**". Change the color to **blue** by clicking on the color patch, then choose **blue** from the available colors. Set the LineStyle to **Hidden** by clicking in the *LineStyle* field. If hidden isn't available, select "other" to open the *Line Style* window. Now click on the **Load** icon and load it from the *Load LineStyles* window.

4. On your own, make four additional layers: Center (gray & center), Dimension (red & continuous), and Phantom (green & phantom). Upon completion, be sure and select the **OK** button at the bottom of the *Layers Manager* window. We'll use these layers in a minute. These steps are reviewed in the graphic on the next page.

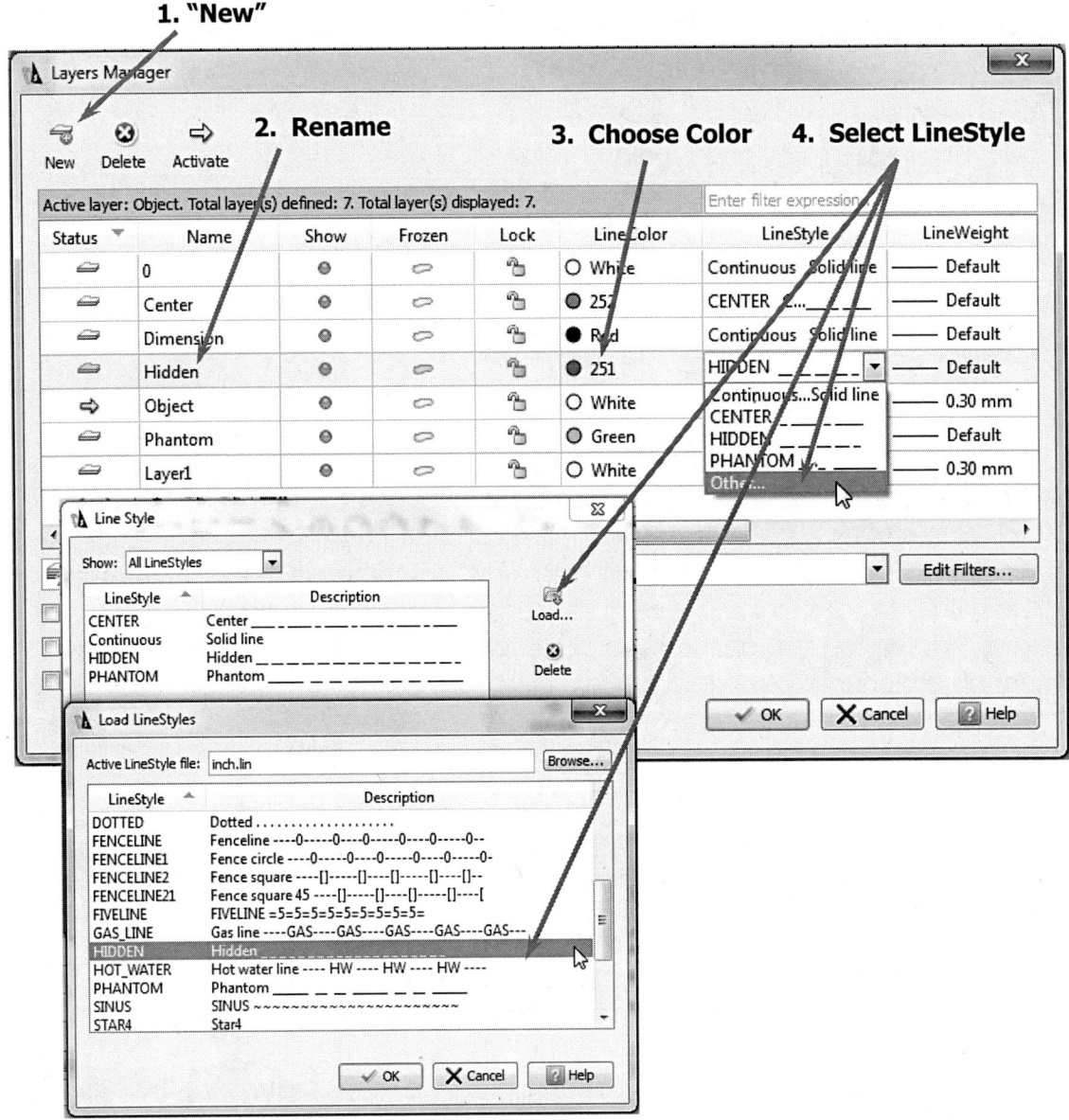

5. **Save** the drawing. Notice the current layer is displayed in the **Layers** toolbar. Anything you draw at this point will be placed on the current layer, and will inherit that layer's color and line style. You can change the current layer by clicking on the arrow next to the current layer and selecting a different one from the list (see graphic on next page).

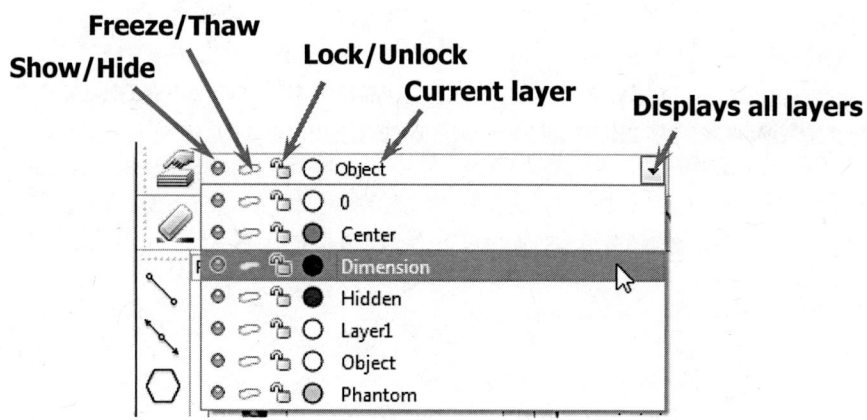

6. The symbols to the left of each layer name mean the following:

- **Show/Hide** – Hiding a layer removes it from view. Useful for managing large drawings like house plans. Also useful for hiding construction lines.
- **Freeze/Thaw**- Similar to Show/Hide, but entities on frozen layers are not only invisible, but also protected from being edited.
- **Lock/Unlock**- Locked layers are protected from any kind of modification. Once a layer is locked, entities cannot be added or edited on that layer.

Note in the *Layers Manager* window there are other options as well. For example: LineWeight, PrintStyle and whether or not a layer will print.

7. The fastest way to move entities from one layer to another is to select the entity(s), then pick the new layer from the list in the **Layer** toolbar. Using a **Selection Window** (with no command active), select the clevis. All the entities should be highlighted with the EntityGrips active. On the **Layer** toolbar, click the drop-down list and select the **Object** layer.

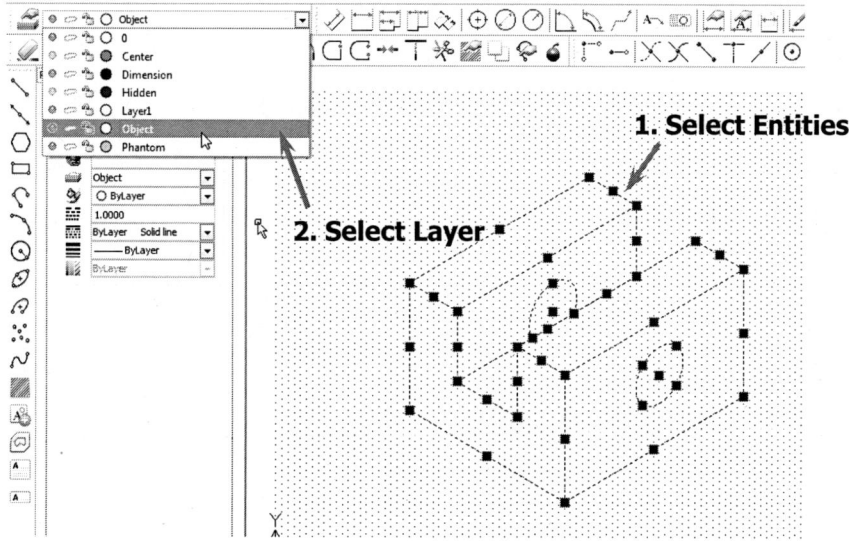

8. On your own, switch to the **Hidden** layer and draw hidden lines in the isometric view of the Clevis to show the hidden edges of the object. Switch to the **Center** layer and create a center line through the hole in the side of the Clevis.  Your drawing should look like the one below:

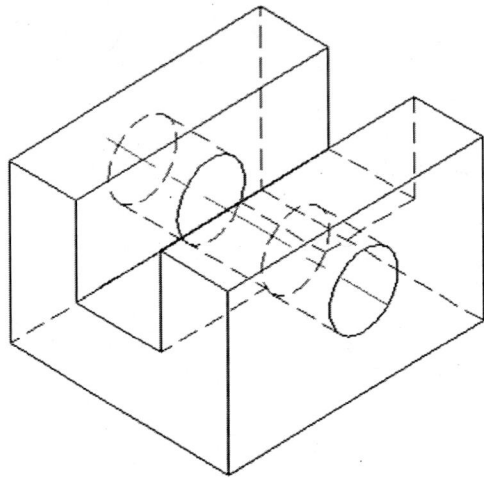

9. If you want to preserve these layers for future use, **Delete** the drawing of the clevis and save the drawing as "Mechanical**.dwt**" (instead of .dwg). This creates a template of your own making. The next time you start a new mechanical drawing use **Mechanical.dwt** (instead of standard.dwt), and the layers you just created will be present and ready to go.

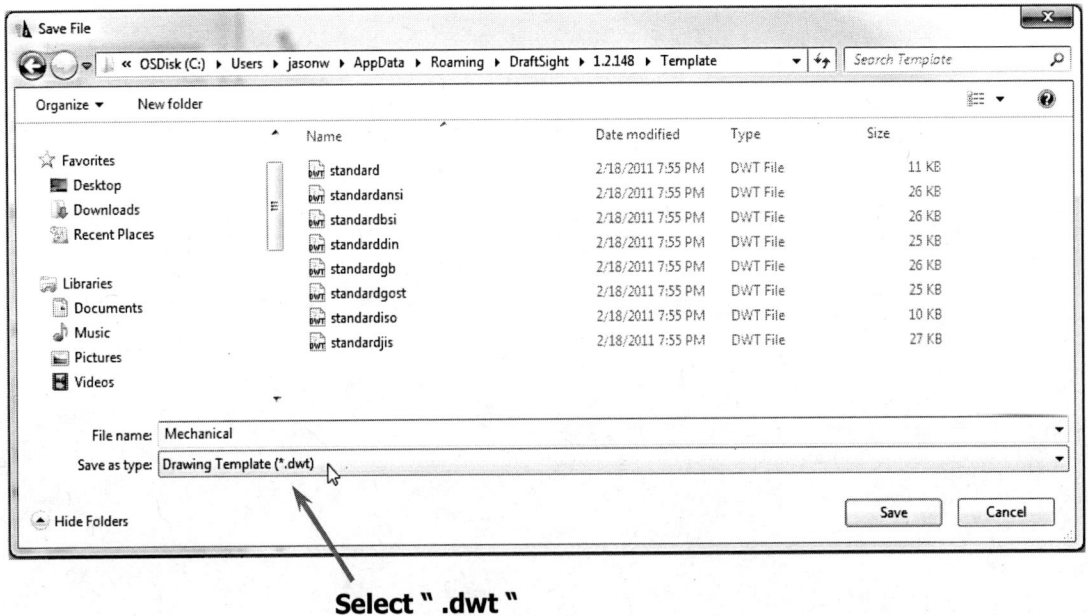

Select " .dwt "

## Using Construction Lines for Multi-View Drawings

As you are aware, 2D drafting has a fundamental problem:  **Nothing in the real world is two-dimensional!**  A couple of the ways drafters compensate are by drawing isometric views (as in the example on the previous page), or more often by creating multiple views of objects to show features in the third dimension.  The later is based on the principals of **orthographic projection**. While it is not in the scope of this text to teach orthographic projection, we will cover some of DraftSight's tools used to create multi-view drawings. Study the figure below, a multi-view drawing of the clevis done previously, with the isometric view retained at half-scale for reference:

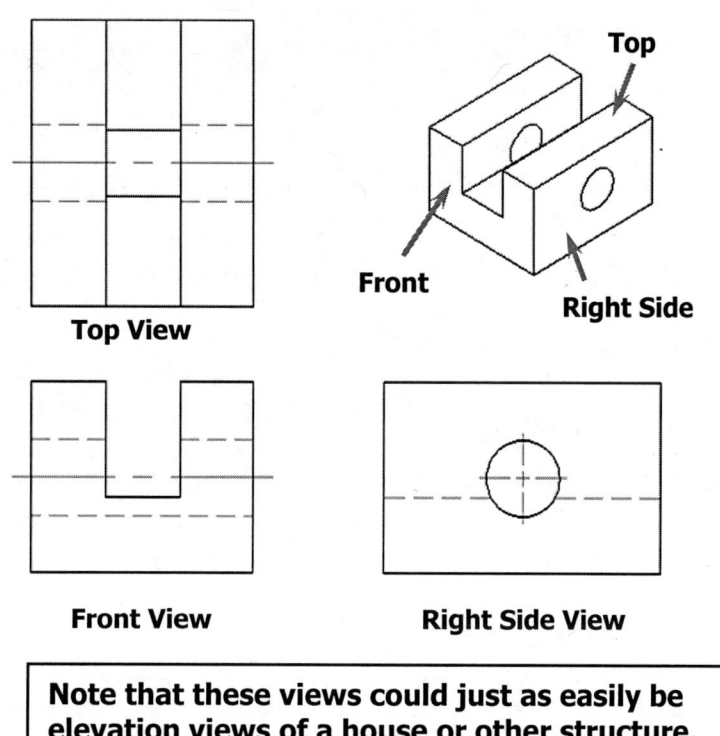

Top View

Top

Front

Right Side

Front View

Right Side View

Note that these views could just as easily be elevation views of a house or other structure.

Notice several things:

1. How the views are aligned with each other.
2. The center and hidden lines that represent round and hidden features, respectively.
3. The ability to show greater detail in the multi-views vs. the isometric view.
4. The logic of the orthographic layout:  The right side view is to the right of the front view, while the top view is above the front view (this is commonly called 3rd-angle projection and is used for drawings in the U.S.).

How was this multi-view drawing created using DraftSight? Several methods you've already learned could be employed to keep the views aligned, including **Snap** and **Grid**. However, each has its limitations. A more versatile method is to use the **Line** (or **Infinite Line**) command to create construction lines to be used as guides to align drawing views. Let's give it a try:

1. **Open** Clevis.dwg (if it isn't already open). **Move** the isometric view up and out of the way. Using the dimensions on the drawing below, create the front view in the lower left-hand portion of the drawing area on the **Object** layer.

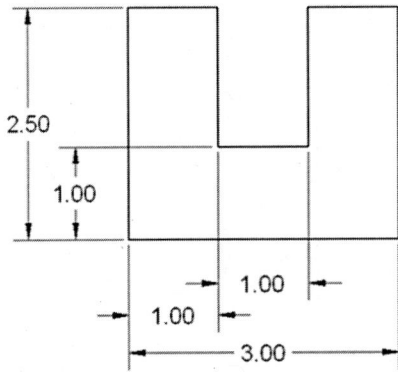

2. Switch to the **0 layer**. Click on the **Infinite Line** icon in the **Draw** toolbar. As the name suggests, infinite lines have no beginning or end, just a midpoint which is used to place them. Using **ESnap**, place a construction line at the lower right-hand corner of the front-view. For the "next position", turn on **Ortho** and click to the right side of the view. Place two more horizontal construction lines at each intersection.

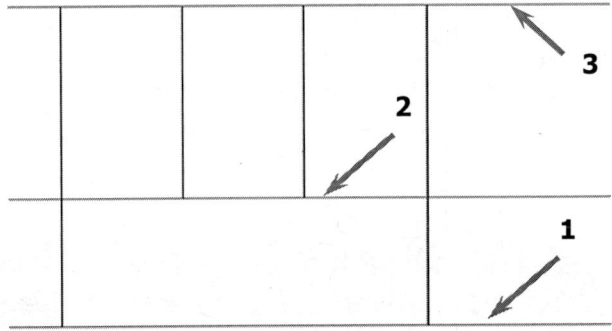

3. Using the construction lines as a guide and the dimensions given below, create the right-side view of the clevis. Hint: Use **offset** to make the vertical lines.

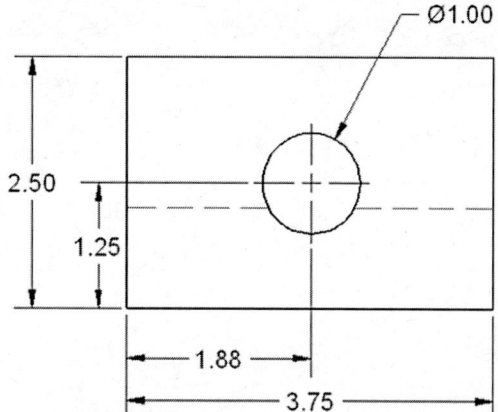

4. Draw a "fold line" at 45 degrees with its endpoints positioned directly above the right-side view you just created. Run vertical infintie lines from the right-side view to the fold line (see below). Run horizontal construction lines from each intersection along the fold line.

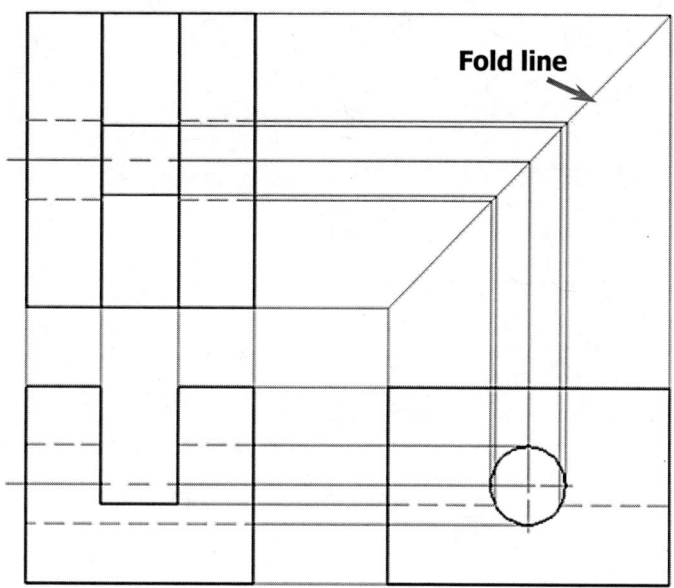

5. Finally, return to the front view. Run vertical infinite lines from each intersection. The top view is formed where these lines meet the horizontal lines coming from the fold line. Trace-over or **trim** the infinite lines (thus turning them into regular lines) at the applicable intersections in order to create the top view. Use the appropriate layers for the hidden and center lines. **Hide** the **0 Layer** in order to remove the remaining construction lines from view. **Save** the drawing.

## Chapter 8 Suggested Learning Exercises

Continue your Unit 2 Project...

### *Mechanical Project (Pocket Tool)-*

**Open** Pocket Tool.dwg. Create layers for **hidden** and **center** lines. Make a side and top view for each of the objects shown below. Do not dimension.

> *Tip:* If the hidden and centerlines don't appear as such, type "**SETGBLLSCL**" in the command window and try a value like **.5** for the scale factor.

### 1. Large Flat Screwdriver

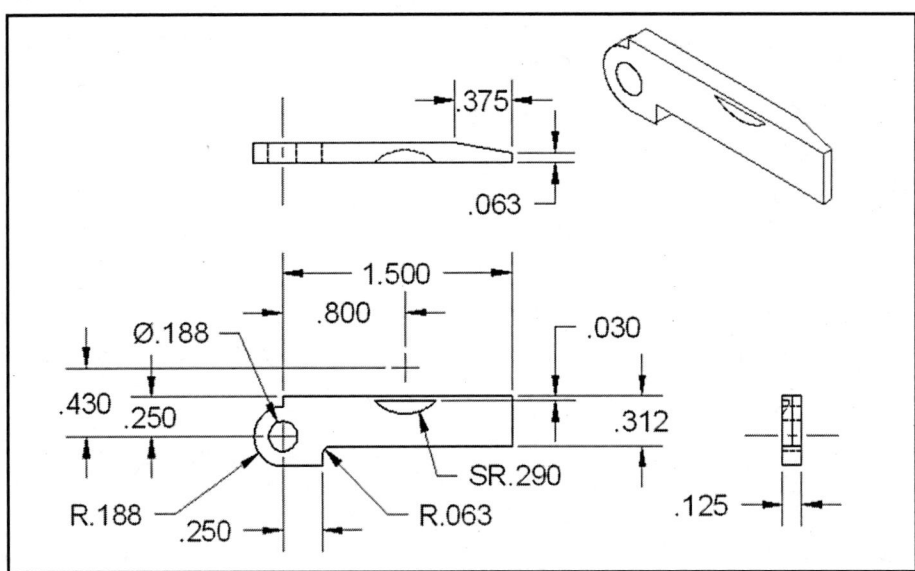

### 2. Phillips Screwdriver

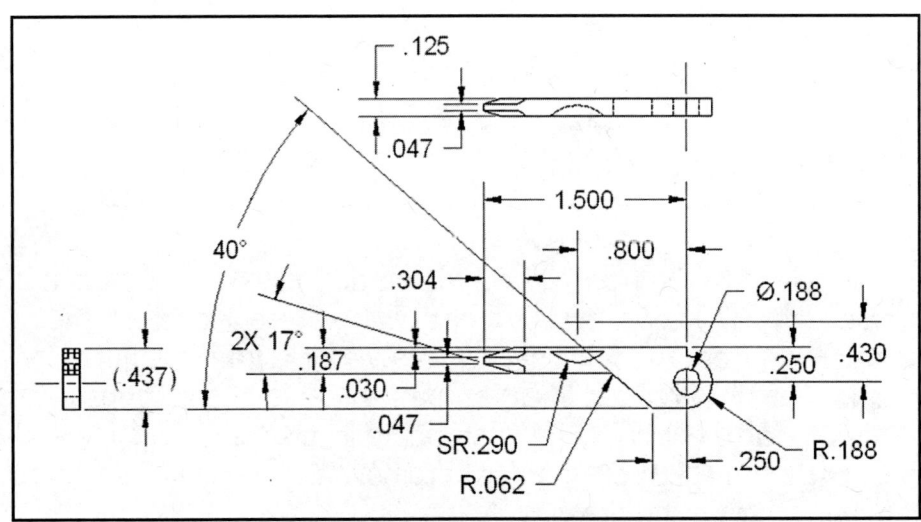

## *Architectural Project (Garage)-*

**Open** Garage.dwg.  Create a **hidden** layer for the footings and foundation.
Draw at least two elevation views of the garage as shown below.  When finished,
**rotate** the front elevation and place it next to the side one.  Do not dimension.

> *Tip:* If the hidden lines are too dense to actually appear as hidden, type
> "**SETGBLLSCL**" in the command window and try a value like **20** for the scale.

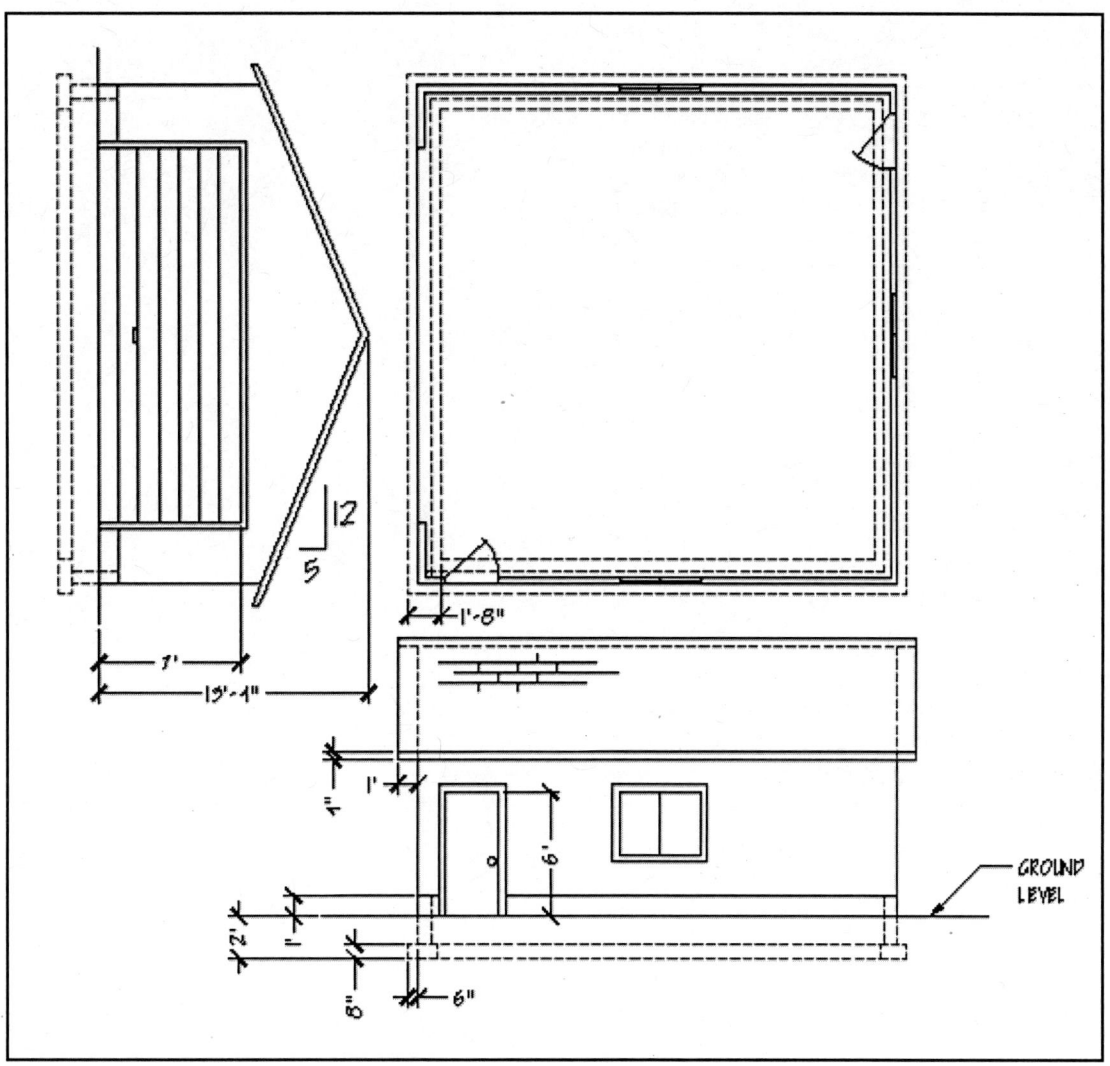

**NOTES:**

## Chapter 9- Creating Annotations

Objectives:
1. Create and edit text
2. Utilize spell checker
3. Set-up a text style
4. Create hatching
5. Place notes using the leader command

DraftSight has its own built-in word processor for placing notes on drawings and entering data in title blocks. It also has the ability to cross-hatch objects with various patterns for material identification.

## Creating text

1. Start a **New** drawing using the standard template. Select the **SimpleNote** icon from the **Draw toolbar**.

2. The *Insert SimpleNote* window should appear. Here you enter text, specify the insertion point for the text, the style, angle and size. Enter "This text was created using SimpleNote" in the *Text:* field. Select the "OK" button when finished.

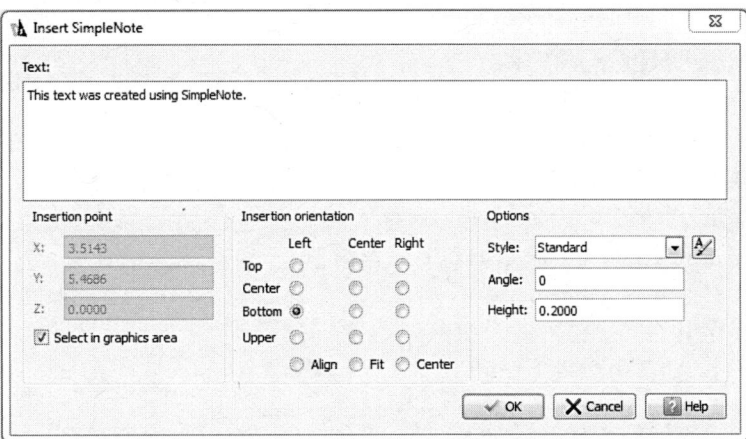

3. If "Select in graphics area" was checked for the **Insertion Point**, DraftSight will now have you place the text using your crosshairs. Click anywhere.

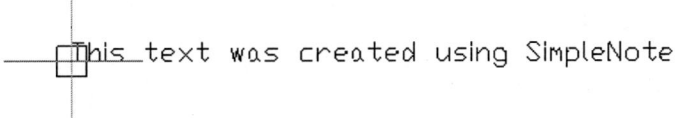

4. Note the default text height was .2". The minimum (and most common) text height for drafting standards is 1/8". Double-click on the text you just created. The *Edit SimpleNote* window should appear. Change the **Height** to **.125"**. Also Change the word "created" to "creeted" and choose OK.

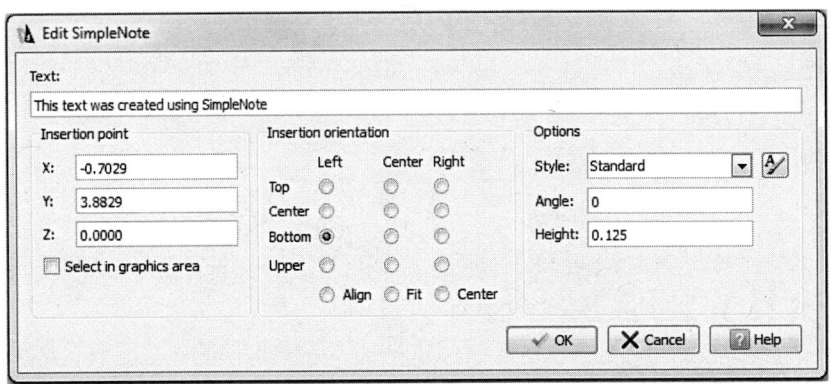

---

***Tip:*** To calculate minimum text height for drawings to be plotted at a scale, multiply the reciprocal of the scale by **.125"**. For architectural scales, first convert the units to decimal inches, and then divide the second number by the first to get the reciprocal. Multiply by .125" as before. Examples follow:
Scale is 1:4, the Reciprocal=4/1, and 4 X .125= **.5"** text
Scale is 1/4"=1' (or .25"=12") the reciprocal=12/.25 (or 48), 48 X .125= **6"** text

---

5. Enter "**SPELLCHECK**" in the command window. When prompted to **specify entities**, select the text you created. The *Spell Check* window should appear and suggested the correct spelling for the misspelled word "creeted". Select "created" from the list and the **Change** button. Next, DraftSight may recognize "SimpleNote" as a misspelled word. In this case select the **Ignore** button. Verify DraftSight corrected the spelling.

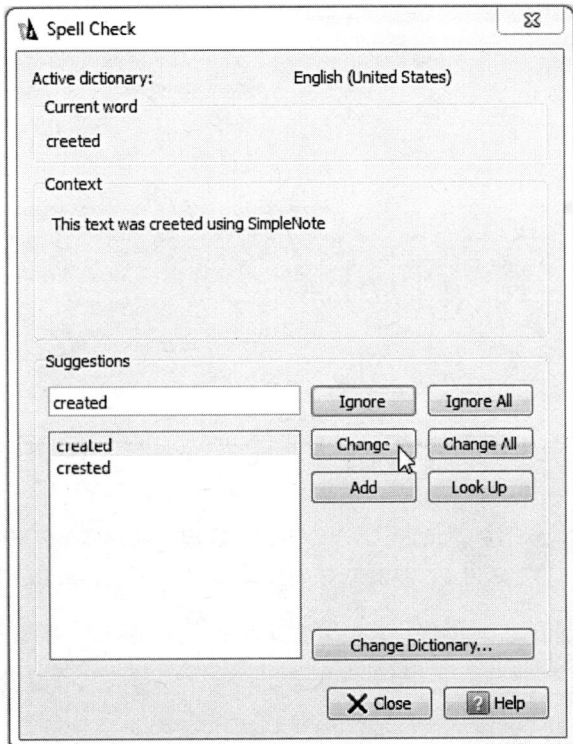

6. On your own, experiment with the **Note** command.  Upon initiating the command, the user specifies a **first** and **second corner**, creating a box where the text will fit inside.  Also, the ***Edit Note*** window has many more options, including: bold, italics, underline, justification, etc., almost like a mini-word processor.

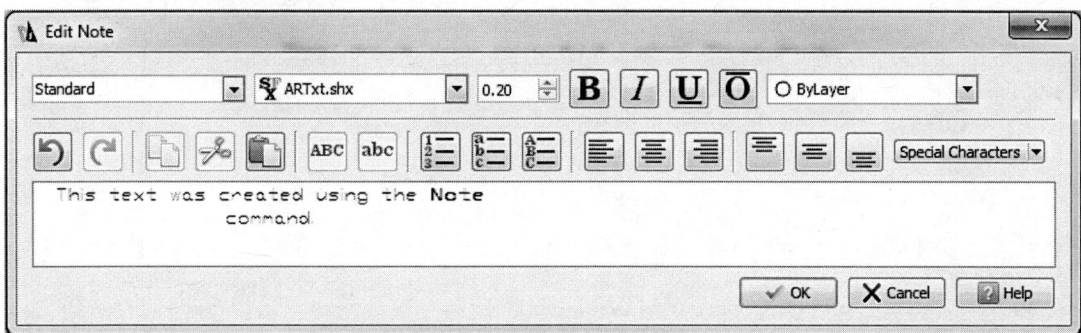

7. If you left-click once on text created with the **Note** command, the entity grips will highlight.  The text box can be adjusted by clicking on the entity grips and dragging them to a new location.

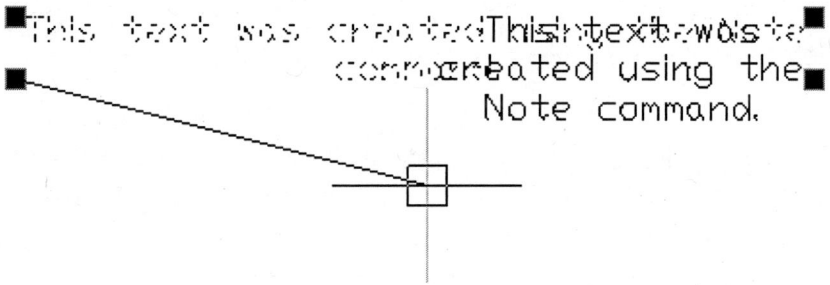

## Text Styles

You may have noticed that the text we entered is, well...kind of weak.  This is DraftSight's default style.  Let's set up a new text style with a bold, easier-to read-appearance.

1. Go to the **Format** menu and select **Text Style**. The ***Options*** window should open to Drafting Styles and Text.  Click on the **New** button next to **Style:** and create a new style called "**ArialBold**".  Also choose **Arial** from the **Font:** list and **Bold** from the **Format:** list.  Note the **Preview** window in the upper-right corner. Be sure and click the **OK** button to close.  Reference the graphic on the next page for help.

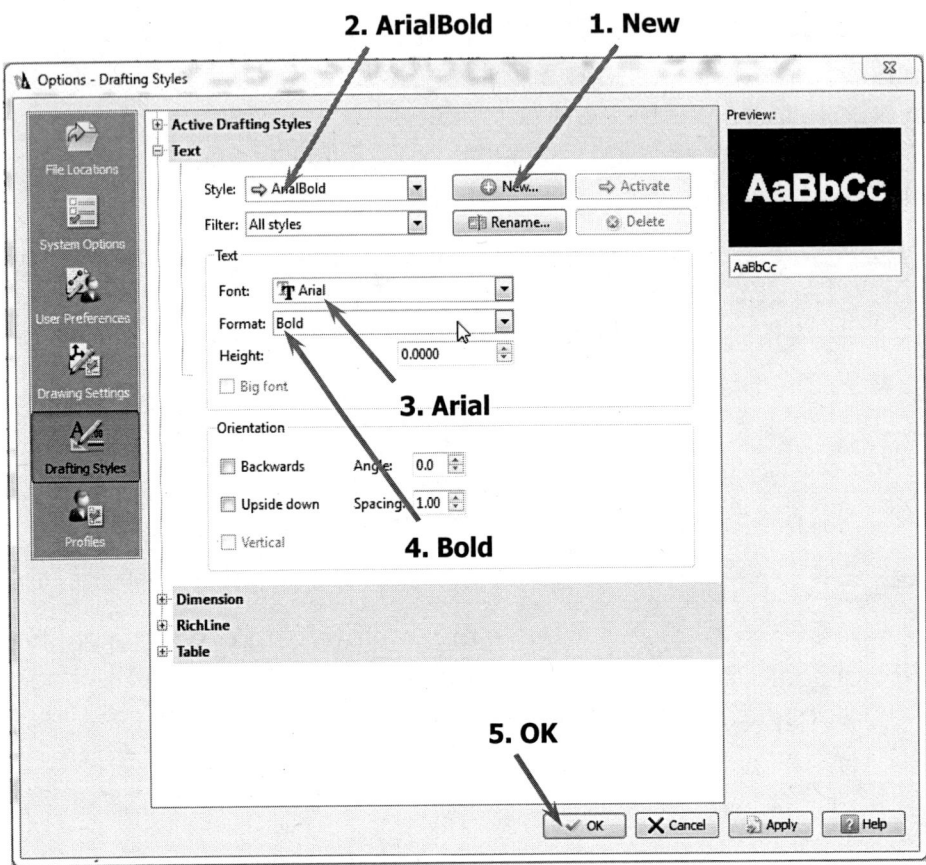

2. Select the **Note** icon in the **Draw toolbar**. After specifying a text box, and once the *Edit Note* window appears, choose the style **ArialBold** we created. On your own and using random text of your choice, experiment with **Justification** and inserting **Special Characters**.

3. If you want to edit text created with the **Note** command, simply double-click on it and the *Edit Note* window will reappear.

# Hatching

The main use for hatch patterns in drafting is to distinguish the materials an object is made of. Typically this is done in a section or "cut-away" view. With architectural drawings hatch patterns are also used to show materials and foliage in elevation views and landscape plans.

1. **Open** Pie Chart.dwg that we created in Chapter 5 (if you can't find it, take a minute and re-draw it). The most common mistake in hatching is not having a totally enclosed area to hatch. **Zoom** in on each corner of the Pie Chart and ensure the lines are touching, otherwise the hatch will fail.

2. Locate and select the **Hatch** icon in the **Draw** toolbar. The *Hatch/Fill* window should appear.

3. The first thing to do is **Specify Points** (or **Specify Entities** can be used if picking a single closed entity like a circle or rectangle). The *Hatch/Fill* window will temporarily dismiss so you can select a point internal to an object. Select the larger portion of the pie chart (Note that DraftSight analyzes the object and highlights it) Press **Enter** to return to the *Hatch* window.

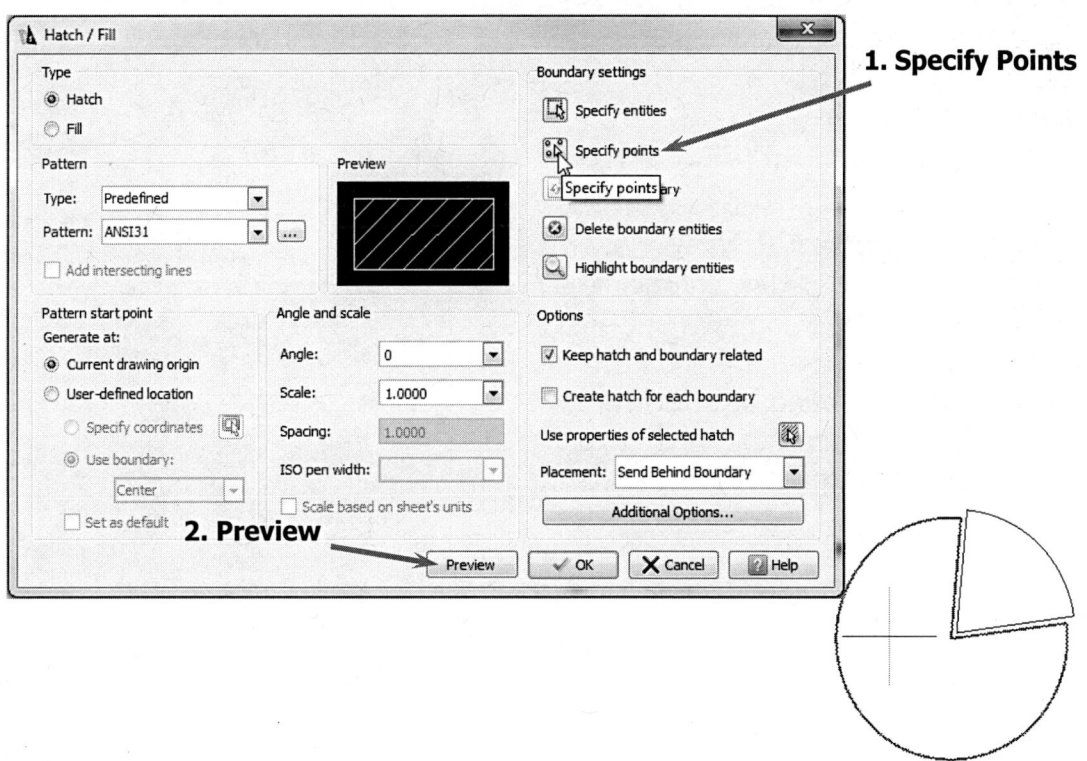

4. Press the **Preview** button. The scale (or density) of the hatch depends on the size of your pie chart. Note the command window; you may either press the **Escape** key to return to the *Hatch/Fill* window or right-click to accept the current hatch. Press **Escape** and adjust the **Scale:** until your pie chart looks similar to the one below:

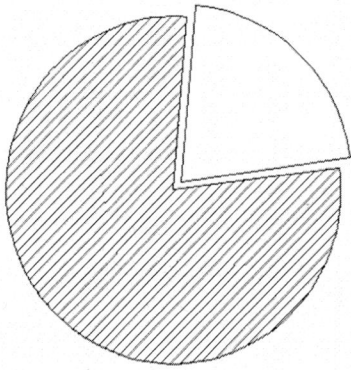

5. The hatch pattern can be modified by clicking on Preview patterns icon next to the **Pattern:** drop-down in the *Hatch/Fill* window.

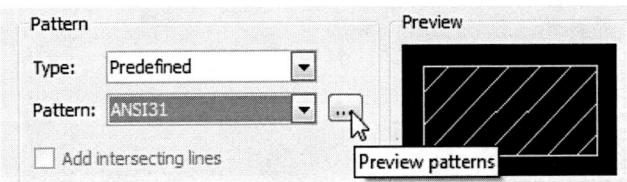

6. The *Select Pattern Style* window will appear. Note the patterns available by selecting the **ANSI** and **ISO** buttons are mechanical in nature, and architectural patterns can be found by selecting the **Sample** and **Custom** buttons. Explore the various patterns that are avaiable.

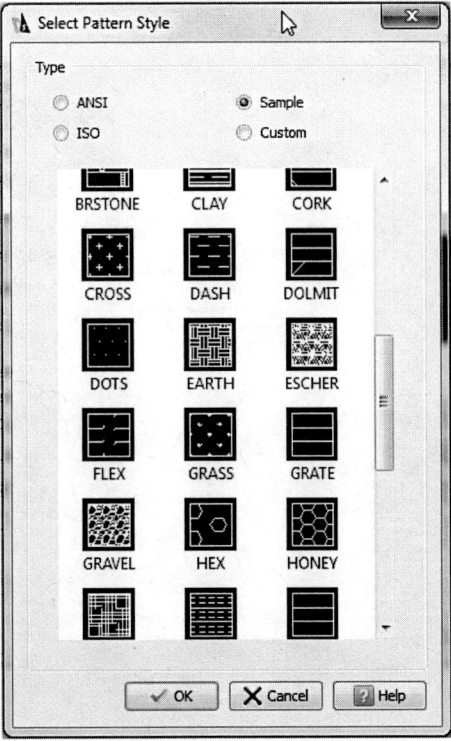

7. On your own, hatch the smaller portion of the pie chart with the **ANSI37** hatch pattern (Note: You can edit the hatch by double-clicking on it). **Save** the drawing. It should look like the one to the right.

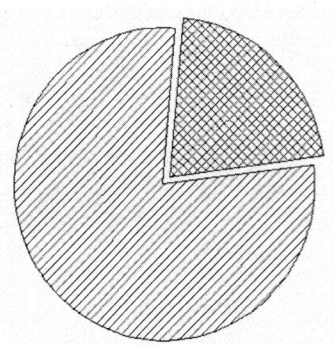

8. Hatch patterns are "associative". This means if you change the size or shape of the object hatched, when done correctly, the pattern will update to fill the new area. Using a **Crossing** window and **entity grips**, stretch the lower right-hand corner of the smaller pie chart. Observe how the hatch pattern automatically adjusts as shown in the drawing to the right. **Undo**.

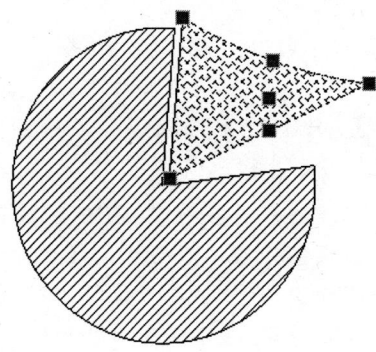

9. Double-click on one of the hatch patterns. Select the **Additional Options** button in the bottom-right corner of the *Hatch/Fill* window. Here you can remove "islands", or areas trapped inside the hatched area that you don't want hatched.

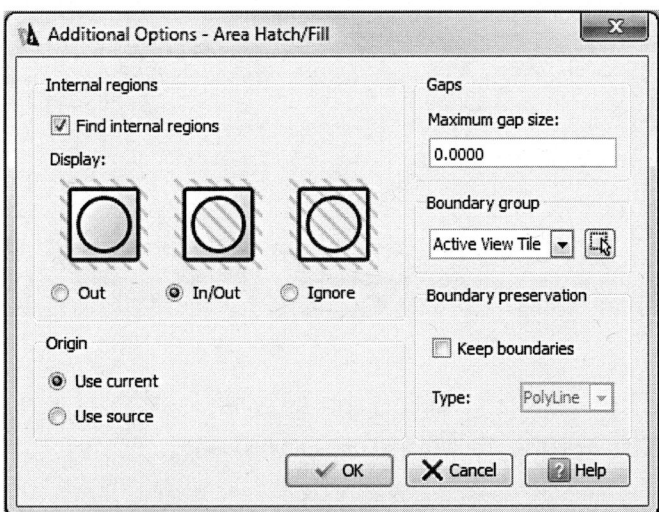

10. Finally, on your own, change the larger portion of the pie chart to the **Hex** pattern and the smaller portion to the **Stars** pattern. Adjust the **scale** so your pie chart resembles the one below. **Save** the drawing.

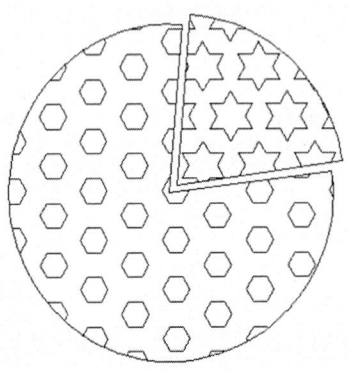

## Leader Notes

Closely related to the text command learned previously in this chapter is the **Leader** command. It is basically a note with an arrow attached to it. Leaders are used to call attention to a specific feature of your drawing.

1. With Pie Chart.dwg open, locate and select the **Leader** icon in the **Dimension** toolbar (to turn on the **Dimension** toolbar, select it from the list that appears when you right click over an existing docked toolbar). Enter "**S**" in the command window for "settings".

2. In the ***Format Leaders*** window, choose the **Arrows/Lines** tab and select **Straight** for the **Leader and line type**. Select **OK**.

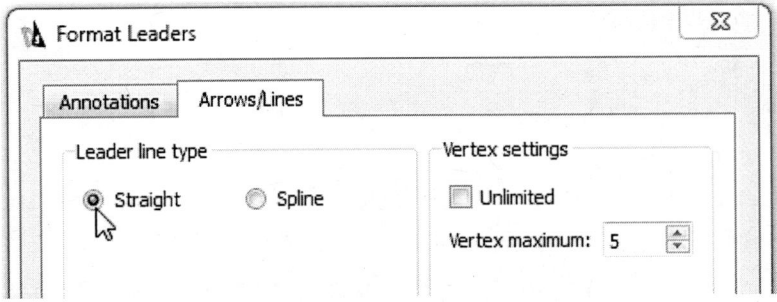

3. For the **start point**, click just inside the smaller (star) portion of the pie chart. It may help to turn off **ESnap** and **Ortho**.

4. For the **next vertex**, go up and to the right at about a 45 degree angle and left-click. For the **next vertex**, turn **Ortho** mode on and go further right and left-click.

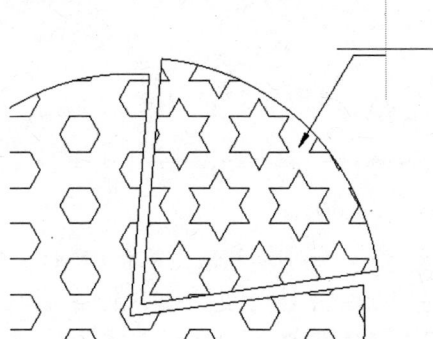

5. When it asks for the text width, press **Enter** to accept the default. Enter "**22% ARCHITECTURAL**" when prompted to **Specify text**. Press **Enter** twice. Now add another leader so it looks like one below.

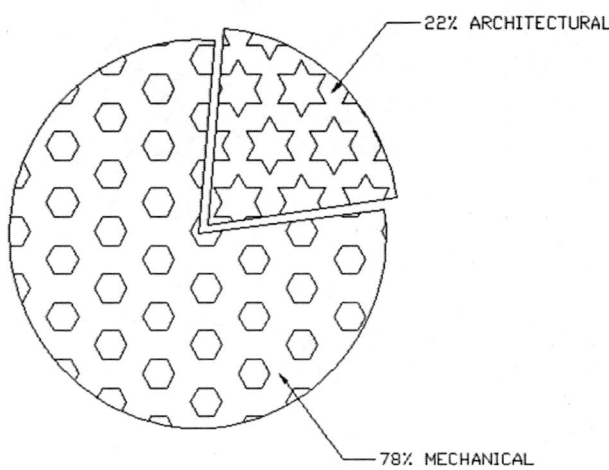

6. On your own, create a new **text style** that uses the "**City Blueprint**" font. Change the "22% ARCHITECTURAL" leader text to this new style. Do this by double-clicking on the text, highlighting it with the cursor in the *Edit Note* window, and selecting the new text style from the pull-down list. The font should change to City Blueprint (reference graphic on next page).

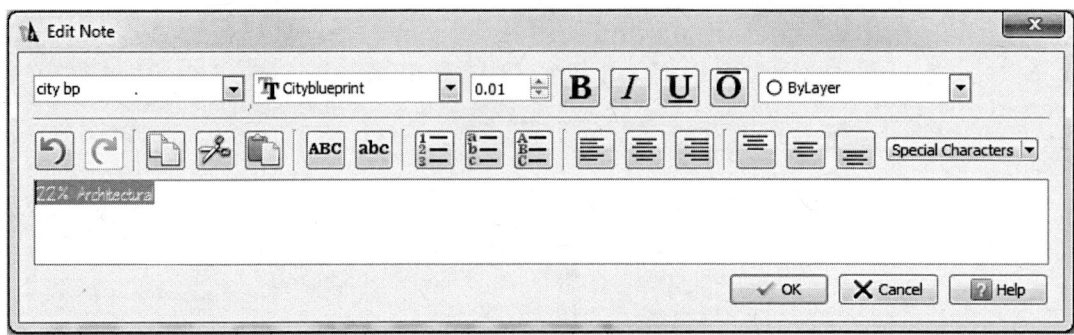

7. Create new **text style** using the "**Arial**" font and change the "78% MECHANICAL" leader text to this style. Add a title to the pie chart using **Arial** and **Note** as shown in the drawing below:

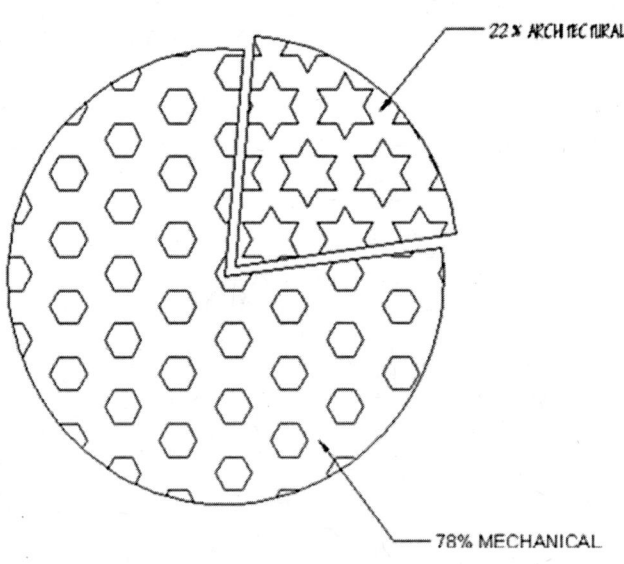

8. On your own, experiment with different leader settings. Find a way to make wavy leader lines like this:

## Chapter 9 Suggested Learning Exercises

Continue your Unit 2 Project...

### *Mechanical Project (Pocket Tool)-*

Open Pocket Tool.dwg and draw the following two items:

1.  Create the drawing views of the **Handle** shown below. Place the text as indicated. Make a new layer called "**Cutting_Plane**" and assign it a **phantom** line style. Create a cutting plane using **Leader** on the new layer. Draw the section view as shown below. **Hatch** the section. Do not dimension.

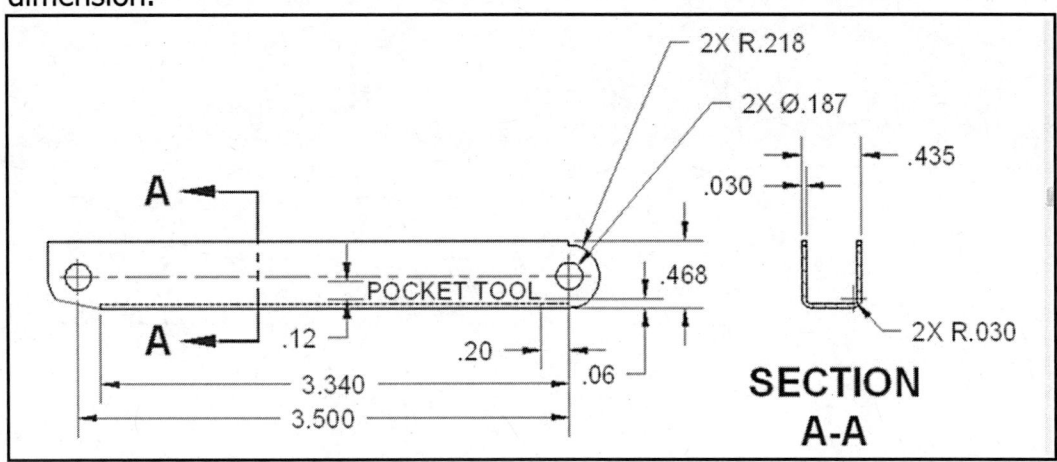

2.  Create the drawing views of the **File** shown below. Use hatch patterns to show the different file markings. Do not dimension, but add the leader notes for the file patterns using the **Leader** command. **Check the spelling**.

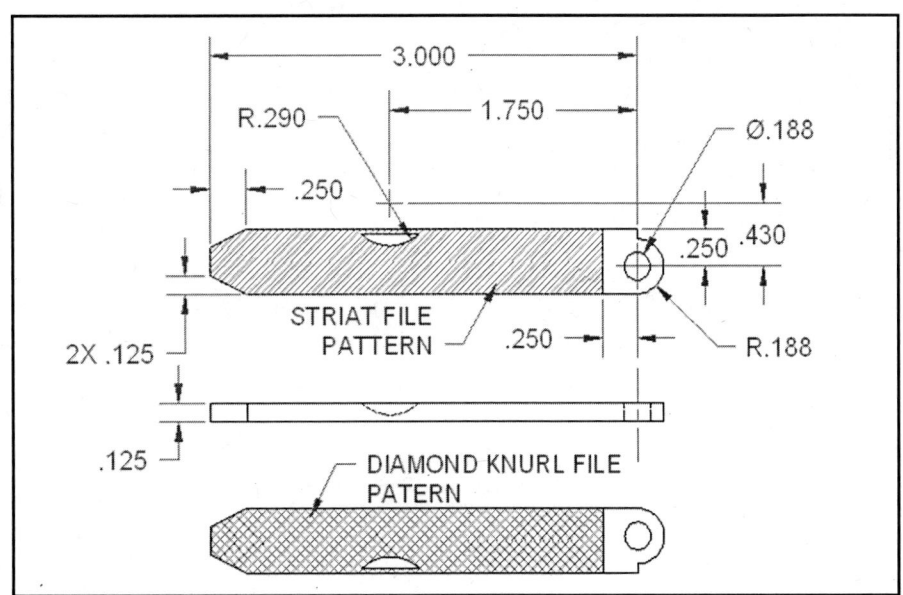

## Architectural Project (Garage)-

Open Garage.dwg.  Make a new layer called "**CuttingPlane**" and assign it a **phantom** line style.  Create a section line on the new layer through the roof, wall and foundation on the plan view as shown. Draw a section view for this cutting plane with accompanying hatches, text and notes near the section line. Do not dimension.

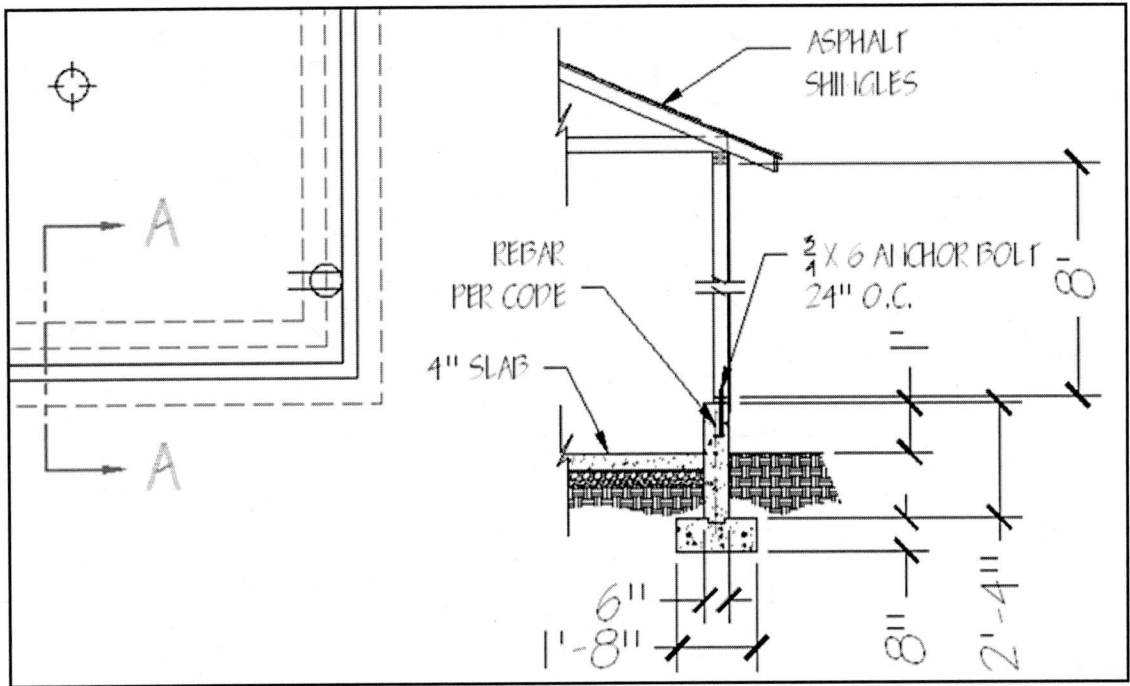

(**Close-up of footing and foundation:** )

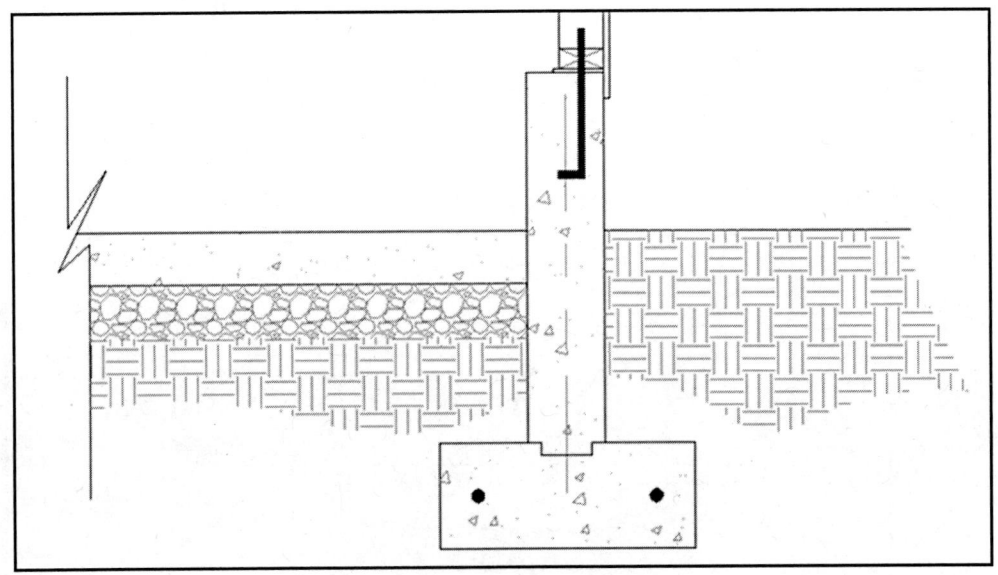

## Chapter 10- Basic Dimensioning

Objectives:
1. Create and edit a dimension style
2. Apply radius and diameter dimensions
3. Apply linear and aligned dimensions
4. Apply angular dimensions
5. Edit dimensions

As stated in the introduction to this text: drafting is a language. Thus far we've learned how to create and edit geometry, set-up drawing views, add notes, and make section views using some of DraftSight's commands. All that remains to complete the communication process it to add dimensions to your drawings. This allows the builder, fabricator or machinist to accurately produce what you designed. We'll start by learning to setup a dimension style based on your dimensioning needs. **Open** Tape Dispenser.dwg from Chapter 7. Activate the **Dimension** toolbar and take note of the icons we'll be using in this chapter:

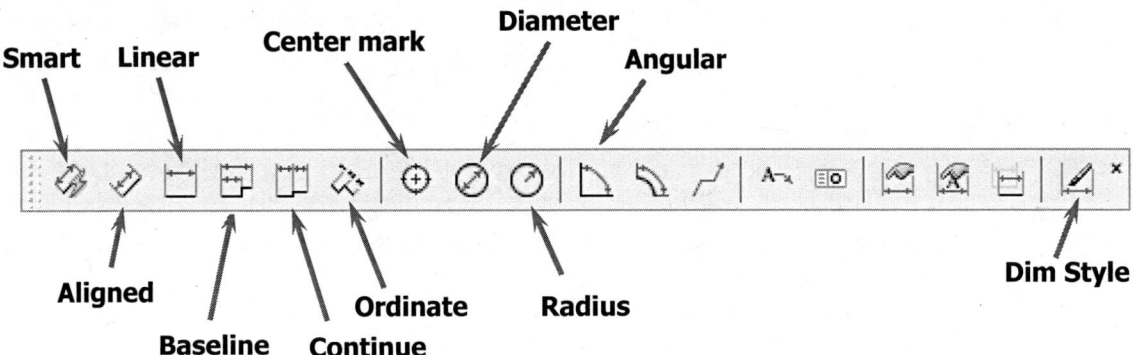

## Dimension Styles

Dimension Styles are used to specify the size and format of your dimensions. It is vital to set them up properly. Dimension Styles save time and can ensure the drawing meets general drafting and corporate standards.

1. Locate and select the **DIMENSIONSTYLE** ("Dim style" for short) icon in the **Dimension** toolbar. The *Options* window should appear in *Drafting Styles* configuration.

2. Note the current style: **Standard**. Also note the preview window. It's kind of hard to see, but displays some of the major attributes of the current style,

such as: Closed arrowheads on the end of the dimension lines, leading zeros on values less than 1, 4-place decimal dimension values, and a simple text font. This default style probably won't meet your needs, so we're going to modify it.

**Preview**

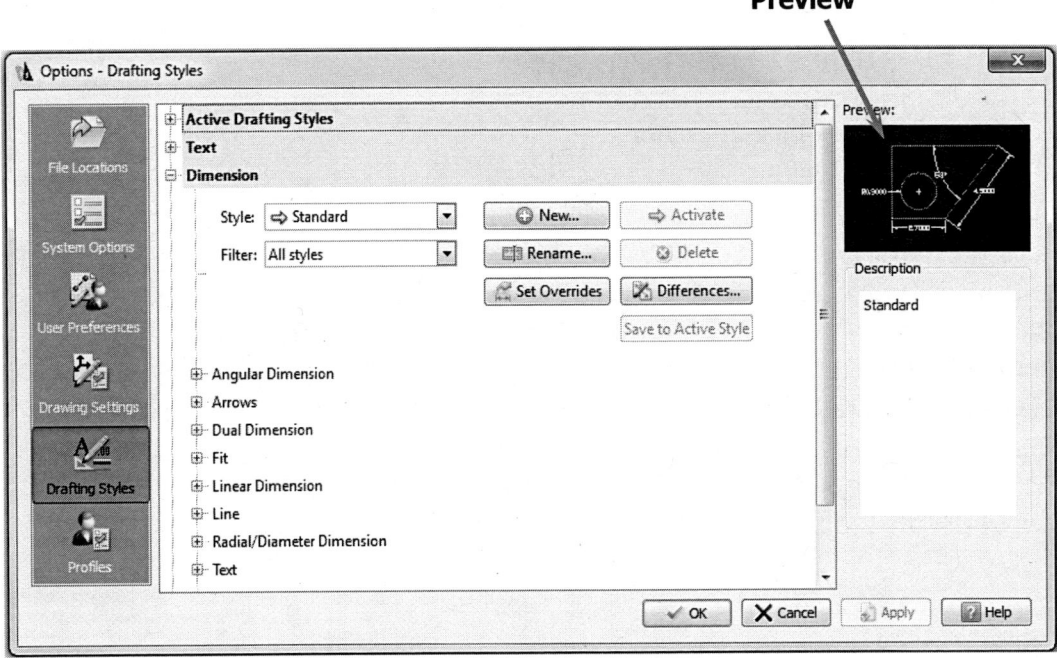

3. There are numerous dimension attributes that can be changed here, but let's start with the **Text**. Select the plus-sign next to **Text** and then the plus-sign next to **Text Settings**. Next select the **Modify Text** icon next to the **Style:** drop-down.

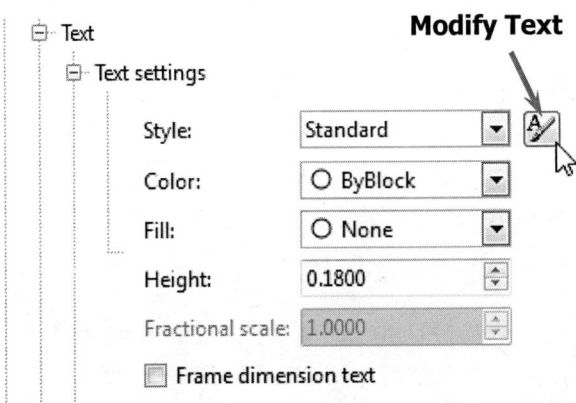

4. Select **Arial** for the Standard Text **Font**. This font will be easier to read than the default font.

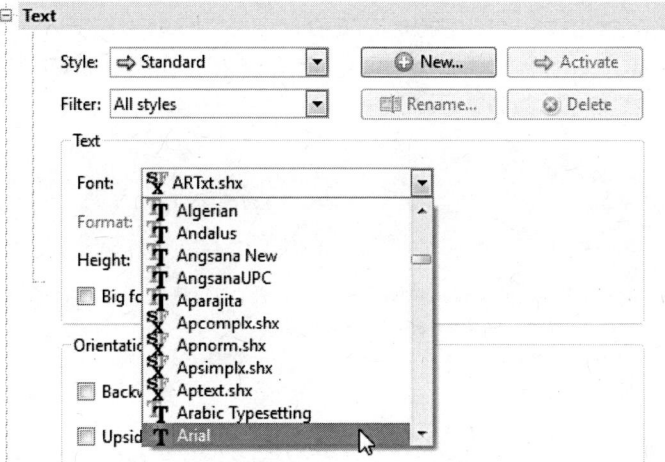

5.  Scroll down and click on the plus sign next to **Dimension**. Change the **Text Height** to **.12"**.   Also scroll up and change the Arrows Size to **.12"**.

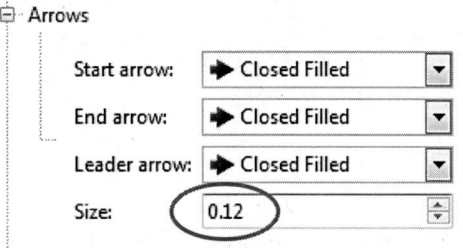

6.  Select the **Fit** and **Dimension scale** settings. The **Scale factor** is where you would enter the **reciprocal of the drawing scale**, just like we did for text height in the previous chapter.  For example, for a drawing at a scale of 1:4, you would enter **4** here.  For ¼"=1', you would enter **48**.  This multiplies all other dimension parameters by this value (e.g., text height, arrow size, etc.). The tape dispenser is small enough to fit at 1:1 scale, so leave the value at **1** in this case.

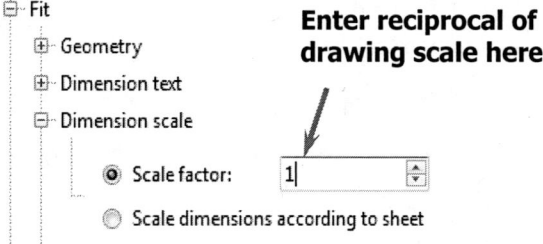

7.  Access the **Linear Dimension** settings. Leave the **Format** as **Decimal** (but note it could be changed to **Architectural** if desired). For mechanical drawings, the number of decimal places indicates the dimension tolerance.

Change the precision to three place decimal (**0.000**). Hide the leading zeros. Repeat this step for Angular dimensions (FYI: Only Metric drawings use zeros before the decimal point).

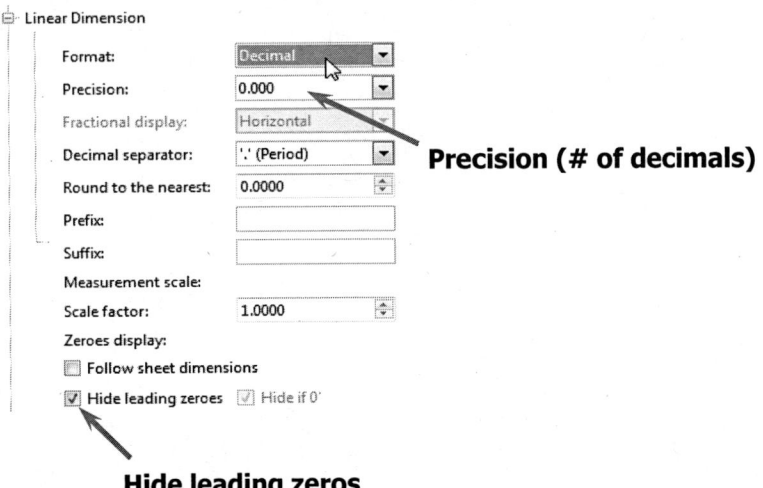

**Precision (# of decimals)**

**Hide leading zeros**

8. Go to **Line, Extension line settings**. Set the **Distance past dimension lines:** value to **.12"**.

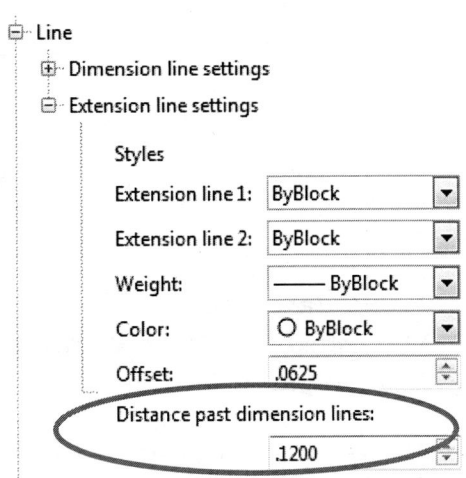

9. Finally, go to the **Radial/Diameter Dimension** settings and change the **Center mark display** to "As centerline". As you toggle this option between "As centerline" and "Ad mark", watch the result in the preview window. Select the **OK** button to dismiss the **Options** window and **Save** the drawing.

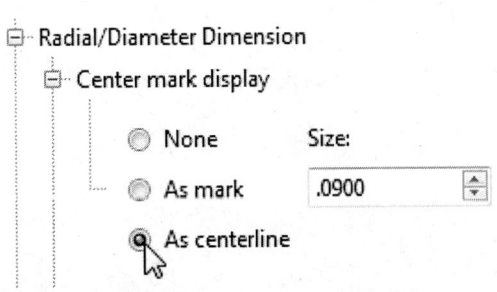

# Diameter and Radial Dimensioning

Before we start by dimensioning the several round features on the tape dispenser, create a **Dimension layer** to place the dimensions on. Use the continuous Line Style, and a color of your choice.

1. Activate the **Diameter** command in the **Dimension** toolbar. Pick the .75" hole in the center of the dispenser for the "**curved entity**". Click above and to the left, just outside of the tape dispenser's profile, to place the dimension. Note that DraftSight created center lines to mark the center of this feature.

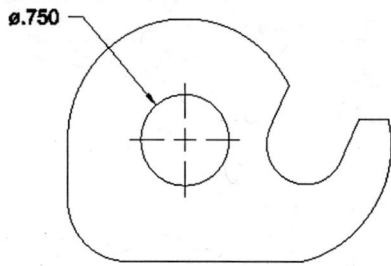

2. On your own, create a new **dimension style** called "**Radial**", based on **Standard**. Change the **Center mark display** to "**As mark**". Activate this new style by choosing "**Radial**" from the **Style:** drop-down list and selecting the **Activate** button.

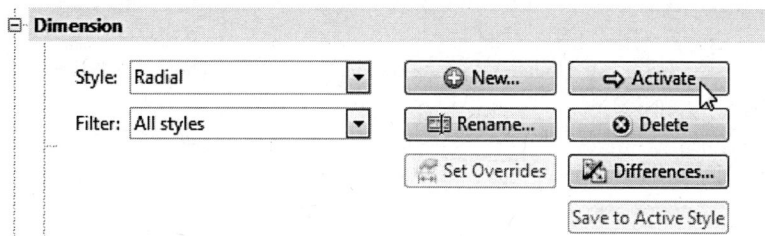

3. Next, select the **Radius** icon. Proceed to dimension the radii as shown below:

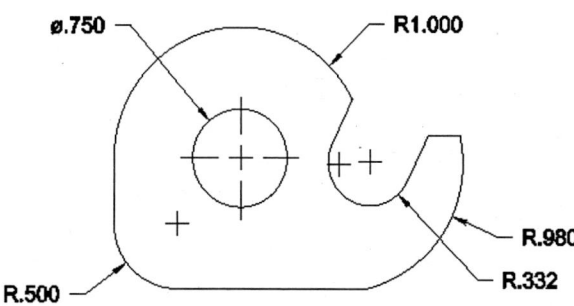

4. Notice that depending on where a dimension is placed, DraftSight automatically creates marks at the center of most arcs and circles. However, if you need a center mark without creating a corresponding dimension, the **CenterMark** command is available. Delete one of the dimensions you placed and create a center mark in its place. **Undo** twice to restore the deleted dimension.

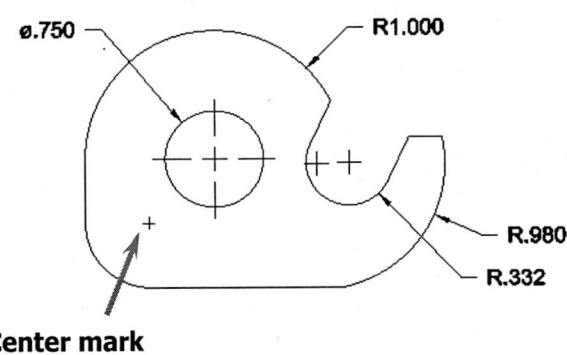

Center mark

## Linear and Aligned Dimensioning

1. Activate the **Standard** dimension style. Select the **Linear** dimension icon. DraftSight requires the **first extension line position**. This is where you want the dimension to originate from. Using **ESnap**, pick the lower end of the vertical centerline for the Ø.750 hole. For the **second extension line origin**, pick the lower end of the vertical line on the left side of the part. Drag the dimension down and click to place it.

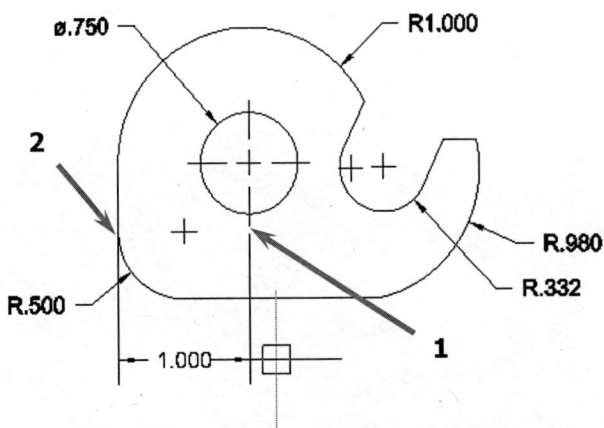

2. On your own, place the remaining linear dimensions shown in the drawing below. The difference between creating a vertical or horizontal dimension is the direction you sweep the mouse while placing the dimension (left/right sweep = vertical, up/down sweep= horizontal). To avoid extension and dimension lines crossing, start with the shorter dimensions first. Also, dimensions can be manipulated using **Entity Grips** after placement.

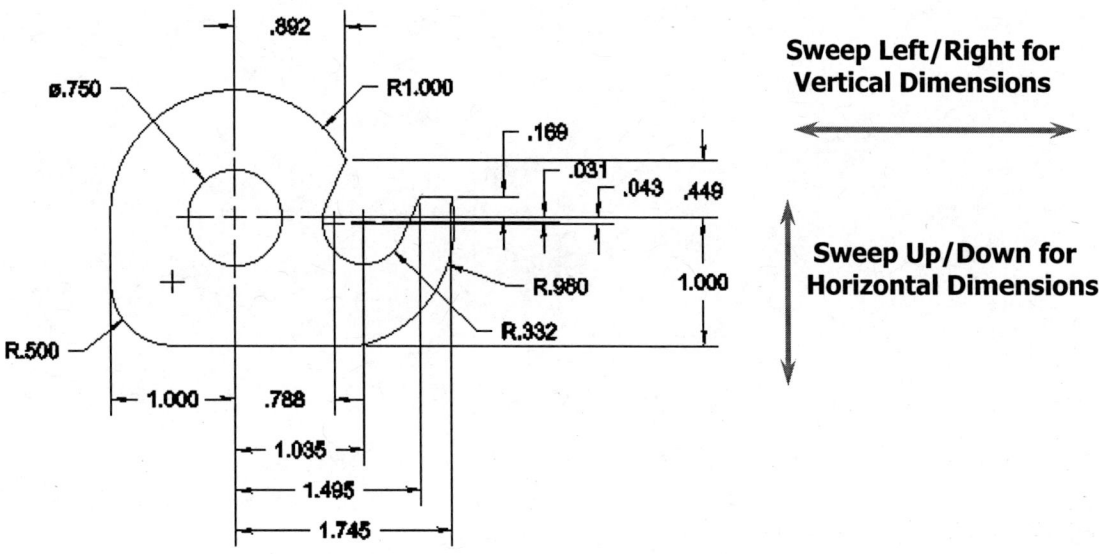

**Sweep Left/Right for Vertical Dimensions**

**Sweep Up/Down for Horizontal Dimensions**

---

*Tip:* Use **GRID** and **SNAP** for equal spacing between dimensions.

---

3. If the length of a diagonal line is required, use the **Aligned** dimension command. Select the icon. For the first and second extension line origins, pick the endpoints of the diagonal line to the right of the R.332 arc. Place the dimension as shown in the drawing below:

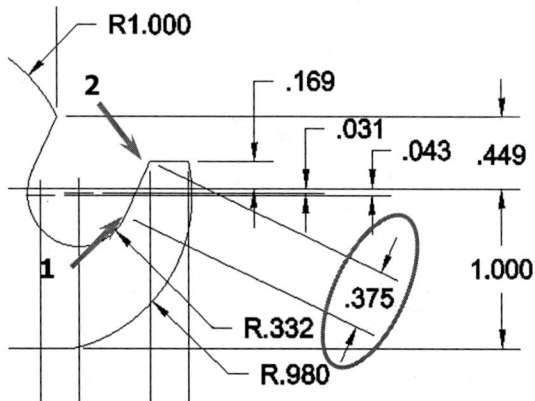

## Angular Dimensions

1. Select the **Angular** dimension icon. Select the diagonal line to the left of the R.332 arc. Next, pick the horizontal line at the bottom of the tape dispenser drawing.

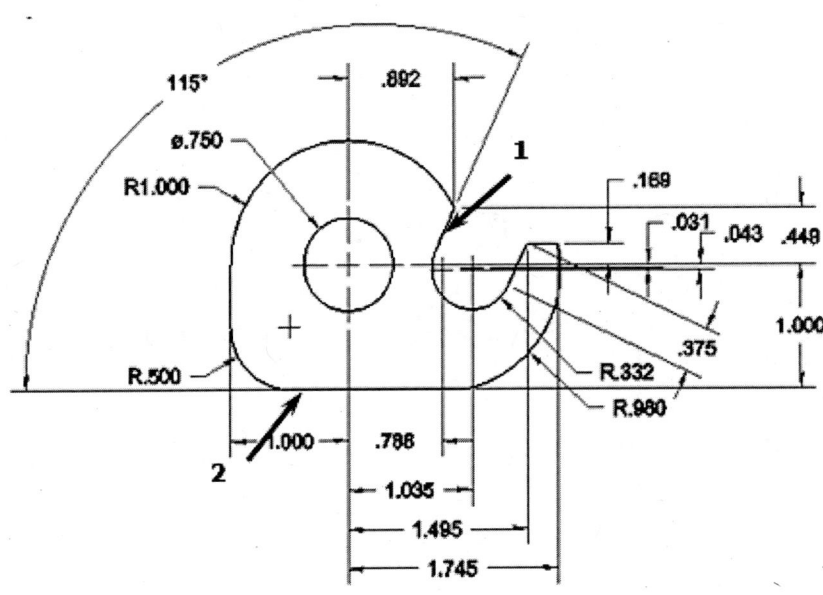

2. Since this angular dimension isn't required to build the part, but is nice to know, let's make it a reference dimension by placing it in parenthesis. To edit the dimension, double-click on it. The **Properties** window should appear (if it isn't open already).

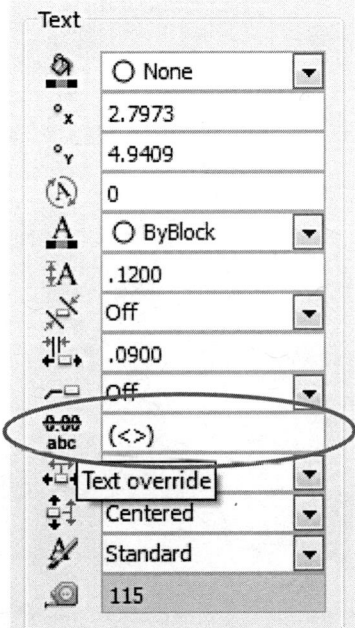

3. Notice the many dimension parameters you can change. Scroll down to the **Text** section. Find the **Text override** field and enter **(<>)**. This tells DraftSight to "insert the actual measurement here, between the parenthesis". The dimension should now read "**(115°)**".

4. The text can be changed during the dimension creation process too. Delete the .375 aligned dimension we made earlier. Initiate the **Aligned** dimension command, and select the endpoints of the diagonal line like we did previously. Before placing the text, type "**t**" for text. Enter "**2X <>**" in the command window and press **Enter**. Place the dimension. This should yield a dimension of "**2X .375**".

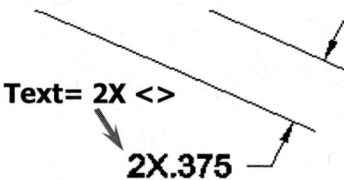

5. Experiment with some of the other commands in the **Dimension** toolbar. **Smart** dimension combines linear, aligned and radial dimension commands. The **Baseline** dimension command is used mainly in mechanical drawing. It can save time by only having to pick a dimension origin (or "datum") once. Baseline dimensioning prevents tolerance stack-up. The **Continue** dimension command is used primarily in architectural drafting. It dimensions from one feature to another (sometimes called "**chain**" dimensioning). **Ordinate** is similar to **Baseline**, but is much more compact and saves a lot of room on the drawing. **Save** the drawing and exit when you are finished.

**Baseline Dimensioning:**

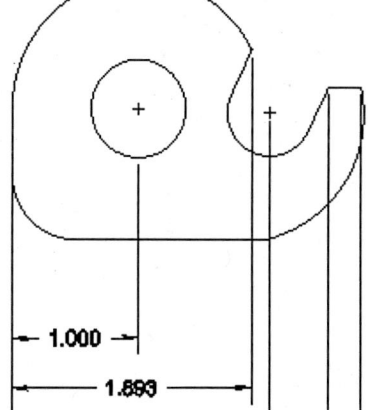

**Chain Dimensioning:**

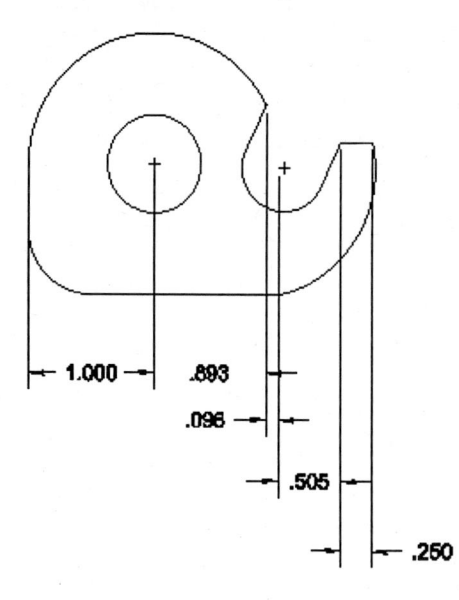

## Chapter 10 Suggested Learning Exercises

Dimension your Unit 2 Project...

### *Mechanical Project (Pocket Tool)-*

Open Pocket Tool.dwg.  If you haven't already, create a **dimension** layer.
Modify the **Standard** dimension style to: Arial text, arrow size & text height=
.12", three place decimal, and hide leading zeros.

1.  Dimension the drawing views for the **Large Flat Screwdriver** as shown:

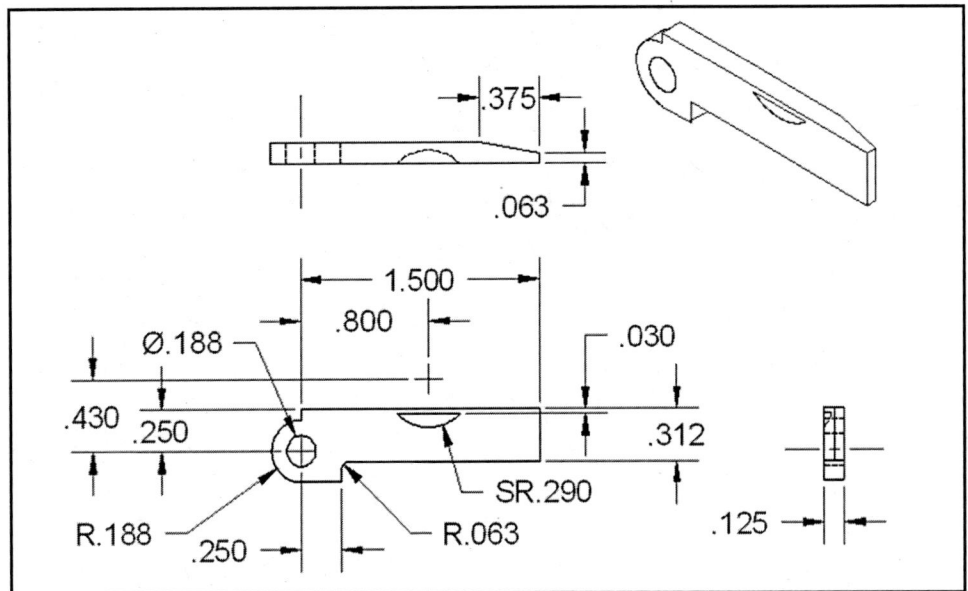

2.  Dimension the drawing views for the **Phillips Screwdriver** as shown below:

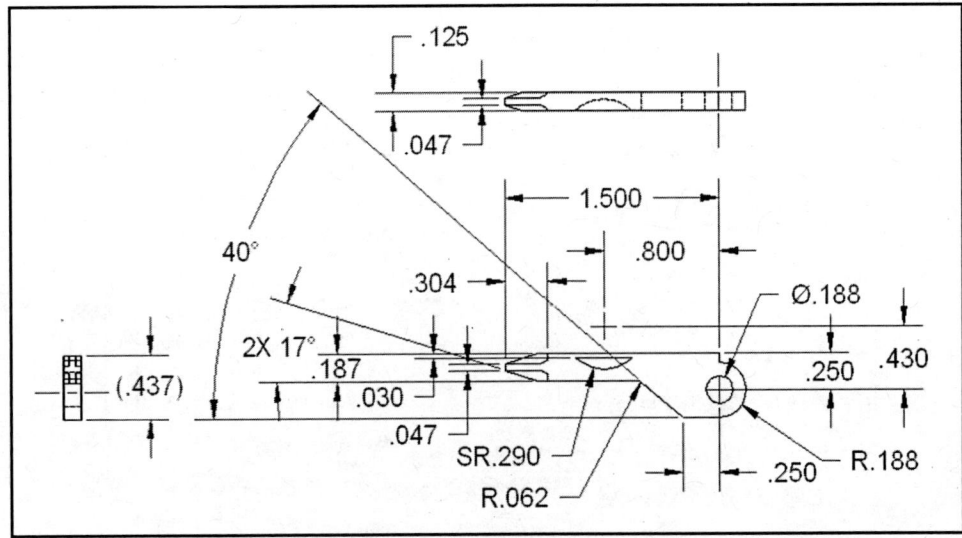

3. Dimension the drawing views for the **File** as shown below:

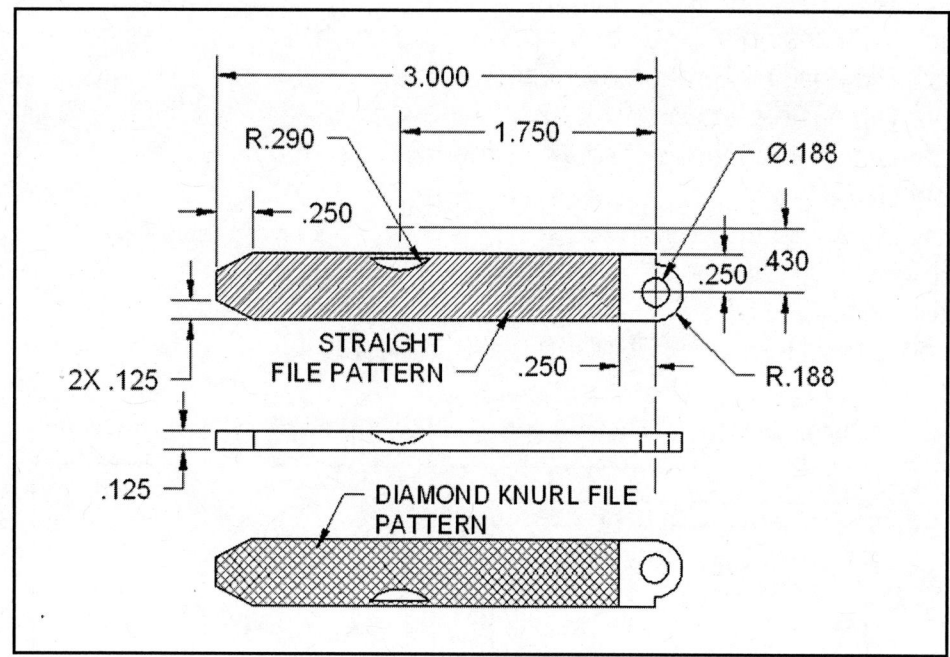

4. Dimension the drawing view for the **Knife Blade** as shown below (add the note for the thickness too):

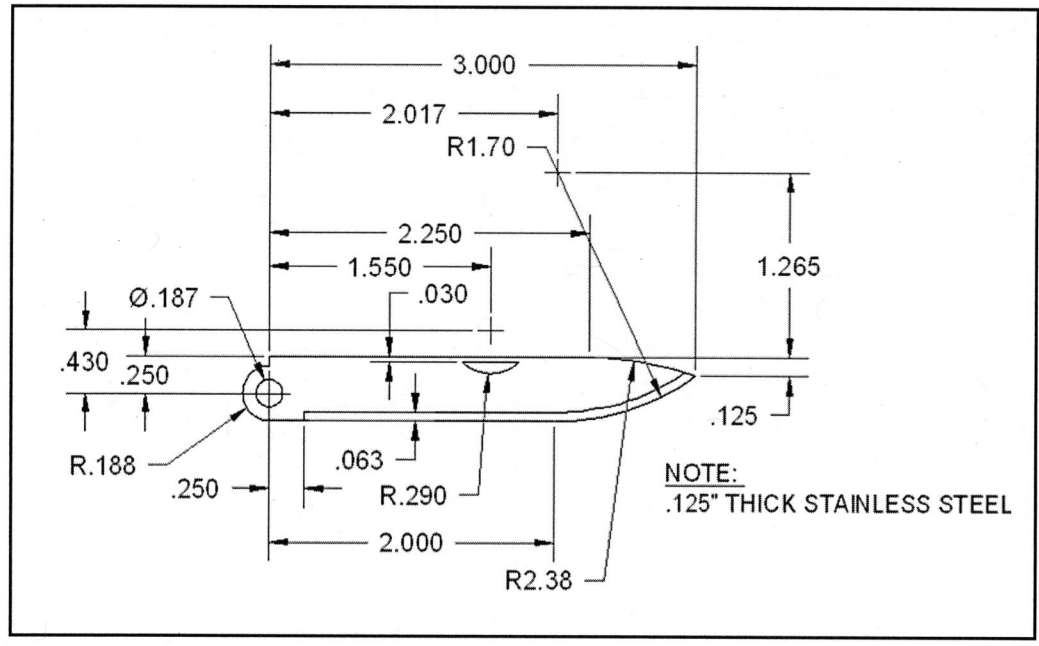

## *Architectural Project (Garage)-*

Open Garage.dwg. If you haven't already, create a **Dimension** layer. Modify the **Standard** dimension style to the following parameters:

- Linear Dimension Format= Architectural
- Linear Dimension Precision= 0'-0"
- Linear Dimension Zeroes Display= Hide if 0' and 0"
- Arrow size= 1/8"
- Arrow style= architectural tick
- Text font= City Blueprint
- Text height= 3/16"
- Dimension scale factor (Fit)= 48

Proceed to dimension the plan, section and elevation views as shown below:

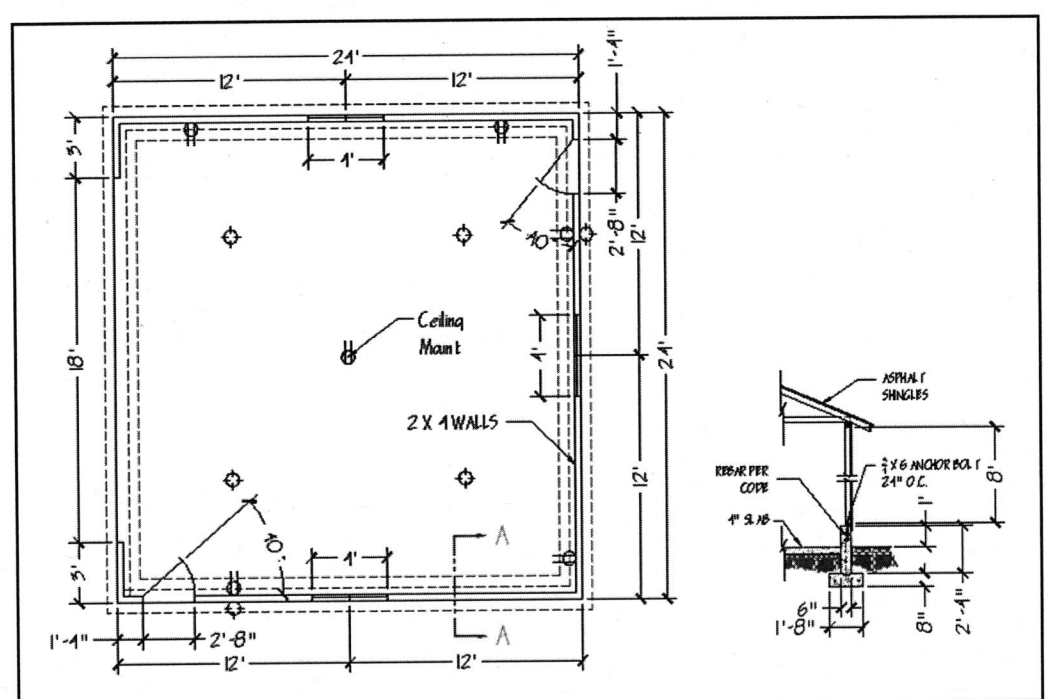

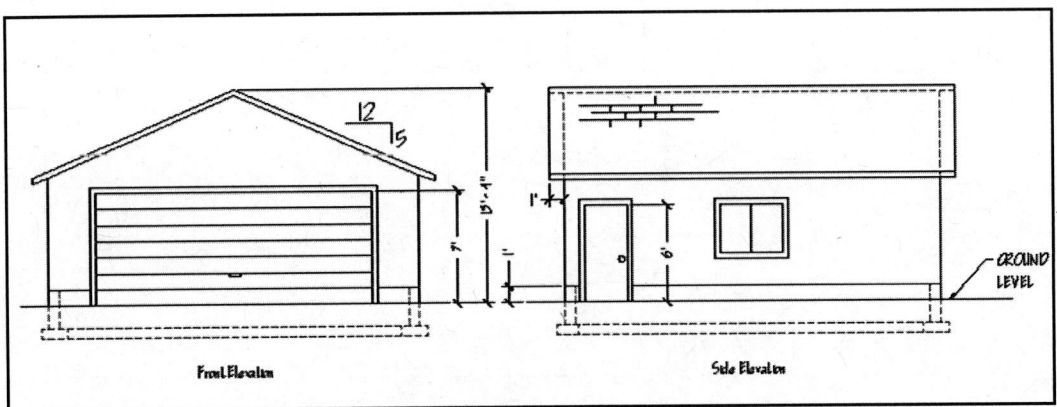

## Chapter 11- Printing and Auxiliary File Creation

Objectives:
1. Choose a printer and paper size
2. Define an area to plot and set the plotting scale
3. Preview a plot and send to the printer/plotter
4. Create files for off-site review and for use with a CAM system

One of the last steps in the Computer Aided Drafting process is printing out a paper copy of the drawing for review and eventually fabrication/construction. Additionally, industries using Computer Aided *Manufacturing* (CAM) systems may desire an electronic drawing file of the geometry (in addition to a drawing) in order to facilitate building parts designed with CAD.

## Printing

Also called "plotting", the ability to create a paper version of a CAD drawing is critical. Even in a digital age, many players in the design-build cycle still prefer a piece of paper in-hand. It would be nice if all the designer had to do was click on the print icon to accomplish this, but because of the nature of CAD drawings, there is more to it  than that. To learn about more about printing, **Open** the Tape Dispenser drawing from the previous chapter.

1. Select the **Print** icon in the **Standard** toolbar.  The ***Print*** window should open.  Note the three options on the top portion of the window:

    **Quick print-** This option fits what is on the screen to the default paper size and prints it to the default printer.

    **Use previous settings-** If active, this option just uses the same settings you used the last time.

    **Manual Setup-** Allows the user to specify the printer command settings.

Select the **Manual Setup** button and choose a printer from the **Name:** drop down list (consult your class facilitator to determine a preferred printer for this exercise).

2. The dispenser is small enough to fit on an 8.5 X 11 piece of paper (called "Letter" or "A-Size") at full scale. Select **Letter** from the list next to **Paper size:** and **1:1** from the **Scale:** drop-down list.

3. Next, select **Landscape** as the drawing orientation (if not selected already, check the preview window to determine the orientation). You'll find it by clicking on the **Additional Options** button and then choosing **Landscape** under *Geometry Orientation*.

4. Next, we need to define an area to plot. **All geometry** prints all entities on the drawing. **Drawing boundary** will only print all that which is inside the current drawing boundary. **Current view** will print the existing drawing area display. Probably the most useful is **Specify**, go ahead and select it and the **Specify Window** button.

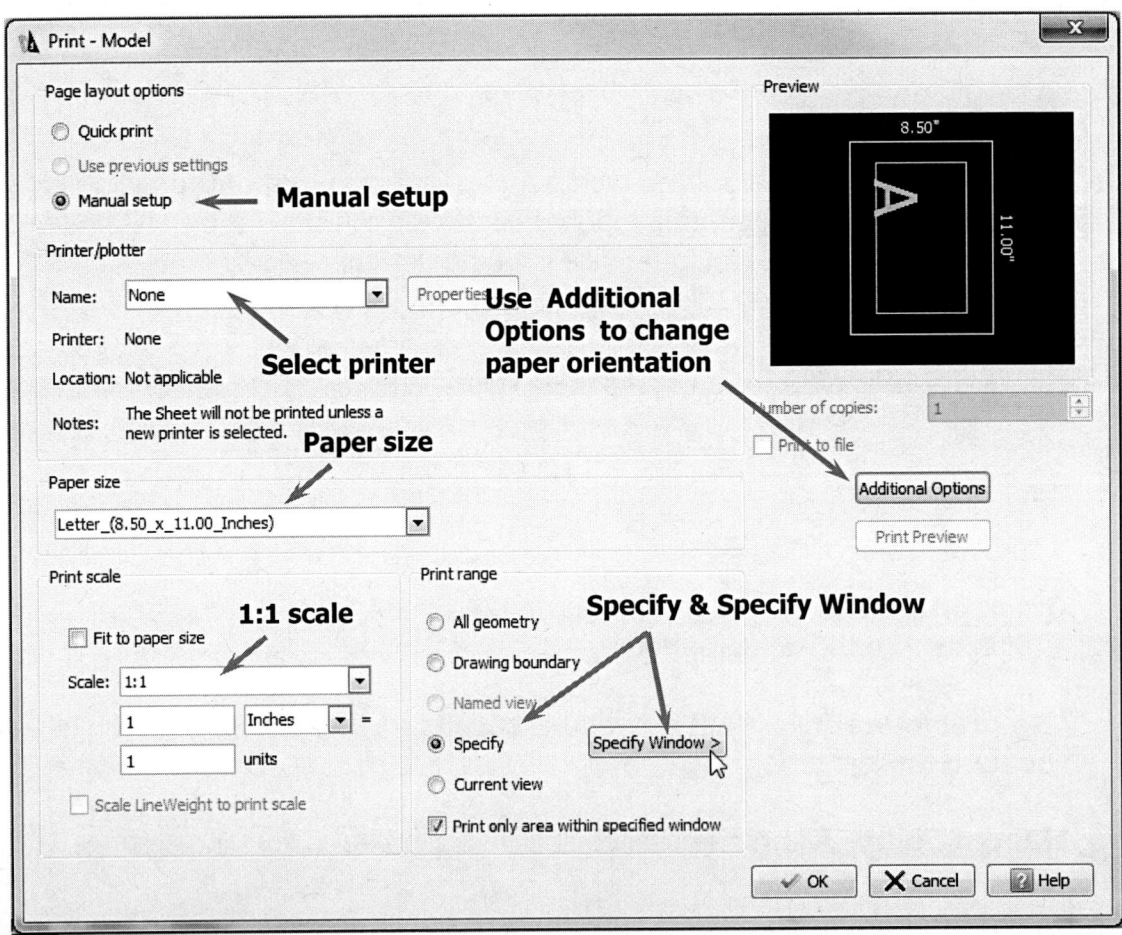

5. DraftSight temporarily returns to the drawing area to select a window to plot. Position the crosshairs and left-click just above and to the left of the dispenser for the first corner. Sweep down and to the right. Left-click when the dispenser fits just inside the window for the second corner.

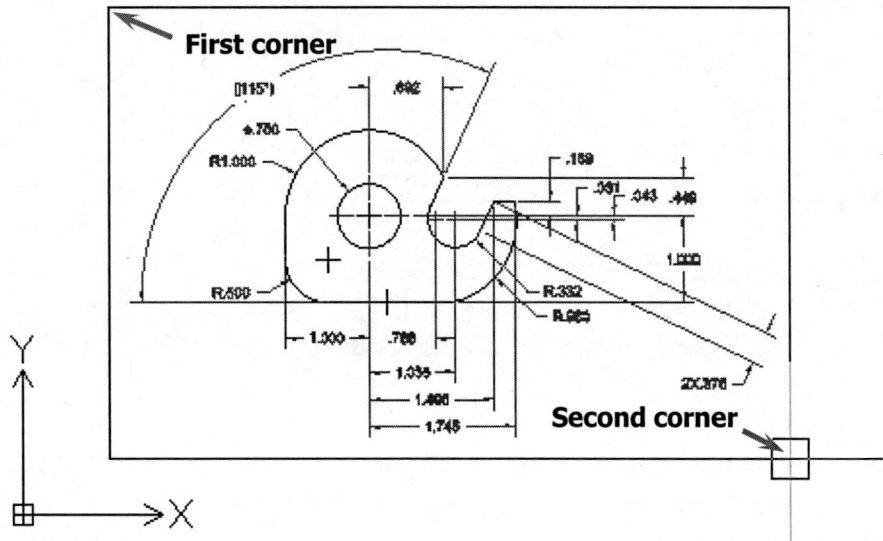

6. Finally, select the **Print Preview** button. The *Print* window temporarily dismisses and allows you see a full preview of how the drawing fits on the selected piece of paper. If it looks good, select the **Prin**t icon and pick up the drawing at the printer. If it needs to be adjusted, press the **Escape** key (or the red "X" icon) to exit the preview and return to the *Print* window.

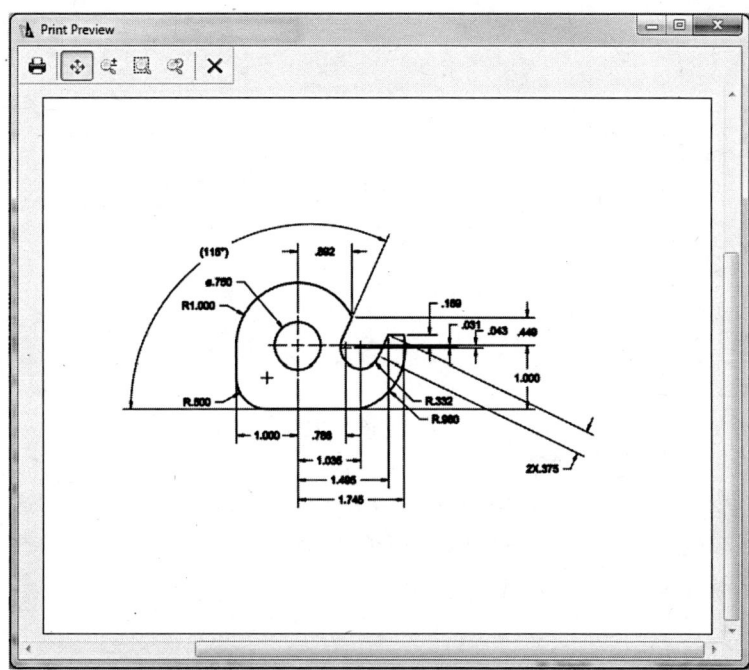

## Creating electronic files for review

DraftSight has the ability to "print" drawings not only to paper, but to files which are can be electronically transmitted and viewed by anyone. This is useful when working with others who need to review your drawings, but who do not have a copy of DraftSight (or don't want to learn to use it). Two common formats are .pdf (Portable Document Format, free viewer available from Adobe®) and .jpg.

1. Select the **Print** icon as before. Pick **PDF** in the **Name**: drop-down list. Set the paper size to **ANSI_A_(11.00 x 8.50 Inches)**. Set the **Scale** to **1:1** and specify a window to print, like we did in the previous section.

2. Note the **Print to file** option is already checked. When selecting PDF for the printer, DraftSight knows you want a PDF file as the output, not a piece of paper. View a full **Print Preview**; if it looks acceptable proceed to "print" the PDF by selecting the **Print** icon in the preview window.

3. DraftSight will prompt you for a name and file location in which to place the **.pdf** file. Name it "TapeDispenser" and select **Save**.

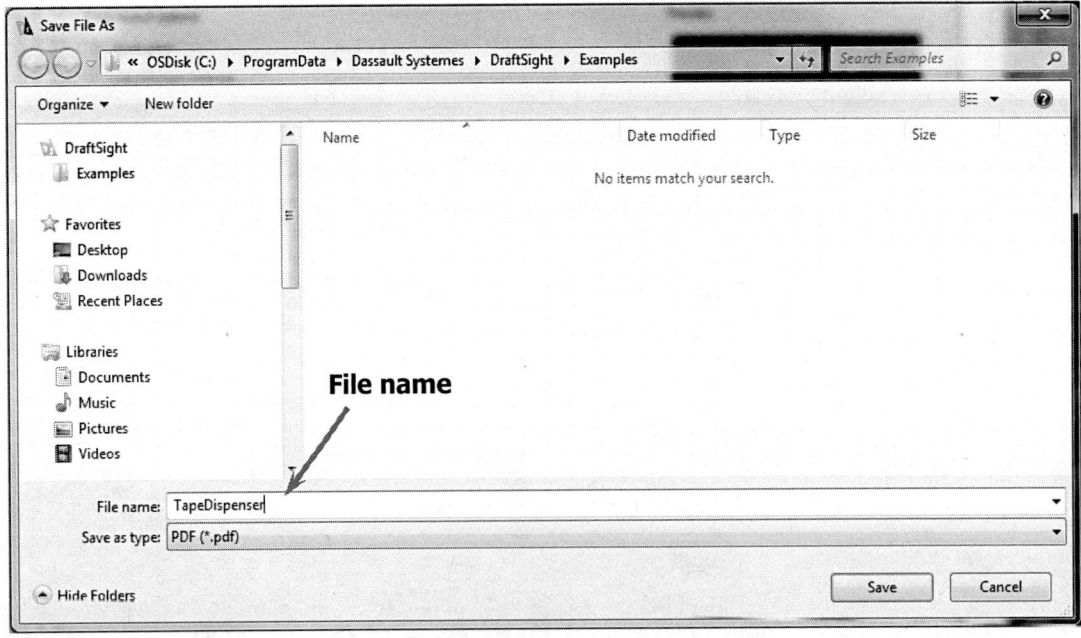

4. Open and examine the saved .pdf file with Adobe® Acrobat® viewer. Similarly useful is the **eDrawing**, which can be viewed and manipulated with a Dassault Systemes free viewer. On your own, explore eDrawings using the File>Publish eDrawings command (if your computer is so equipped).

## Other Electronic Files

DraftSight is a "vector" based program. This means all geometry consists of trackable X and Y coordinates. However, DraftSight can also create and import "raster" files like the aforementioned JPG. These are useful for integrating your drawings into artwork, like a brochure or poster. Importing raster images can be a mess though. Raster files aren't made of lines and curves, rather they are made of millions, of little dots (pixels). These files are imported by finding the **Insert** menu and selecting **Reference Image**. The *Select File* window should open and allow you to choose from any number of raster files. It's best to just trace the raster file on a new layer, then delete the raster file from the drawing area (or hide its layer) when you're finished with it.

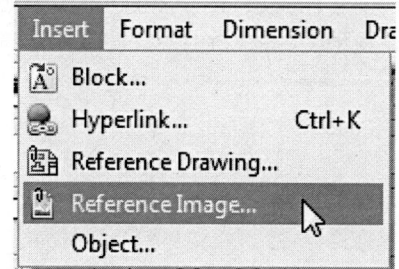

For electronic vector files used in manufacturing, most CAD & CAM programs accept DraftSight's native .dwg format. Another popular choice is the **.dxf** file . DXF files as well as different versions of DWG files can be created by going to the **File** menu and selecting **Save As...**. Remember, it is critical the geometry be drawn full-scale and **exactly** how you want it to be built.

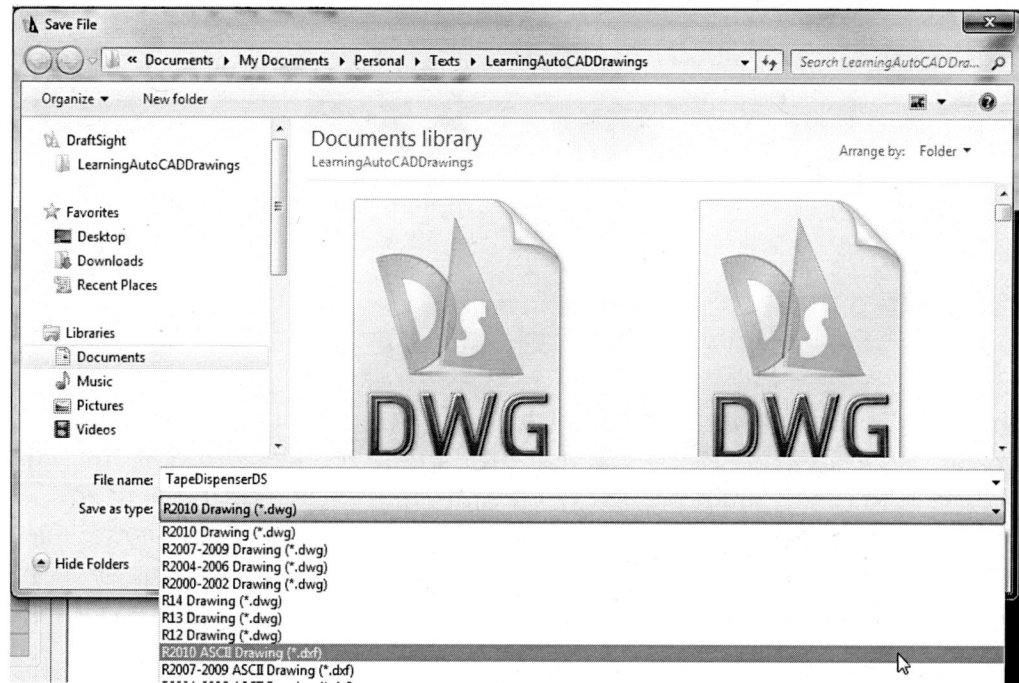

## Chapter 11 Suggested Learning Exercises

Plot your Unit 2 Project...

### *Mechanical Project (Pocket Tool)-*

1. **Open** Pocket Tool.dwg. **Plot** the drawing views of the **Large Flat Screwdriver Phillips Screwdriver**, **Handle** and **Knife Blade** and on A-Size pieces of paper at a scale of **1:1**. Center the plots, and preview them before sending each one to the printer.

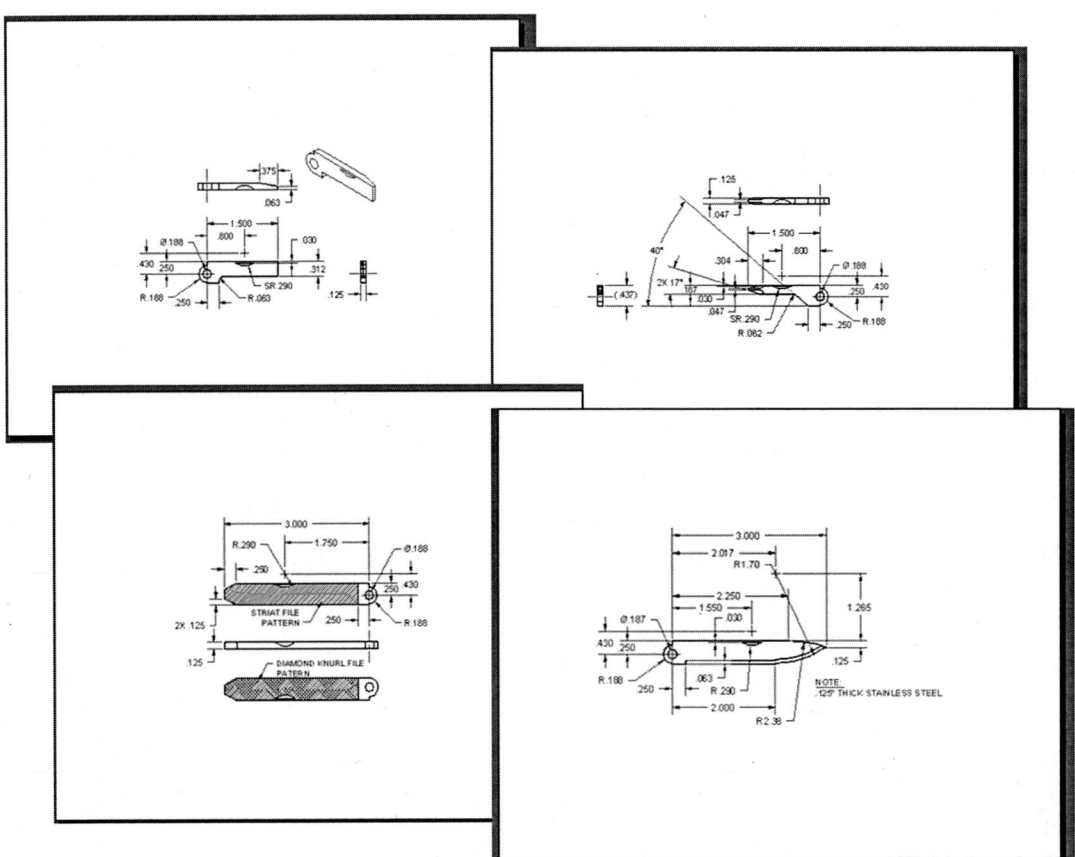

2. With others in your class, take a brief tour of the machine shop in your educational facility (if available). Inquire regarding the kinds of files that can imported in to their CAM program(s). If time permits, export a file from DraftSight into a CAM program (it helps to freeze the dimension, centerline and hidden layers first). Have the machine shop import the file and prepare it for machining on a Computer-Numeric Controlled (CNC) machining center.

## Architectural Project (Garage)-

1. **Open** Garage.dwg. **Plot** the drawing views of each elevation, the section and plan views of the garage on A-size pieces of paper at a scale of **¼"=1'**. Center the plots, and preview them before sending each one to the printer.

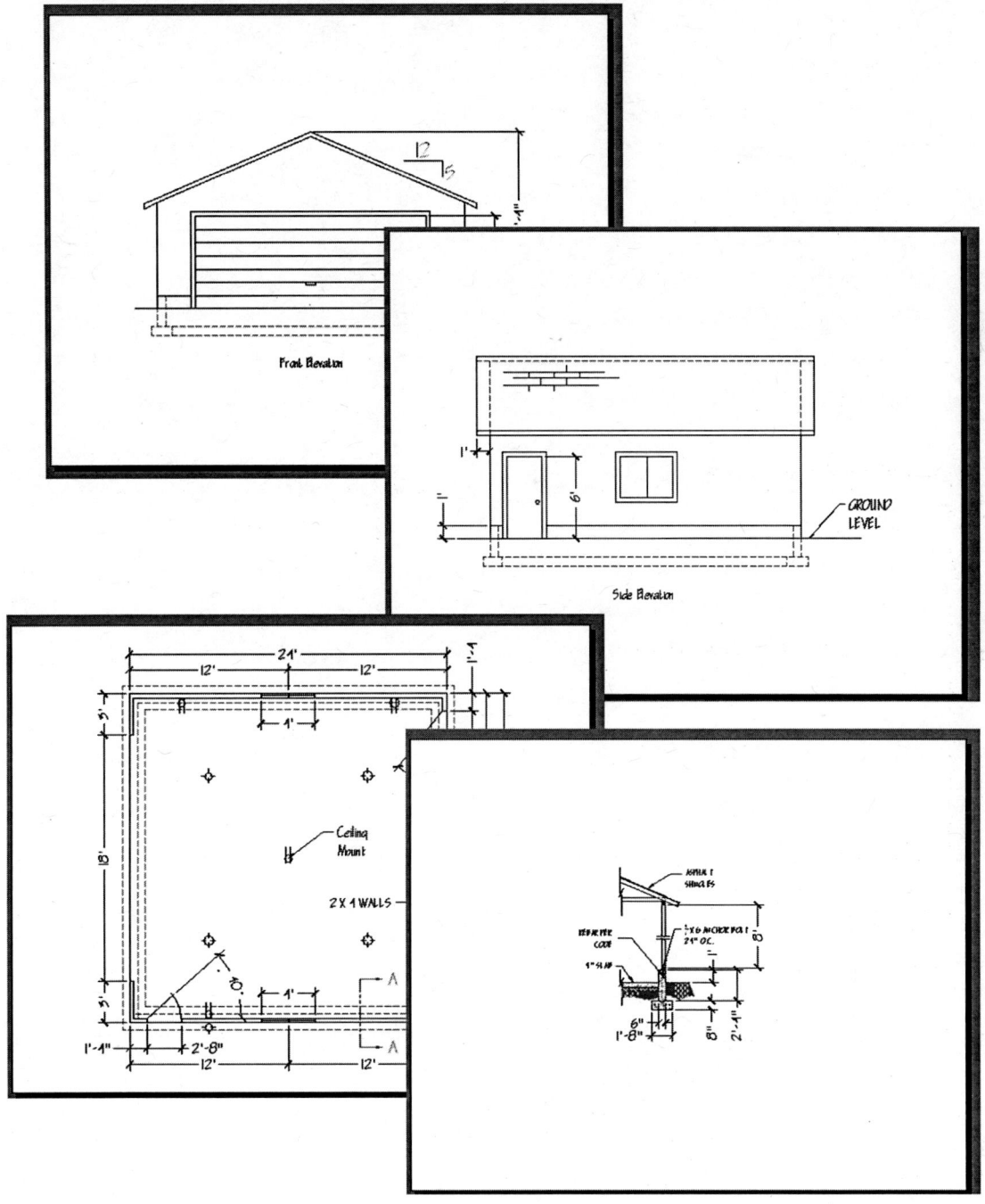

**NOTES:**

# Unit 2 Review

1. Complete the crossword puzzle using the clues provided:

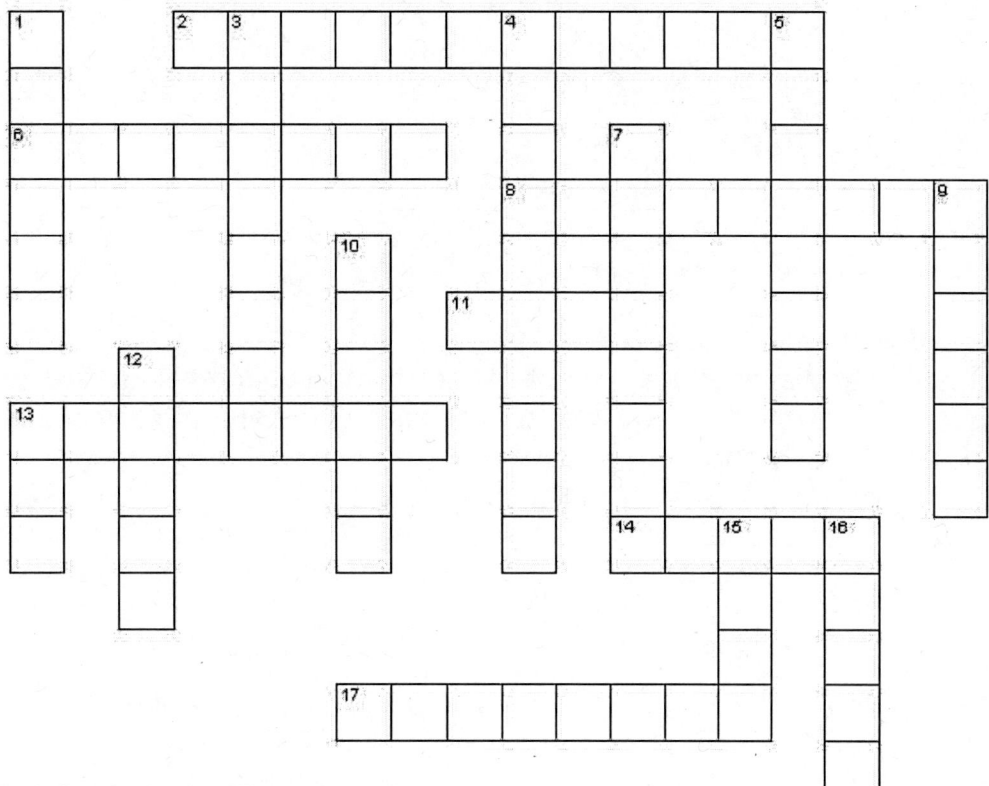

**Across**

2 Method of projecting the different views of an object

6 Coordinate entry method used to create and edit geometry based on the drawing origin (0,0)

8 Type of drawing view that appears to be 3D.

11 Drawing aid that displays a field of equally-spaced points on the screen

13 Dimension command used to specify a hole size

14 Drawing aid that locates geometry features like endpoints, midpoints, center points, etc.

17 Dimension command used when all dimensions originate from a common feature or origin

**Down**

1 Command used to place a note on a drawing which refers to a specific location on an object

3 Coordinate entry method used to create and edit geometry based on the last point specified (@X,Y)

4 Value used to specify the dimension scale, based on the print scale

5 Dimension command which references the previous feature, or chains features together

7 Diagonal line used to reflect orthographically projected views

9 Line type that indicates a round object

10 Drawing management tool used to organize entities by their line type or function

12 Command used to create patterns which often specify construction materials

13 File extension commonly used for exporting geometry to a CAM program

15 This command initiates a mini-word processor of sorts for placing advanced text on a drawing

16 Coordinate entry method used to create and edit geometry based on an angle and distance from the last point specified (@d

2. From memory, provide the name of the command associated with the indicated icons found in the Dimension Toolbar:

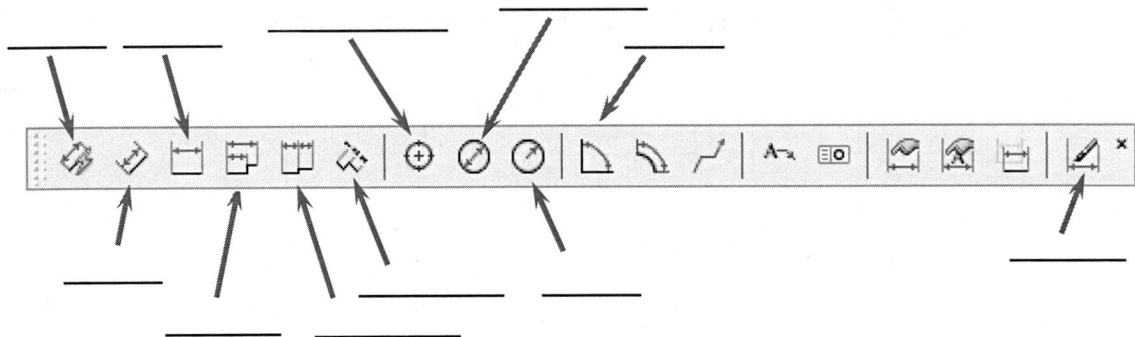

3. Name the entity snaps that exist at the points labeled in the figure below. Multiple alternatives are possible, but use each of the entity snaps in the following list only once:

   o Endpoint
   o Midpoint
   o Center
   o Tangent
   o Quadrant
   o Intersection

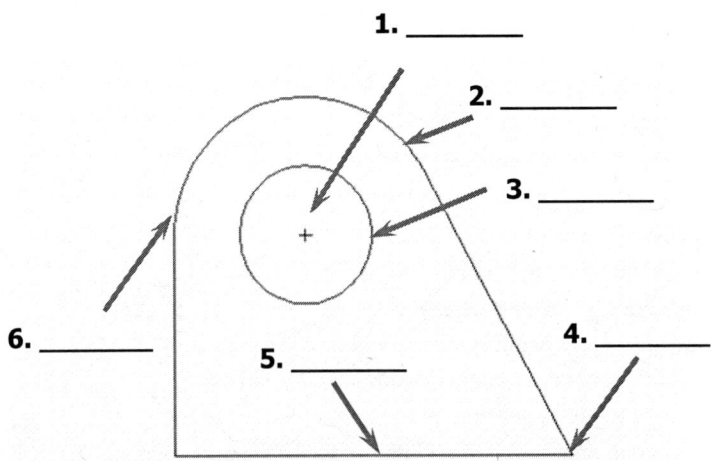

# Part B. Specialized Skills

The following modules are designed to meet learner needs in specific areas. The facilitator should be consulted in choosing applicable modules to meet these needs. Unit 3 contains modules that will mainly help mechanical drafters. Unit 4 modules are architectural in nature. Either way, the Unit 2 project will be relied on heavily in both units.

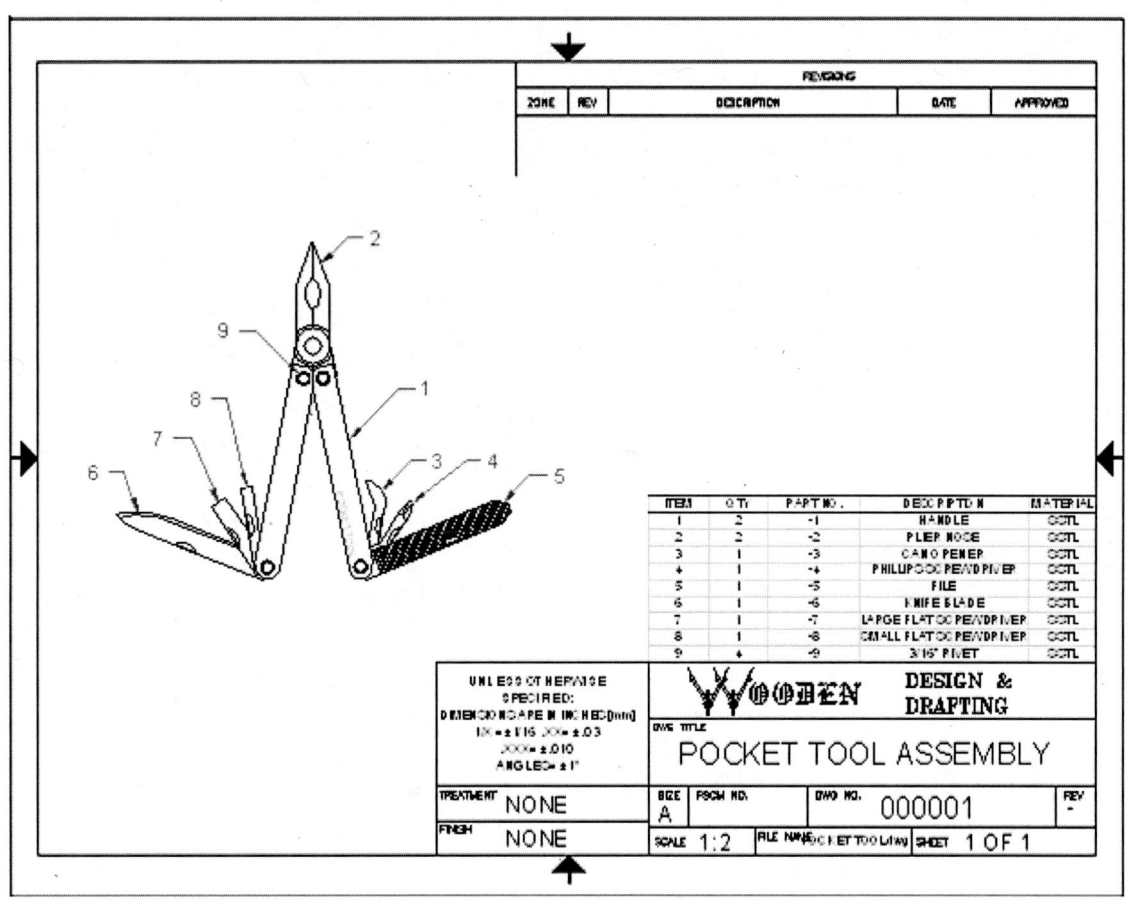

**NOTES:**

# Unit 3- Specialized Mechanical CAD Skills

## Module M1- Mechanical Drawing Templates

Objectives:

1. Set drawing units
2. Set a drawing's boundary
3. Create layers for mechanical drawings
4. Select a mechanical text style
5. Create dimension styles for mechanical drawing
6. Import a title block
7. Save as a drawing template

This module is intended to reinforce some of the basic concepts learned in Chapters 8-10 for the mechanical drafter. If you currently work for a firm that uses CAD for mechanical design, you may want to ask for the company's drawing template (most companies will have a standard template so that all drawings are set-up the same way) in which case this module can, for the most part, be skipped. If you are not yet employed at a firm using CAD, or plan on using DraftSight as a means of self-employment, read on!

## Drawing Units

The first step to consider when creating a template is the units of measurement. Most design and manufacturing firms in the Untied States use decimal inches. We'll also cover some metric and dual-dimensioning techniques in this module.

1. Start a **New** drawing using the standard template (or one that you may already have made in Chapter 8).

2. Choose **Unit System** from the **Format** menu. The *Options* window will appear. Choose the appropriate unit **type** and **precision** for your industry, both for length and angle. It is recommended that for **Length** the settings **Decimal** and **0.000** should be specified. For **Angle, Decimal Degrees** and **0** is usually sufficient (as shown in the graphic on the next page).

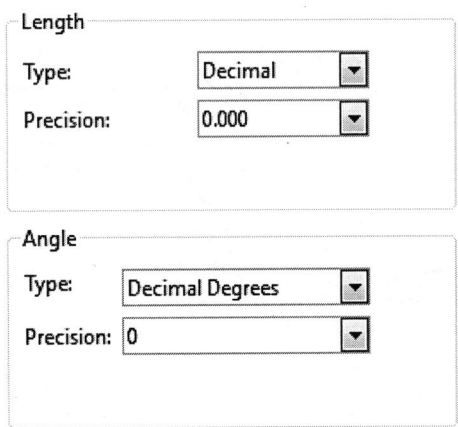

3. Select the **Help** button at the bottom of the window if you'd like to learn more. Press **OK** when finished.

# Drawing Boundary

The second step in creating a mechanical drawing template is to set the drawing boundary or limits. This value will vary greatly depending on the product being drawn (surgical devices vs. industrial equipment for example). Fortunately, the boundary can be changed easily. In actuality though, drawing outside the boundary has minor consequences. Primarily, you lose the ability to use **Grid**.

1. Select **Drawing Boundary** from the **Format** menu. Press **Enter** to except the default **0,0** for the lower left corner. For the upper right corner enter "**44,34**". This creates an ANSI E-Size drawing boundary. You may specify more or less than this depending on your anticipated line of work, but an E-Size is typically the largest drawing used in industry. As mentioned previously, **always draw objects full size when using CAD**. This means you may have to "scale up" the drawing area as required, e.g. a ¼ scale E-size drawing area would be 176,136 (four times 44 & 34).

```
: DRAWINGBOUNDS
Default: (0.000,0.000)
Options: OFf, ON or
Specify lower left corner»
```

```
Default: (12.000,9.000)
Specify upper right corner» 44,34
```

2. **Zoom** to the **Bounds** (enter "**Z**", then "**B**" in the command window- these are shortcut commands). Move the cursor to the upper right-hand portion of the drawing area. Note the coordinate display should read something close to **(44,34,0)**. If desired, set up a **Grid** and **Snap** at an interval you might expect to use. Turn on the grid to view the new drawing boundary. If the spacing is too small, DraftSight will state "Grid too dense to display" in the command window. As you zoom in, the grid will eventually appear.

## Creating Layers

Typically, layers within a mechanical drawing are closely related to their assigned line types. We'll create a number of common layers used in mechanical drafting.

1. Select the **Layers Properties Manager** icon in the **Layers** toolbar.

2. Create the layers and line styles shown in the figure below. **Assign colors** at your discretion. If you prefer a white background* in the drawing area, pick darker colors. The opposite is true for a black background. Be sure to press **OK** when finished.

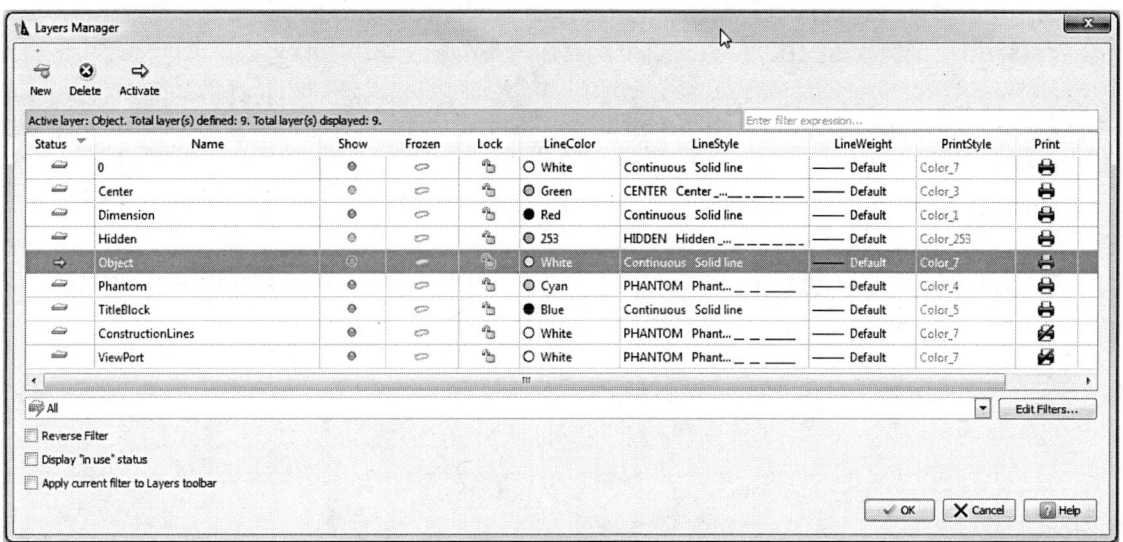

---

**\*Tip:** To change DraftSight's colors, go to the **Tools** Menu and select **Options**. Pick the **Systems Options** icon, then choose **Display** & **Element Colors**.

3. Now would be a good time to **Save** your work. From the **File** menu, select **Save As...**. The *Save File* window should appear. Select **Drawing Template (*.dwt)** in the **Save as type:** drop-down list. DraftSight automatically assumes you want to place the drawing in the Template directory on the hard drive. **Save** the template in a location recommended by your facilitator.

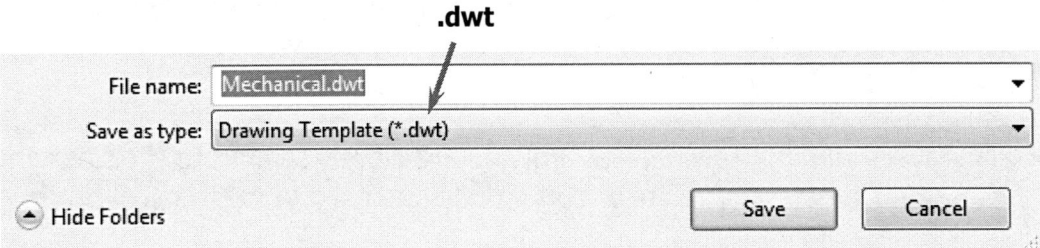

## Setting a Text Style

The default text font in DraftSight can be difficult to read, and isn't all that aesthetically pleasing. It is recommended that you change it:

1. From the **Format** menu select the **Text Style** command.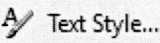

2. Choose an easy to read, neutral font. **Arial**, and some of its variations work well. Others to consider are Tahoma and Verdana. Leave the **Height:** at .0000, as that can be specified later.

3. Select the **OK** button before closing. **Save** the drawing template **(.dwt)**.

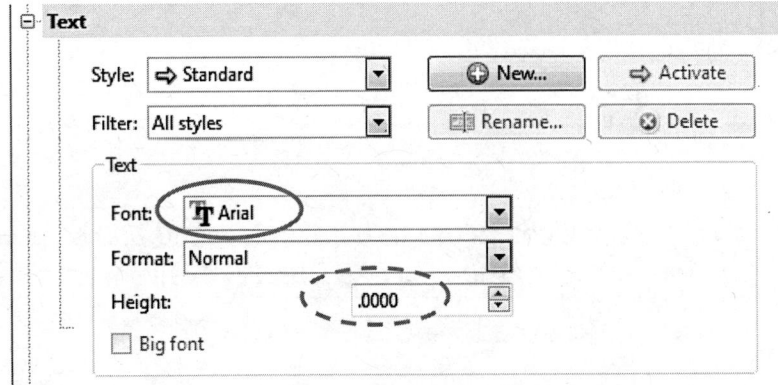

## Dimension Styles

Perhaps the most grueling part of making a mechanical drafting template is creating the dimension styles. It is also perhaps the most necessary, since dimensioning is a vital means of properly communicating design intent. Again, the specifics are closely related to the industry in which you plan to work. Make necessary adjustments, as the following is mostly suggestion:

1. From the **Dimension** toolbar select the **Dimension Style** icon.

2. Inside the *Options* window, make the following changes:

   a. Angular Dimensions, Angular Dimension Settings, Precision: **0** and **Hide leading zeros.**

   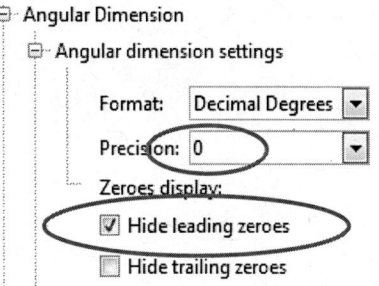

   b. Arrows, Size: **.12**

   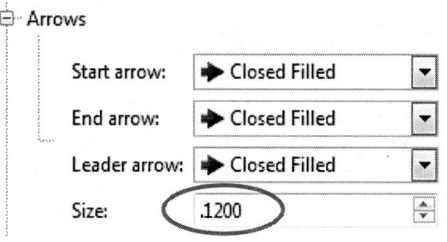

   c. Linear Dimension, Precision: **0.000** and **Hide leading zeros**.

   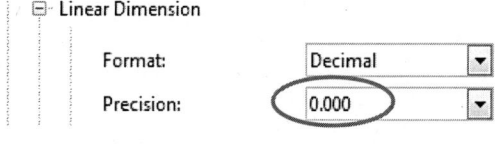

   d. Line, Extension line settings, Offset: **.05** and Distance past dimension lines: **.12**

   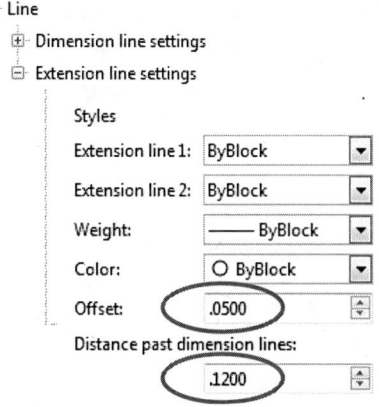

e. Text, Text settings. Height: **.12** and verify the font Style: is **Arial**.

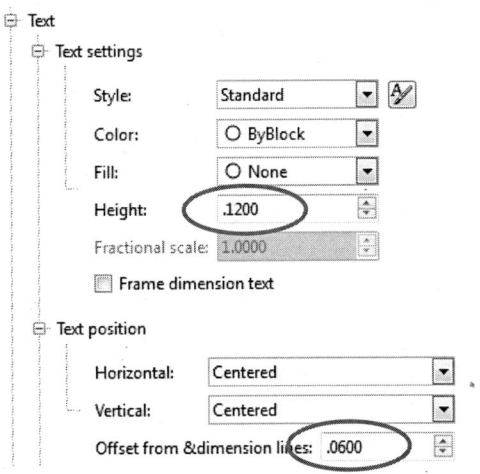

f. Text position, Offset from dimension lines: **.06**

3. Observe the updates in the preview window as the changes are made. When finished, be sure and select **OK** to save the changes. You may also periodically select the **Apply** button to save the settings without exiting.

4. We will now create a new dimension style for dimensions requiring less precision. Standard tolerances are determined by the number of decimal places that make up a dimension value. Select the **Dimension Style** icon again and **New**. Enter **Standard 2 place** for the name of the new style. Press **OK**.

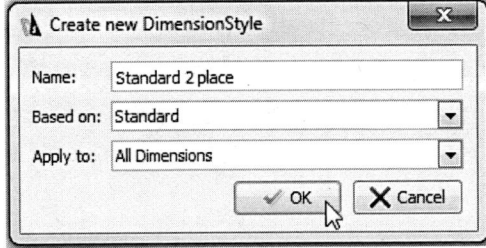

5. Go directly to **Linear Dimension** and change the **Precision:** to **0.00**, click the **Apply** button.

6. We will now create a third style for dual-dimensioning in both inches and millimeters. Select **New** and name the new style **Dual** and Based on: **Standard**. Press **OK**.

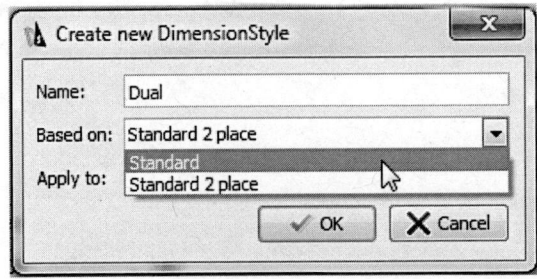

7. Select the Dual Dimension line. Check the **Show dual Dimensions** box. Note the Multiplier value of **25.4** (1 inch = 25.4mm). Press the **Apply** button.

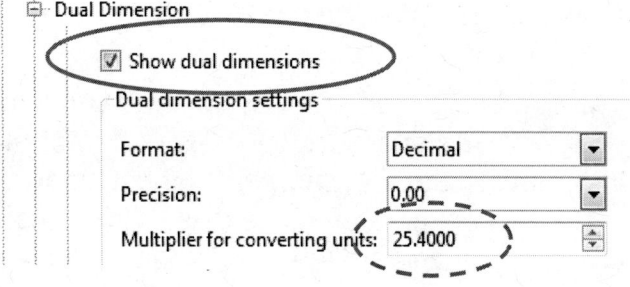

8. Now set up a dimension style for printing half-scale drawings. This effectively means all the values need to double in size (text height, arrow size, etc.). Select the **New** button. Name this one "**Half Scale**", based on **Standard**, and press **OK**. Go to the **Fit** line, **Dimension Scale** and enter **2** for the **Scale factor:** (the reciprocal of ½ scale = 2 ). Select **Apply**.

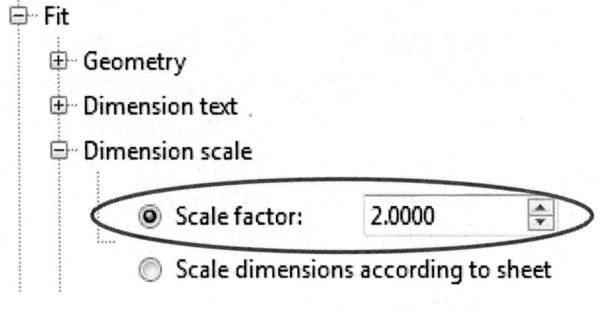

9. Finally, create a style for a specific tolerance (as opposed to a general tolerance designated by the number of decimal places in the dimension). Click on the **New** button and name this one "**Plus 5**" based on **Standard**. Go to the **Tolerance** line, and set the calculation to **Deviation**, precision to **0.000,** and the maximum value to **.005** and hide the leading zeros. Verify there are five dimension styles present. Select **OK** and **Save** the drawing template file.

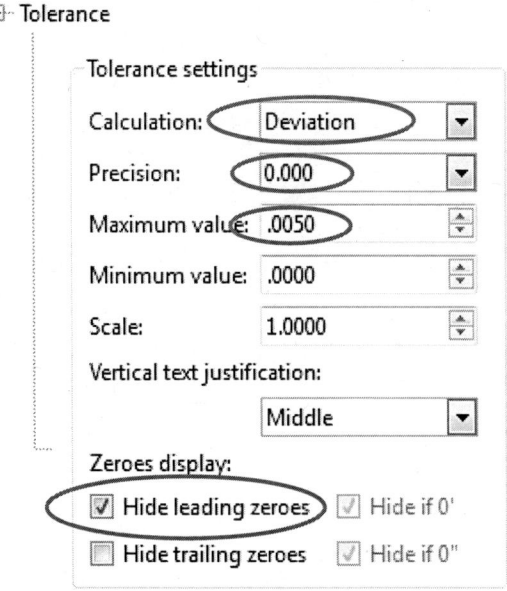

**149**

## Creating a Mechanical Title Block

The title block is an often overlooked and underappreciated part of mechanical drafting. The title block contains vital information, however, such as: contact information, the drawing/part number, drawn date, revision history, drawing scale, and general tolerance data. Other than that, title blocks can be fairly personalized and are left to company preference. The following is a suggestion for capturing a generic mechanical title block that comes with DraftSight, adapt it to your own needs as required.

1. Start a new drawing using your new **mechanical.dwt**. Choose **Block** from the **Insert** menu. **Browse** to the **Examples** folder that comes with DraftSight and choose **C-89764.dwg** and **Open**. This file contains a C-size title block that we'll scavenge (if this file isn't available, work with your facilitator to find another or create a title block from scratch).

2. Before selecting **OK** to dismiss the *Insert Block* window, check the **Explode Block** box. This will break the drawing up into its individual entities.

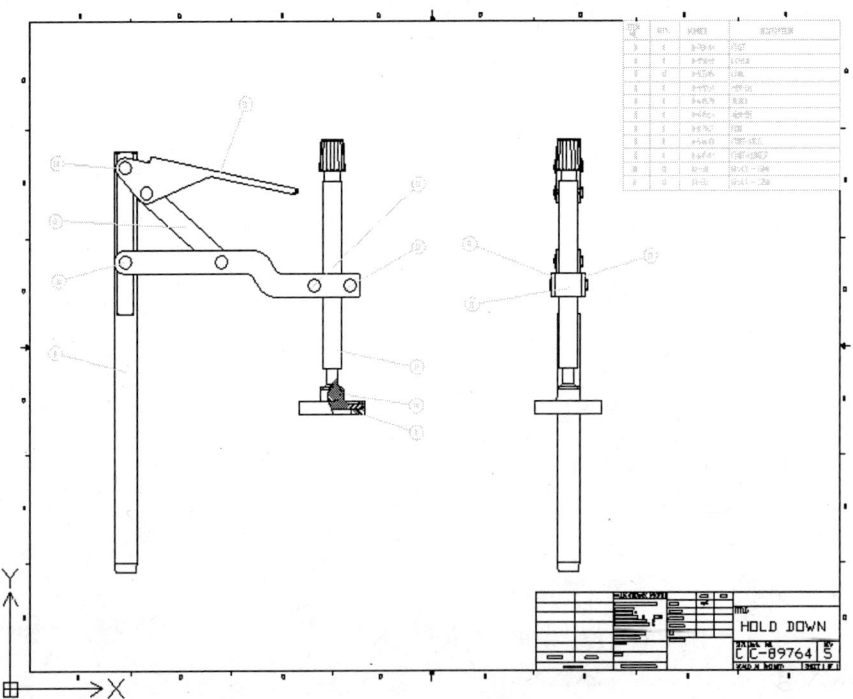

3. You should now see a drawing titled "Hold Down" in the drawing area. All we want is the title block, **Delete** everything else.

4. We'll learn more about **Blocks** in another module. Select the **Explode** command from the **Modify** menu. Pick anywhere on the title block; notice the entire title block is highlighted as it is one entity in its present state (a "block"). Press **Enter** to explode.

5. **Zoom** in on the lower right-hand portion of the title block. Double click on any of the text, notice that either the ***Edit SimpleNote*** or ***Edit BlockAttribute*** window opens*, either way you can edit the text.

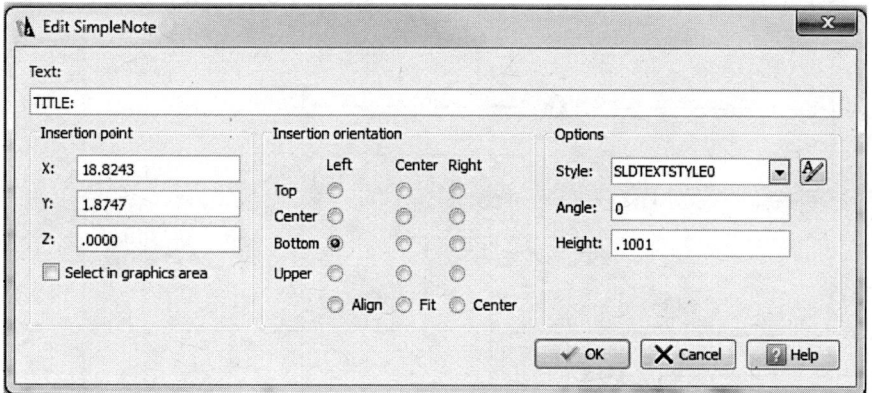

6. Modify the title block to meet your needs (provide your own company name and logo). Place the title block on the TitleBlock layer and **Save** the template.

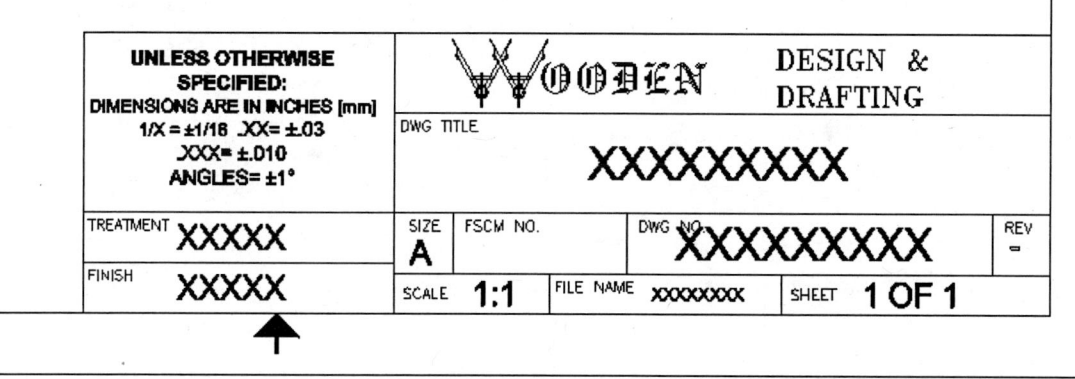

*Tip:* The "X"s in the example above serve as placeholders, prompting you to enter information (except for the tolerance data, where the X's mean something different). They are easy to edit, just double click them. In order to make title block entry even more seamless, research "attributes" in DraftSight's Help utility.

7. On your own, create other sizes of title blocks. Using the C-size title block we inserted in this module, copy and scale the border (but not the text entry area of the title block) by half to create an A-size, double it for an E-size. A B-size fits an 11 X 17 piece of paper, and a D-Size is double that (22 X 34), so Bs and Ds take some stretching as well as scaling. Be sure and **Save** your drawing template file, overwriting **mechanical.dwt** before exiting.

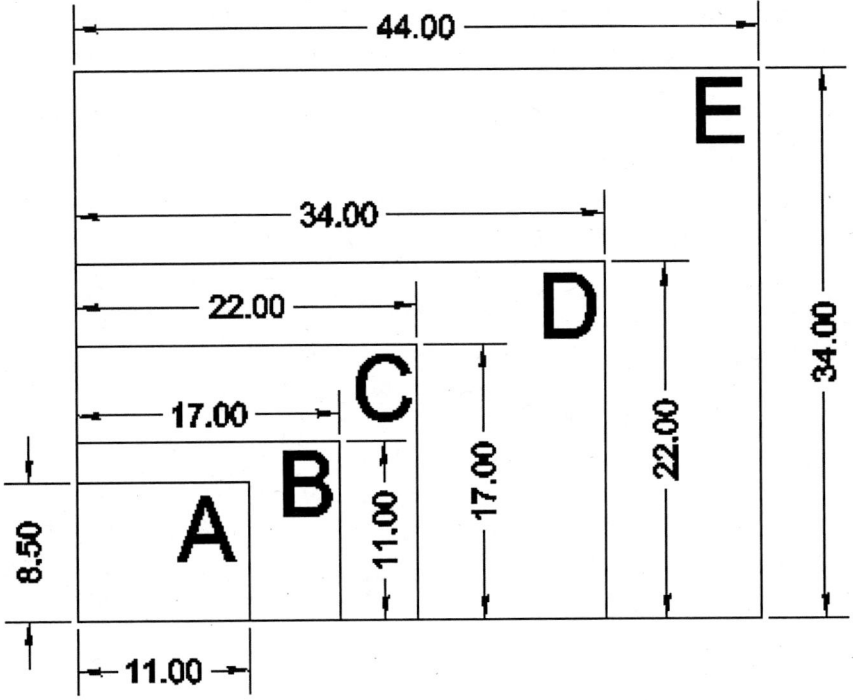

8. Can you think of another way to merge entities from one drawing into another? Instead of using the block command, the **copy** & **paste** commands found in the **Edit** menu work here too just like in any Windows application.

## Module M1 Suggested Learning Exercises

1. Create quarter and eighth-scale dimension styles in both two and three place decimal formats for your mechanical drawing template.

2. Create a +.000/-.005 tolerance dimension style based on the Standard style for your mechanical drawing template.

3. Use your new mechanical drawing template to draw and dimension a drawing from the Additional Exercises located in the Appendix of this text.

## Module M2- Advanced Dimensioning

Objectives:
1. Dimension an object using ordinate dimensioning
2. Apply a geometric tolerance
3. Specify symmetrical, deviation, limits and basic tolerances

This module is intended for mechanical drafters who may have a need to use some of DraftSight's advanced dimensioning capabilities that weren't covered in Chapter 10.

## Ordinate Dimensioning

Ordinate dimensioning allows the drafter to specify the XY coordinates of features from a datum (or 0,0 point) on the drawing view. As you will see, this saves time and valuable space on the drawing area. Many find ordinate dimensioning easier to read than linear dimensioning as well. Open Pocket Tool.dwg to begin.

1. Create a **new layer** called "**Dimord**" and give it a color of your choosing. **Turn off the Dimension layer**. Make **Dimord** the active layer. **Zoom** to the side view of the pocket tool's handle.

2. With the **Standard** dimension style active, select the **Ordinate** dimension icon from the **Dimension** toolbar.

3. Using **ESnaps**, select the center of the .188 diameter hole on the right side of the part for the feature location. **Sweep the mouse** up and down, back and forth. Note the location of the extension line and text changes from vertical to horizontal. A dimension in the X-axis is defined by sweeping the mouse up or down to place the dimension. The Y is defined by sweeping left or right (You may choose instead to type "**x**" or "**y**" in the command window at this point to lock-in the X or Y dimension).

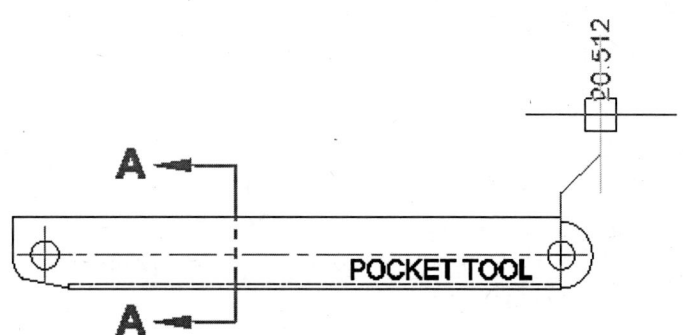

4. **Sweep upward** of the hole center. Note the dimension that appears. This is how far in the X-axis we are from the origin (0,0) of the drawing area. But, we want the hole center to be the datum, or 0,0 point. We can do one of two things: Move the drawing views of the handle such that the hole center lies at the drawing's 0,0 point, or simply make the hole center the ordinate 0,0 point where it currently lies (this is preferred).

5. With the **Ordinate** command still active, enter "**Z**" in the command window. Note that the ordinate dimension text changes to **.000**. Enter "**T**" for text and change the dimension text to "**0**". Place this dimension above the hole as shown below to define the X-axis origin. Repeat for the Y axis (use **Ortho** mode to keep the extension lines straight).

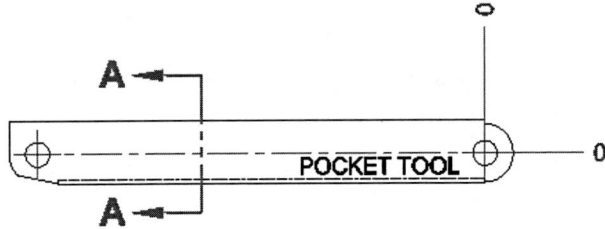

6. Add an X axis dimension to the far left end of the handle (3.718). Note that at first the dimension does not reference the 0,0 point we defined in the previous step. Enter "**R**" in the command window to reference the 0,0 origin.

7. On your own proceed to dimension the handle using ordinate dimensions as shown the figure below. Ensure that every point has an X and Y dimension related to it. If the dimension text ends up too close to another dimension, you can "jog" it by turning off **Ortho** mode. **Save** the drawing.

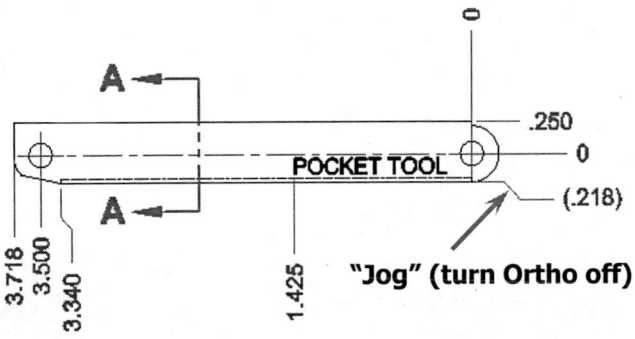

---

***Tip:*** Need to find the area of an object? Go to the **Tools** menu, **Inquiry** cascading menu and select **Get Area**. Use **ESnap** to pick the points that define the area. Press **Enter**, the measured area appears in the command window. Try it!

# Geometric Dimensioning and Tolerancing

As you are probably aware, Geometric Dimensioning and Tolerancing (GD&T) provides great advantages in manufacturing by helping to ensure the interchangeability of components and keeping costs down by reducing scrap. DraftSight offers a range of GD&T dimensioning capabilities.

1. Using the drawing views of the handle in Pocket Tool.dwg once again, **dimension** the radius, diameter and side view on the **dimord** layer as shown in the drawing below.

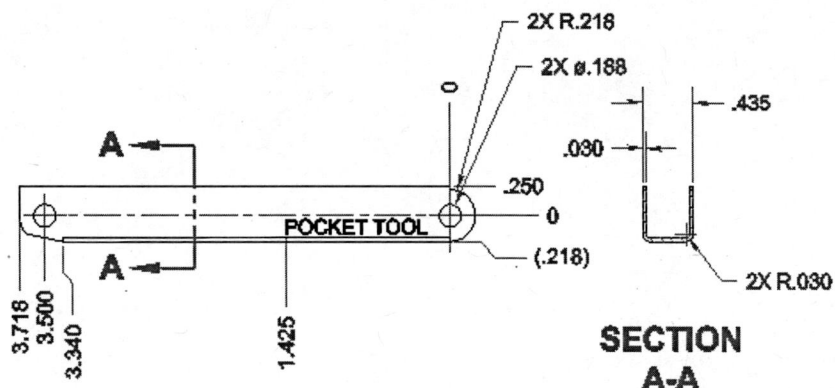

2. Next, select the **Tolerance** icon in the **Dimension** toolbar. The *Geometric Tolerance* window should open. The blank fields represent the parts of a feature control frame. Make the following entries, and press **OK** when you're finished:

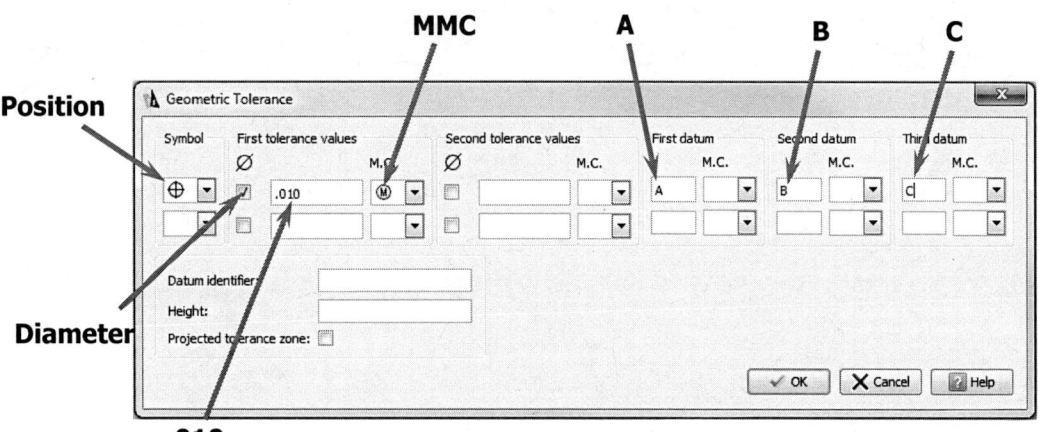

3. Place the feature control frame under the 2XØ.188 dimension like on the drawing shown at the bottom of the page.   Use **EGrips** to adjust dimension locations if needed.

4. Since three datums were referenced in the feature control frame, we need to identify the datum features. Select the **Smart Leader** icon in the **Dimension** toolbar.  Type "**S**" for settings.  The *Leader Settings* window will appear. Under the **Annotations** tab, select **Tolerance** for **Type**.  Under the **Arrow/Lines tab**, select **Datum triangle filled** for the **Arrow Style**. Press the **OK** button.

**Tolerance**

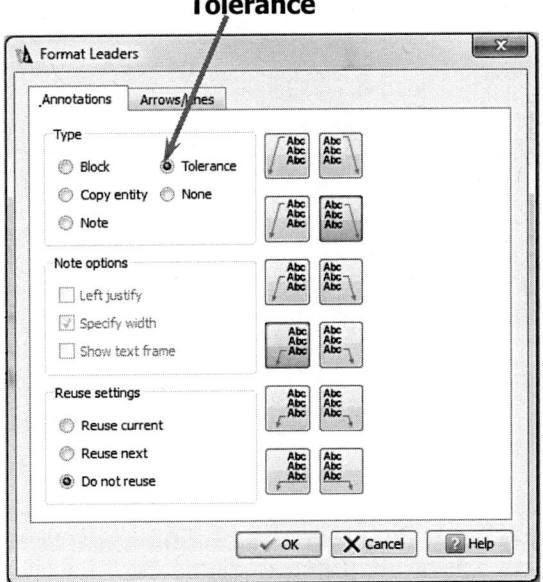
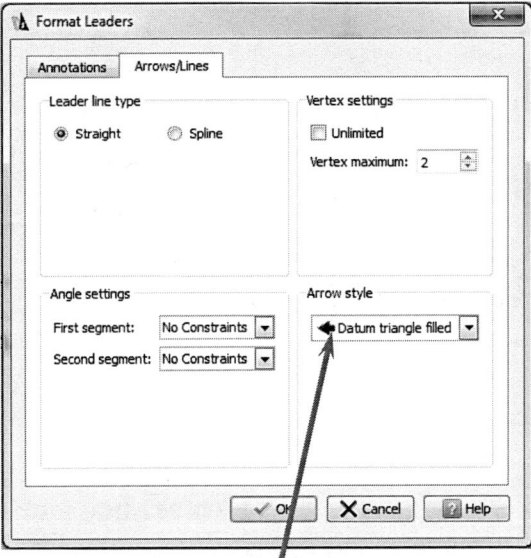

**Datum triangle filled**

5. The *Geometric Tolerance* window will now appear. Enter "**A**" in any one of the datum fields and press the **OK** button. Use the drawing below as a guide to place datums A, B & C.

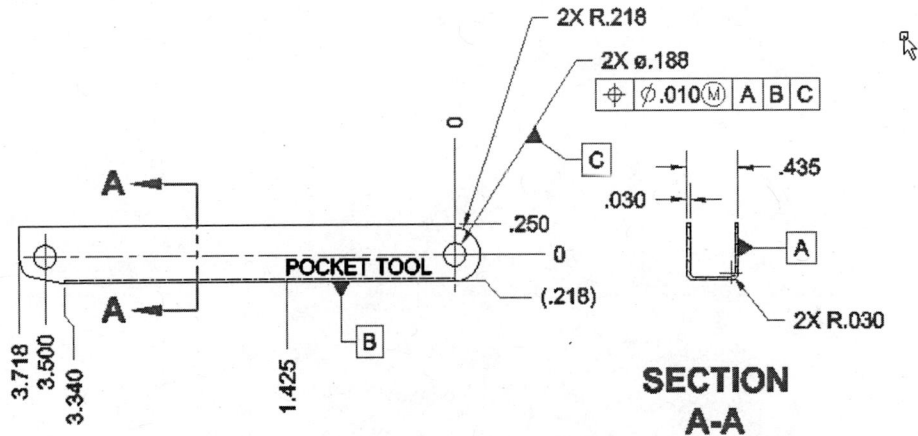

6. As you may know, the location dimensions associated with the feature control frame must now be "**Basic**". This is indicated by placing a box around these dimensions. In this case, there is only one dimension to worry about. Double-click on the 3.500 dimension to access the dimension's properties. Scroll down to the **Tolerances** area of the *Properties* window. In the *Tolerance display* field, select **Basic** from the drop-down list.

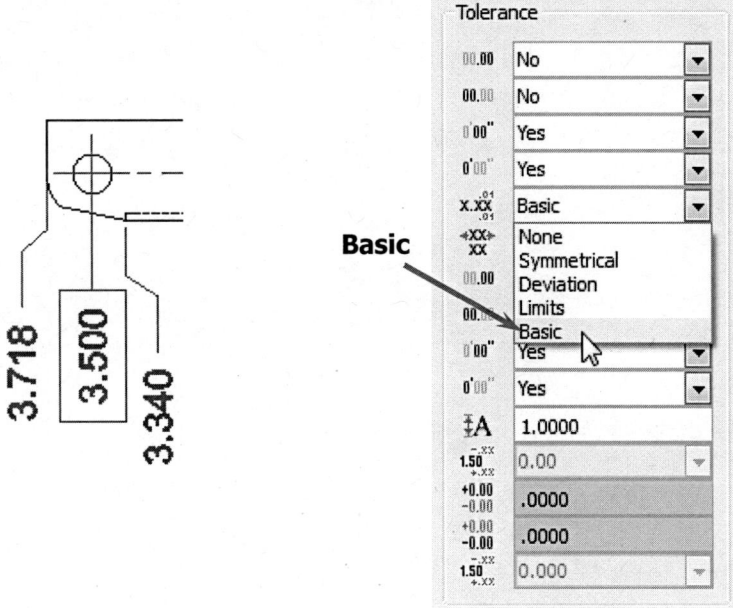

7. Note that you can specify tolerances in symmetric, deviation and limits fashion using this technique as well (instead of creating a dimension style for such as covered in Module M1). **Save** the drawing.

## Module M2 Suggested Learning Exercise

1. Use ordinate dimensioning and Geometric Dimensioning & Tolerancing to re-dimension at least one other part of the Pocket Tool (an example follows):

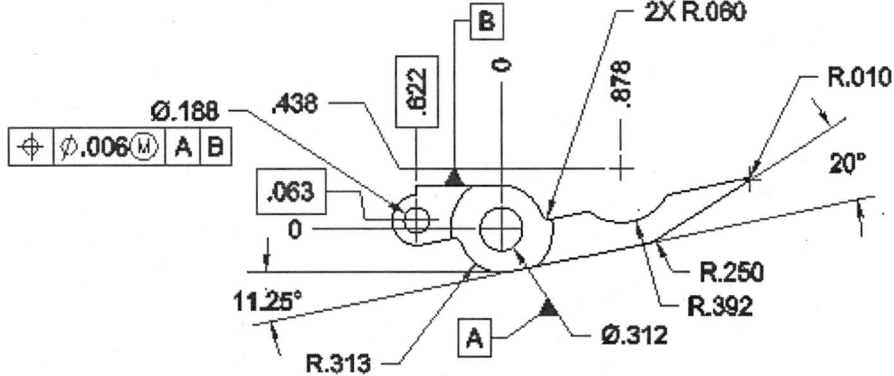

**NOTES:**

## Module M3- Assembly Drawings

Objectives:
1. Define a block
2. Insert a block
3. Explode a block
4. Insert a title block
5. Create a parts list
6. Plot from paper space

This module will demonstrate the value of blocks and their uses by creating an assembly drawing of the Unit 2 Mechanical Project; the pocket tool.

## **Defining Blocks**

Blocks are a useful way to group and manage objects within a drawing. A logical method for blocking objects follows that the entities which make up a part within an assembly should be grouped as a block. As you will see, a block acts as one entity, even though it may be originally made up of several entities.

1. **Open** Pocket Tool.dwg from Unit 2. **Zoom** all the way out. Note there are several drawing views of parts of the pocket tool scattered around the drawing area. **Zoom** in on the three drawing views of the large flat screwdriver. **Hide** all layers except for the object layer (or the layer the visible geometry is on).

2. Select **Define** from the **Draw** menu and **Block** cascading menu. This opens the ***Block Definition*** window.

3. In the *Name* field, type "**LargeFlatScrewdriver**". For the **Base Point**, click on the **Select in graphics area icon** and pick the center of the Ø.188 hole in the side-view of the screw driver (use **ESnaps**). For the **Block entities**, click on the **Select in graphics area** icon and window the side view of the screw driver (see next page).

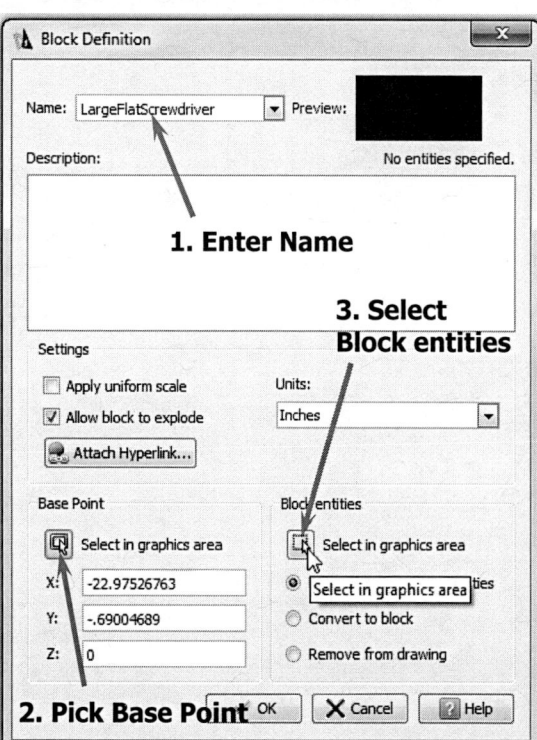

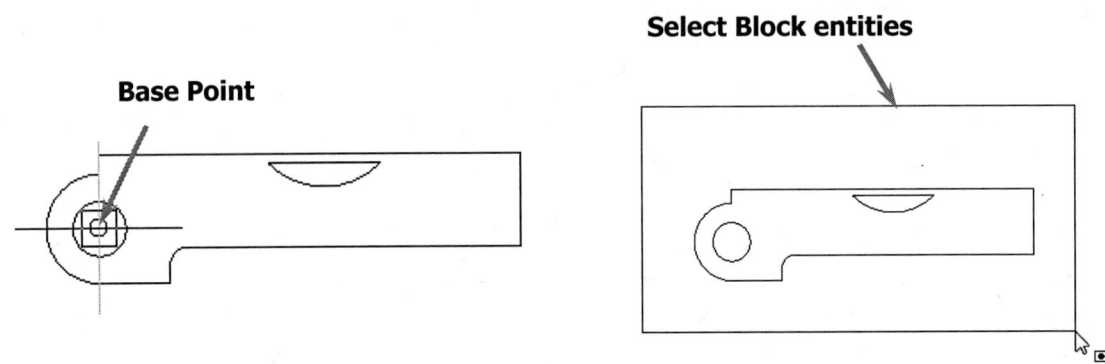

**Base Point**

**Select Block entities**

4. Note there are other options for what to do with the **Base entities**. You can preserve them (leave as-is), convert them to a block, or remove them from the drawing (delete them). For this exercise, just select **Preserve as separate entities**. Choose "**OK**" when finished.

5. It may seem like nothing happened, but the block is stored away in the drawing for future use. We'll get to that part in a minute. In the meantime, make blocks of the front views of the small flat screwdriver, knife blade, handle, and plier nose as shown below. Name each accordingly, and use hole-centers for base points. **Save** the drawing.

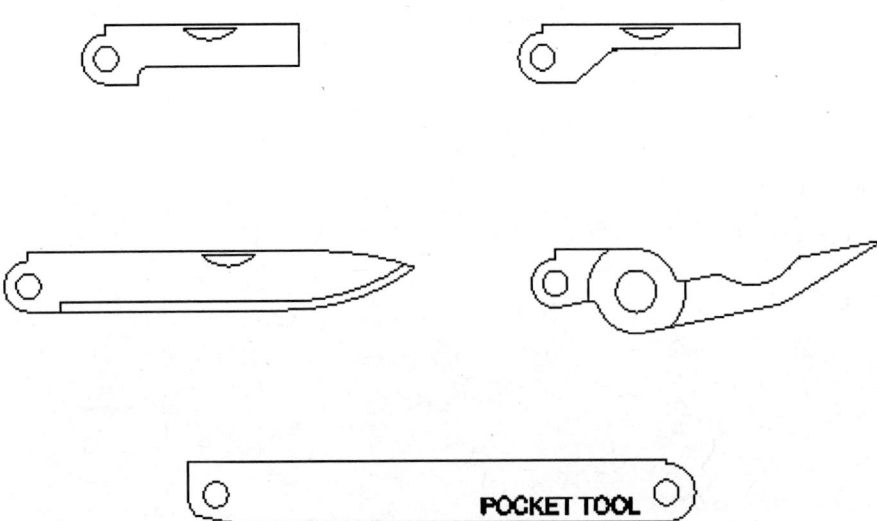

POCKET TOOL

## Inserting Blocks

1. **Pan/Zoom** into an unused portion of your drawing area, away from the drawing views of the pocket tool components. From the **Insert** menu, select the **Block** command. The *Insert Block* window should appear. From the *Name* drop-down list, select **Handle**. Note the handle is shown in the small preview window.

2. Select **Specify later** for **Position**. Leave the other parameters as shown in the figure below. Note that you can adjust the Scale, Rotation and whether or not the block is "exploded" (returned to its original state) prior to insertion. Click on the **OK** button.

3. The *Insert Block* window dismisses so you can place the block. Note the crosshairs are attached to the base point you specified earlier for the handle. Click an empty portion of the drawing area to **Specify destination** for the block of the handle. Now just for fun, select the block of the handle. How many entity grips does it have? How many entities is it now? Where does the entity grip happen to be?

4. Next, we'll make a mirror image of the handle.  Pick the **Mirror** icon in the **Modify** toolbar.  For the mirror line, pick the two hole centers of the handle.  Enter "**Yes**" to delete the source entities.

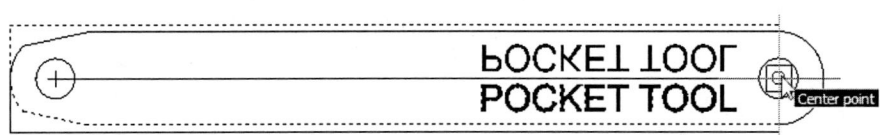 

5. Locate and select the **Explode** icon in the **Modify** toolbar.  **Select the mirrored Handle and press enter**. Besides the text righting itself, what else did exploding the block do?  (Hint: try selecting it.)

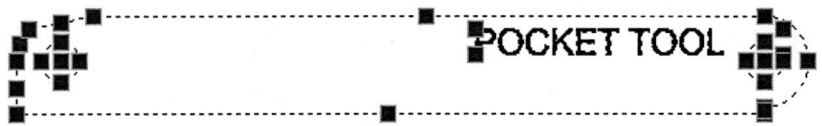

6. Now **insert** the block of the knife blade at the center of the right hole in the handle.  Specify an insertion angle of 260 degrees.

7. On your own, **insert** the Large and Small Flat Screwdrivers at angles of 225 and 200 degrees respectively.  **Insert** the Plier Nose on the other end of the Handle, rotated 180 degrees. Your drawing should look like the one below:

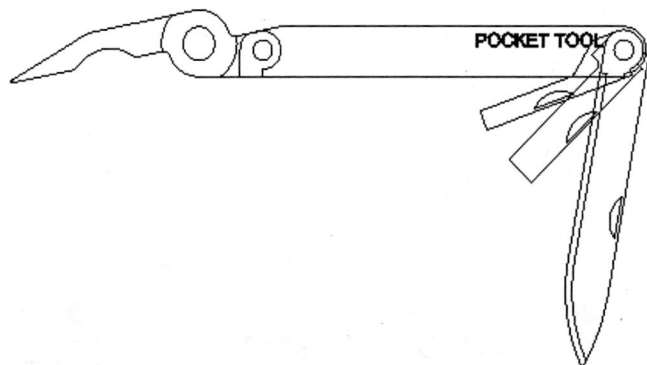

8. **Insert** another block of the plier nose, sharing centers with the previous one. Using the **Mirror** command, mirror the second plier nose so it sits opposite of the first one (see next page).

9. On your own, **insert** another handle and position it as shown in the drawing below (Tip: The angle between the handles is 23 degrees).

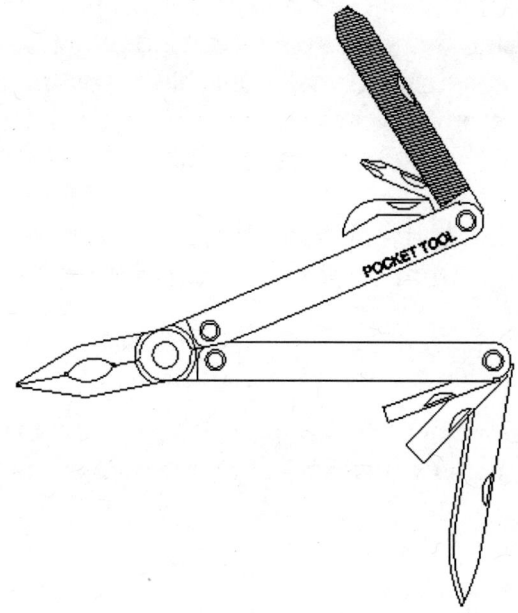

10. Make **blocks** of the Phillips screwdriver, file and can opener. Position them in the assembly as shown above. Try using the **Rotate** command with the **Reference** option, it will help.

11. **Rotate** the entire assembly so the pocket tool is upright. **Explode** the blocks making up the parts and clean things up, deleting/trimming geometry hidden by the handles and other parts. Add rivets in each of the handle holes (∅ .250"). Your drawing should look like the one below when you are finished. **Save** the drawing.

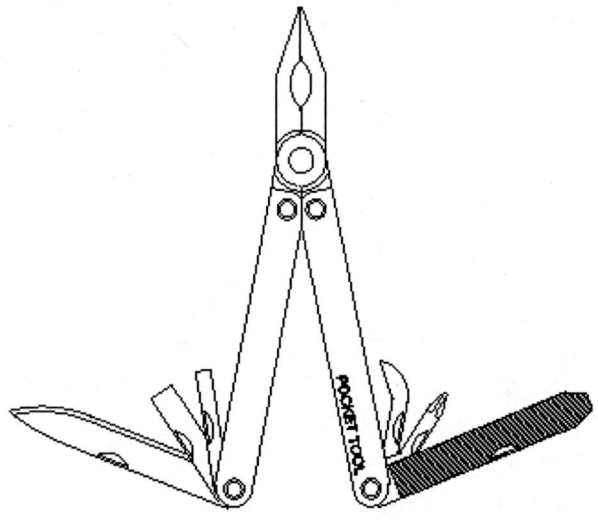

## Inserting a Title Block

Thus far we've been using blocks *internal* to drawings. You may have noticed the **Browse** button inside the *Insert Block* window. This allows you to basically merge two drawings. Normally title blocks would be readily available from the template you started the drawing with. In this case however, we need to borrow a title block from another drawing started with your template.

1.  Leaving Pocket Tool.dwg open, **start a new drawing** using the **Mechanical** template from Module M1. **Save** it as "**temp.dwg**".

2.  Switch to Pocket Tool.dwg. From the **Insert** menu, choose **Block**.

3.  When the *Insert Block* window appears, select the **Browse...** button and find **temp.dwg**. Uncheck any **Specify later** boxes. Select **Explode Block** and click "**OK**".

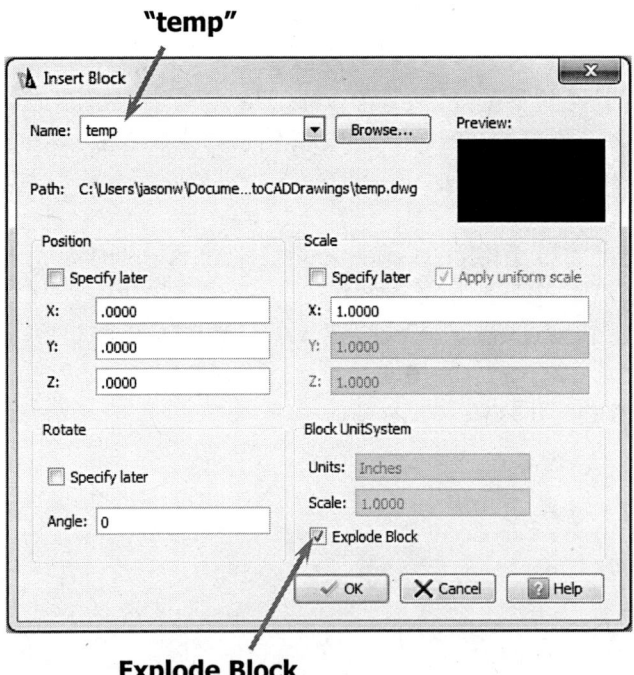

"temp"

Explode Block

4.  Next, initiate the **Insert Block** command again. This time when the *Insert Block* window appears, choose the **Name:** drop down. Your title blocks should be available. Pick the **A-size** title block that one you made in Module M1from the list. Check **Specify later** for **Position**. Click **OK** and drag the A-size title block into place in the drawing area, framing the assembly of the pocket tool (see next page).

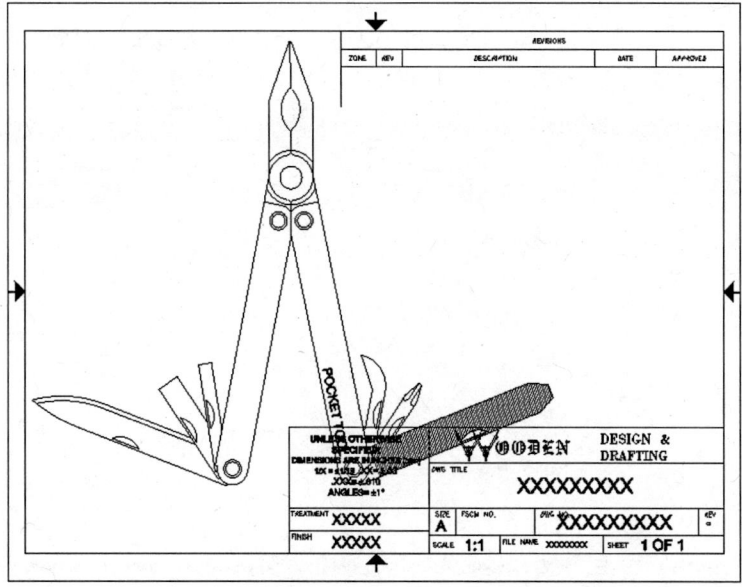

## Inserting a title block in sheet space

Note that in the example above, the assembly is too large to print on an A-Size piece of paper at full scale. To make it fit better, we'll have to print it half-scale compared to the title block. **Sheet space** is the perfect environment to accomplish this. First though, let's annotate the assembly with item arrows in preparation for creating a parts list in the next section. These item arrows will have to be twice as big to be legible on a half-scale drawing.

1. Select the **Dimension Style** icon and then the **New** button. Create a new style called "**HalfScale**" based on **Standard** and click **OK**.

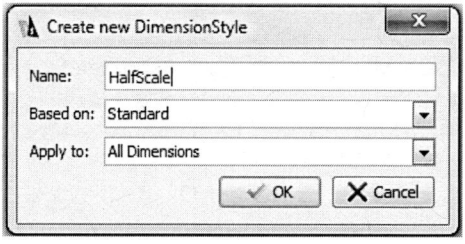

2. Select **Fit** and **Dimension scale.** Enter "**2**" in the **Scale factor:** field. Now activate the new dimension style **HalfScale**. Press the **OK** button when finished.

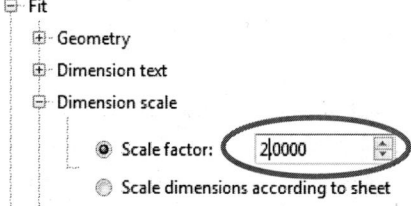

3. **Delete** the title block we inserted around the pocket tool assembly in the previous section. Activate the **Dimension** layer. Using **Leader** label each of the parts of the pocket tool assembly as shown in the drawing below. These annotations will correspond to the item numbers in the parts list.

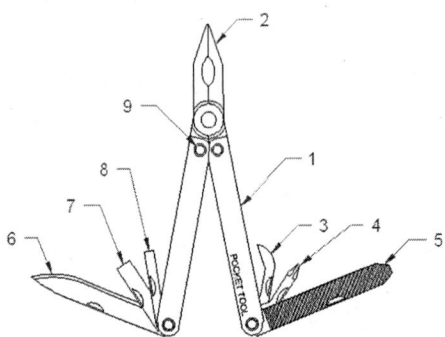

4. Now we will enter **Sheet Space** by selecting the **Sheet 1** tab at the bottom of the drawing area. Note the coordinate system icon takes on the appearance of a triangle, also note the box around the drawing area- this is a **Viewport**. A viewport is a window so you can "look" into model space. Double-click inside the viewport to activate it; **Pan** & **Zoom** so that the Pocket Tool assembly fits nicely inside the viewport (see picture below).

**Active viewport**

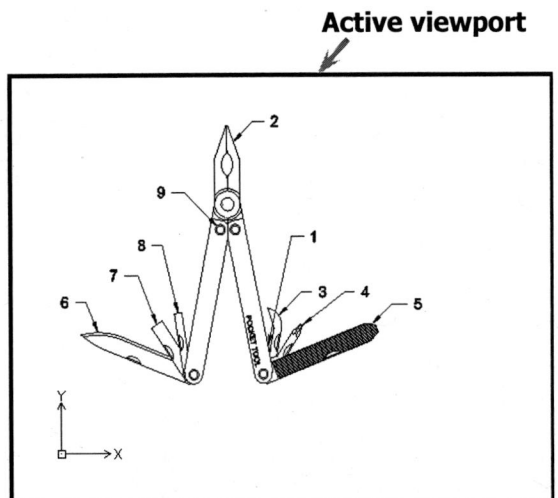

5. Double-click outside of the viewport to de-activate it. Select the viewport with the pickbox, then right-click and select **Properties** from the pop-up menu. In the *Properties* window, choose **1:2** from the **Standard Scale** drop-down list. If you ever zoom inside of the viewport, you will have to repeat this step.

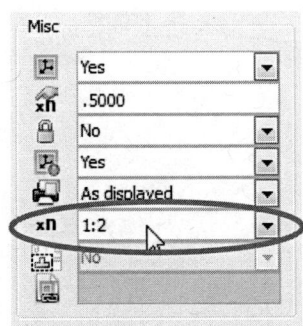

6. Press the Escape key to de-select the viewport.

**Insert** the A-size title block; un-check all the "Specify later" boxes but select **Explode Block**.

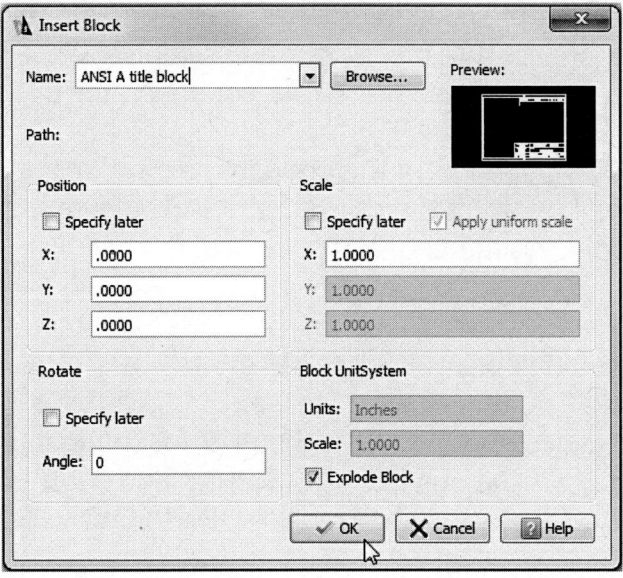

7. The sheet space title block should look like the one in the graphic below. If needed, activate the viewport and pan (do not zoom or you will have to re-set the scale) so that only the assembly of the pocket tool is visible.

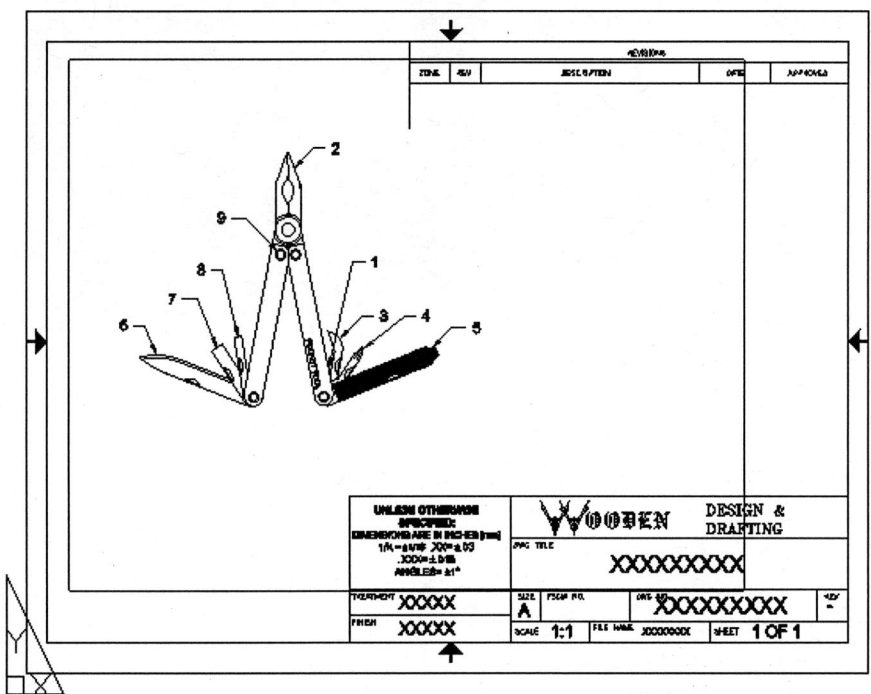

## Creating a parts list using Table

The parts list (sometimes called a "Bill of Materials") is an important feature of any assembly drawing.  It provides the names, part numbers, quantities and material for the components that make up the assembly.  While there are several ways to make a parts list, we'll use the **Table** command for this example.

1.  With Pocket Tool.dwg open from the previous section, make sure the **Sheet1** tab is active at the bottom of the drawing area.  You should see something similar to the graphic on the previous page.

2.  Locate and select the **Table** command from the **Draw** menu.  The *Insert Table* window should appear.  Click the **View table styles** icon next to the **Table Style** name field and change the **Text Height** to **.12**. For the insertion method, select **Set position**. Enter **9** for the **Rows** and **1** for the row height. Enter **5** for the number of **Columns** and set the Column width to **.85**.  Leave the **Cell styles** as shown below. Press **OK**.

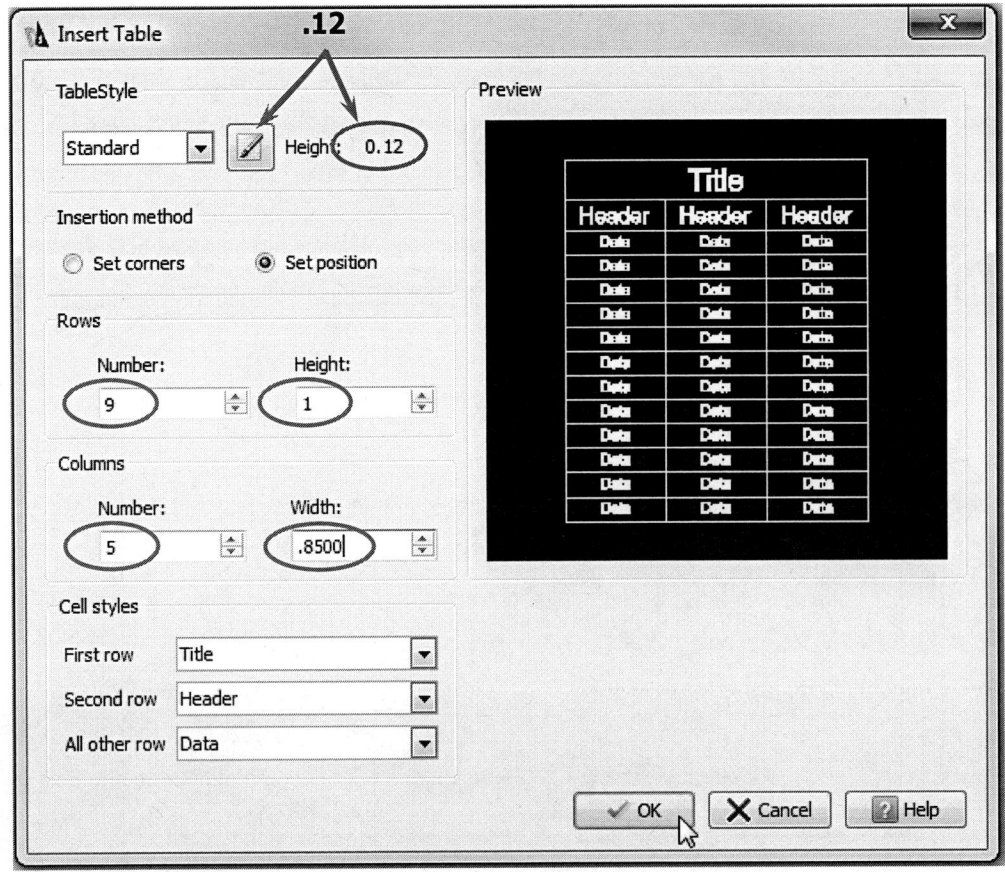

3. Place the table above the title block. The ***Edit Note*** window should appear. Type "**PARTS LIST**" for the title and press the **Tab** key. Type "**ITEM**" to for the first header cell and press the **Tab** key. Continue to enter the information found in the graphic below. Pressing the arrow keys will also take you from one cell to another. If you exit the ***Edit Note*** window and find a mistake, just click on the table, right-click and select **Table edit** from the pop-up menu. Also, use **EGrips** to resize the columns and to place the table as shown below.

| PARTS LIST | | | | |
|---|---|---|---|---|
| ITEM | QTY | PART | DESCRIP. | MAT'L |
| 1 | 2 | -1 | HANDLE | SSTL |
| 2 | 2 | -2 | PLIER NOSE | SSTL |
| 3 | 1 | -3 | CAN OPENER | SSTL |
| 4 | 1 | -4 | PHIL. SCRWDRVR | SSTL |
| 5 | 1 | -5 | FILE | SSTL |
| 6 | 1 | -6 | BLADE | SSTL |
| 7 | 1 | -7 | LRG FLT SCRWDRVR | SSTL |
| 8 | 1 | -8 | SM FLT SCRWDRVR | SSTL |
| 9 | 4 | -9 | 3/16 RIVET | SSTL |

UNLESS OTHERWISE SPECIFIED:
DIMENSIONS ARE IN INCHES [mm]
.1X = ±1/16  .XX = ±.03
.XXX= ±.010
ANGLES= ±1°

WOODEN DESIGN & DRAFTING

DWG TITLE XXXXXXXXX

TREATMENT XXXXX

SIZE A  FSCM NO.

DWG NO. XXXXXXXXX

REV -

FINISH XXXXX

SCALE 1:1  FILE NAME XXXXXXXX  SHEET 1 OF 1

4. Fill out the title block. Move the viewport to the **Viewport** layer (create it if it doesn't exist) and **hide** the layer. **Save** the drawing.

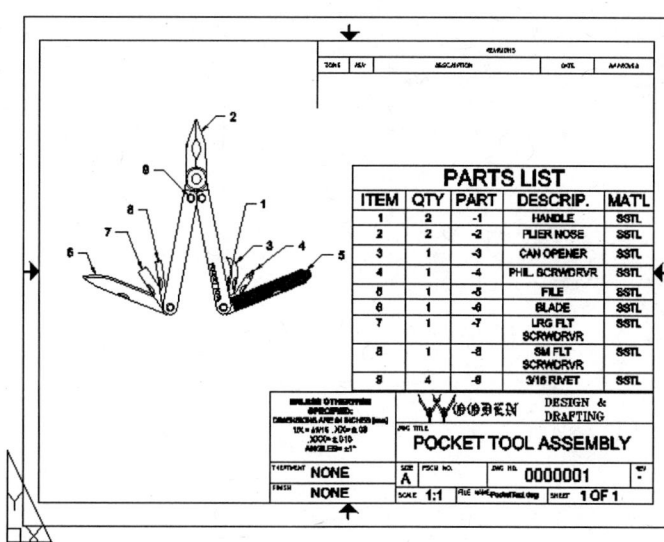

## Sheet Space printing and management

In Unit 2 we learned to plot from **model space** (the environment in which you draw and detail objects). A more capable method exists in the **sheet space** environment. We will set up the assembly drawing of the pocket tool to plot at half-scale from sheet space.

1. Having completed the previous section, with Pocket Tool.dwg open and the **Sheet1** tab selected, select the **Layers Manager** icon in the **Standard** toolbar. Make sure the ViewPort layer is set **not** to print (the viewport should be on this layer). Press **OK** when finished.

2. Select the **Print** icon in the **Standard** toolbar. Choose your printer, an **A size** (also called Letter) paper and a scale of **1:1**. Select **All geometry** for the Print range. Choose **Print Preview**.

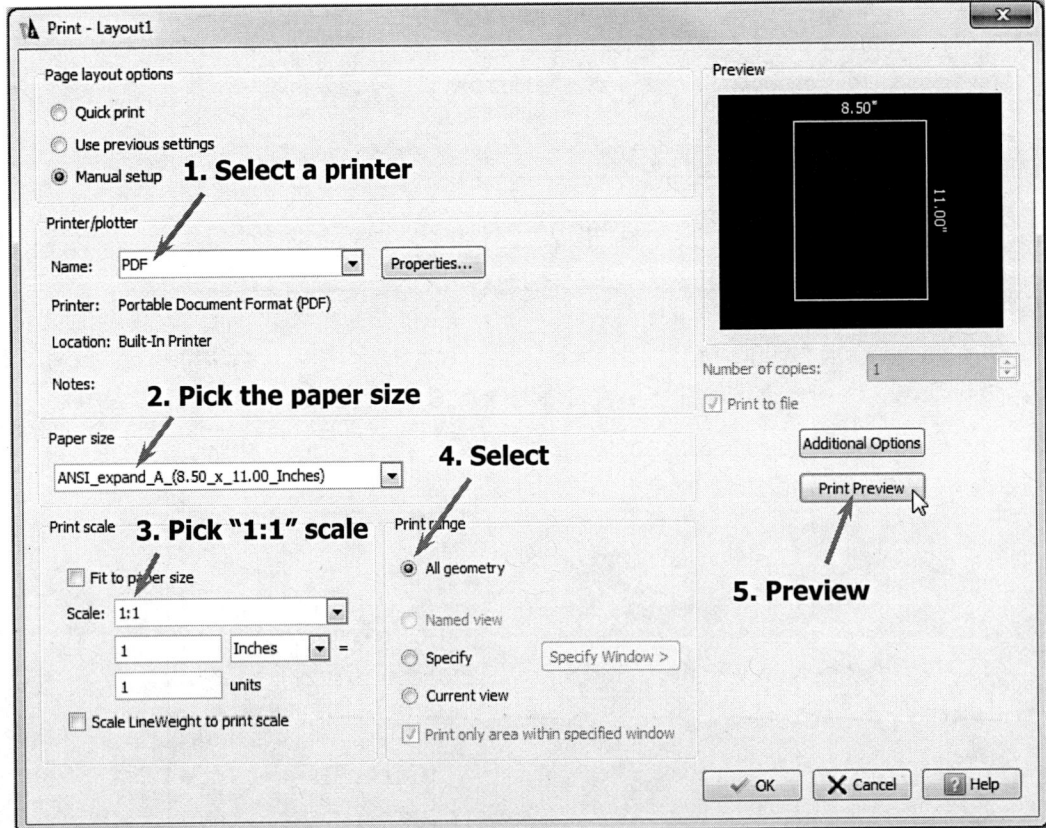

3. If the preview looks acceptable, go ahead and **Print** the drawing.

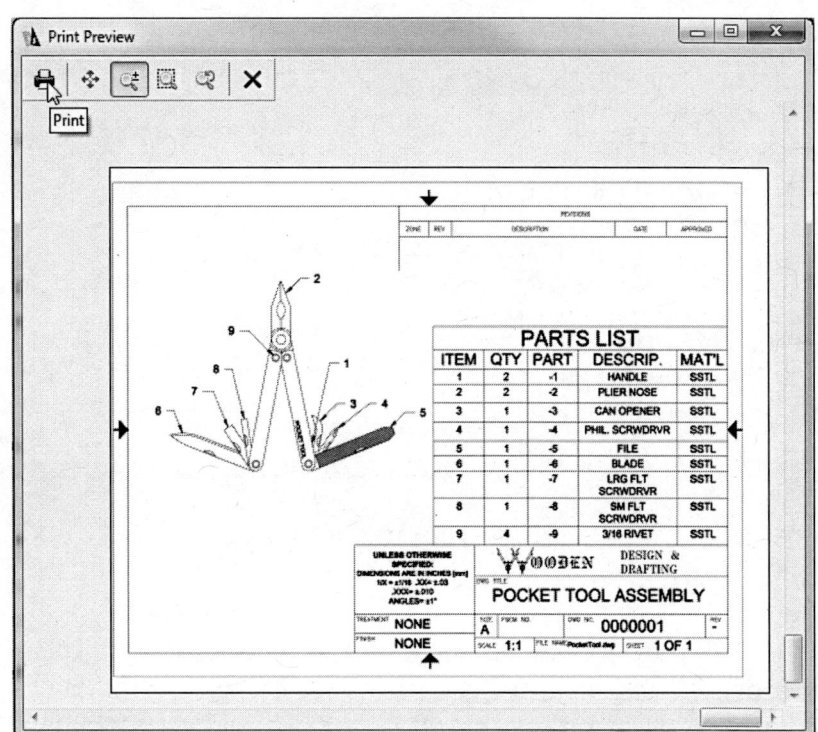

4. Tabs can be renamed. This is done by right-clicking on the tab and selecting **Rename** from the pop-up menu. For mechanical drawings it makes sense to just leave them named after the sheet number (page number) found in the title block.  Sheets can also be deleted, delete Sheet2 by right-clicking on the tab and selecting **Delete** from the pop-up menu.

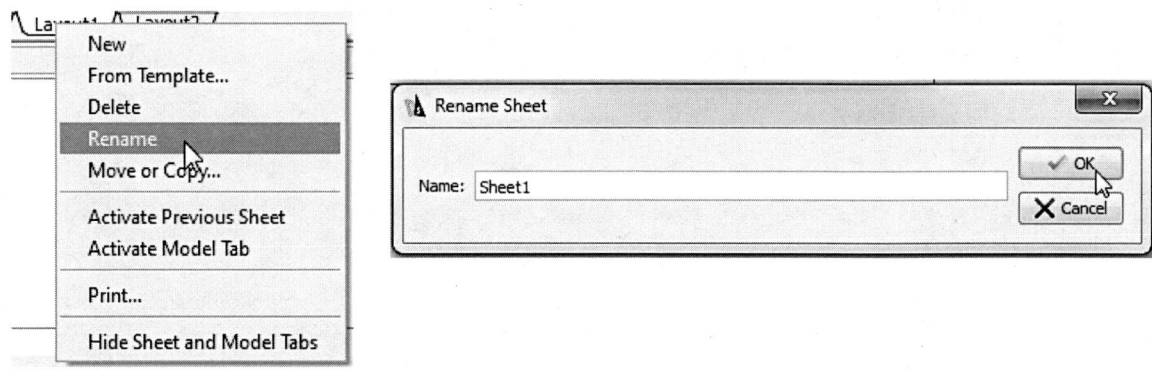

5. **Copy** the **Sheet1** tab by right-clicking on it and selecting **Move/Copy**.

6. In the *Move/Copy* window, check the **Copy sheet** box and select **OK**. Rename the new sheet to "**Sheet2**" and activate this sheet.

7. Go to the **Layers Manager** and **show** the **ViewPort** layer.

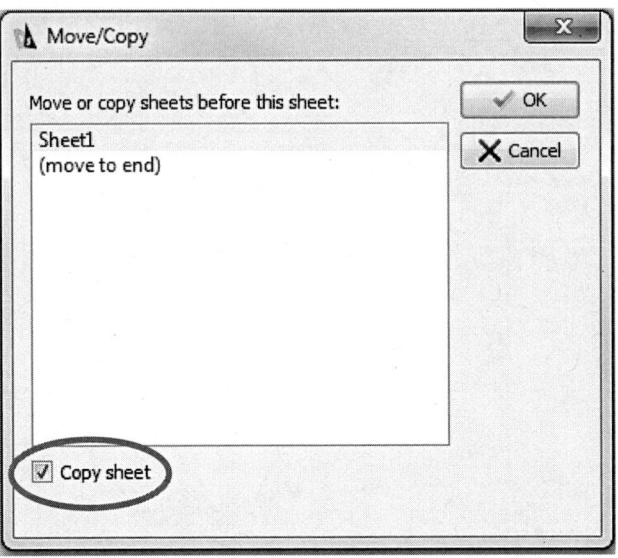

8. **Delete** the parts list on Sheet2. Activate the viewport on Sheet2 and **Pan** to the dimensioned view of the handle.

9. De-activate the viewport and set its scale to **1:1** as described in the previous section. If needed, re-size the viewport using its **EGrips** to remove unwanted geometry. Edit the title block. Sheet2 should now look like the graphic below.

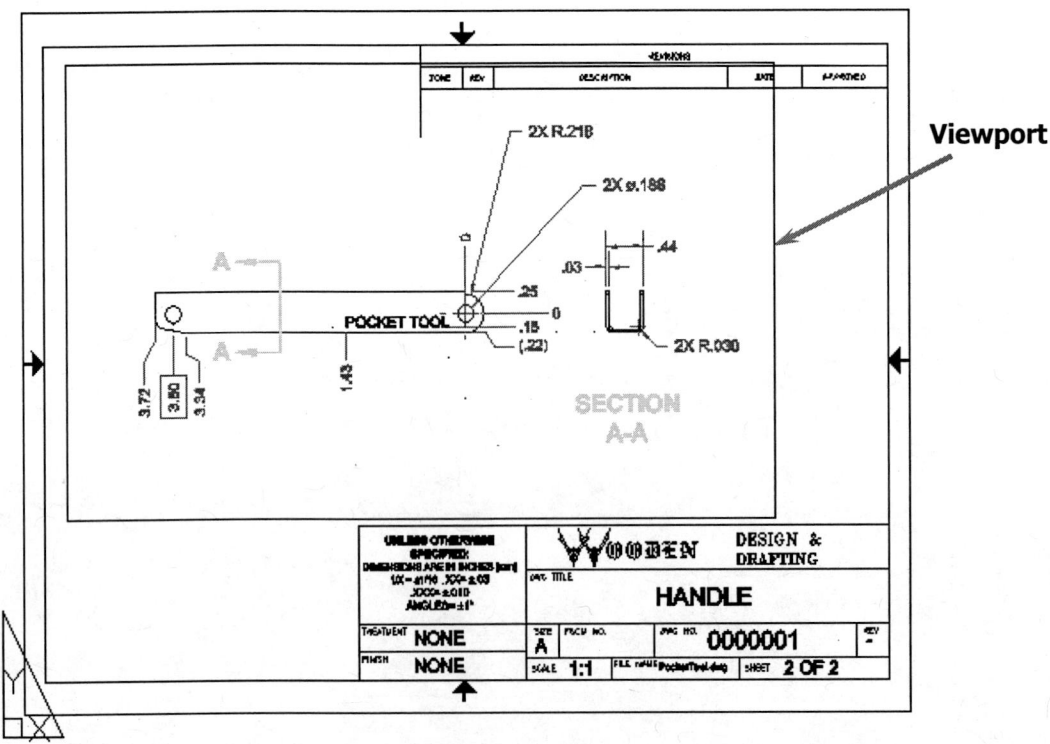

## Module M3 Suggested Learning Exercise

Create new sheets and print each of the drawing views for the remaining components of the pocket tool.

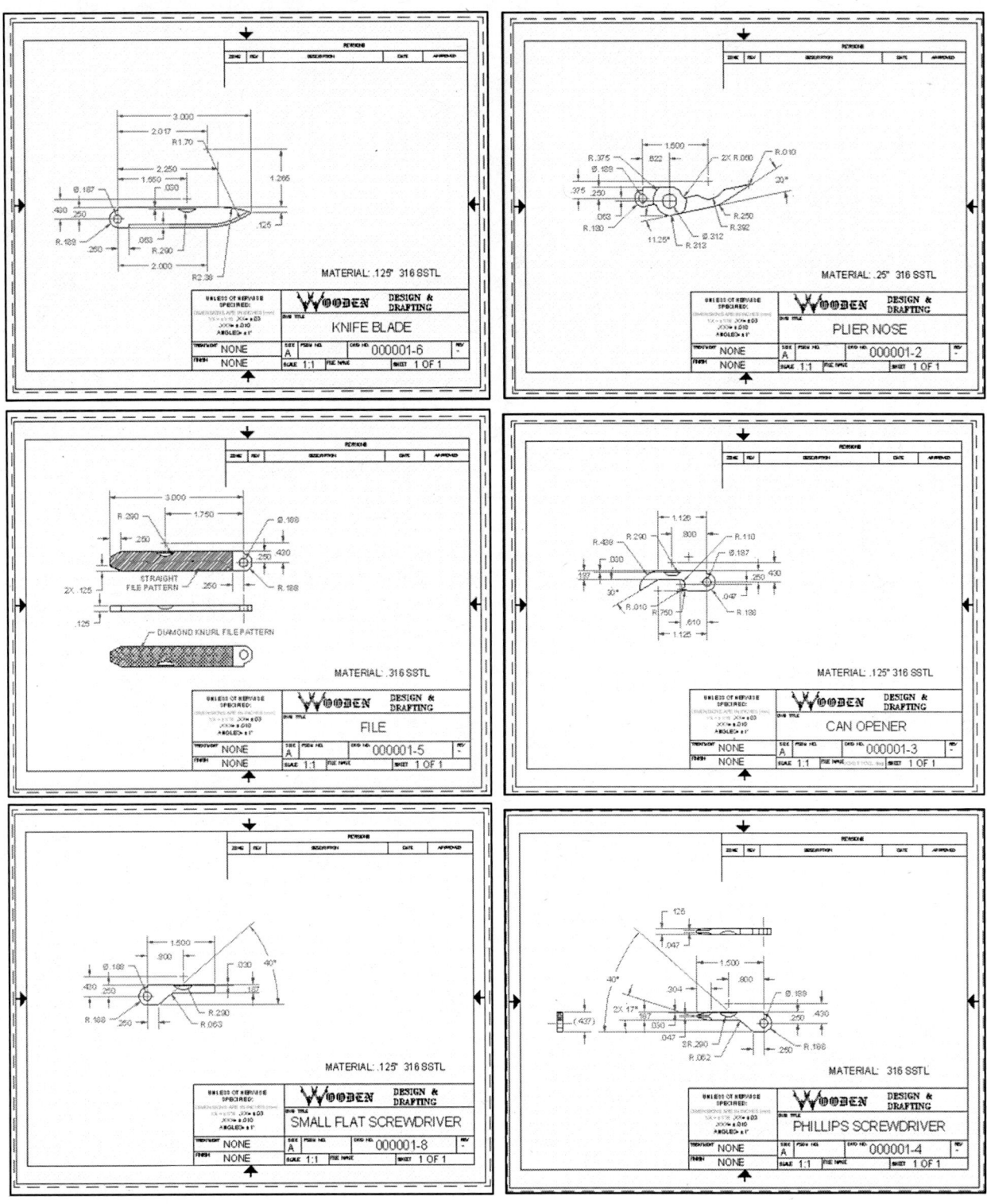

**NOTES:**

# Unit 4- Specialized Architectural CAD Skills

## Module A1- Architectural Drawing Templates

Objectives:
1. Setting a drawing's units and boundary
2. Create architectural layers
3. Set up an architectural dimension and text style
4. Create an architectural title block

This module is intended to build upon of the basic concepts learned in Chapters 8-10 for the architectural drafter. If you currently work for a firm that uses CAD for architectural design, you may want to ask to use the company's drawing template (most companies will have a standard template so that all drawings are set up the same way) and this module can be, for the most part, skipped. If you are not yet employed at a firm using CAD, or plan on using it as part of self-employment, read on...

## Architectural Drawing Units

Most architectural and construction firms in the United States use feet and inches as the unit of measurement for construction drawings. We'll start by defining these units.

1. Start a **New** drawing using the **standard** template.

2. Choose **Unit System** from the **Format** menu. The *Options* window will appear. Select **Architectural** from the drop-down list under Length & Type. Set the precision to **1/4"**. Leave the Angle type as decimal degrees unless you have a reason to do otherwise (e.g. survey work often uses other units). Select the **Help** button if you'd like to learn more. Press **OK** when finished.

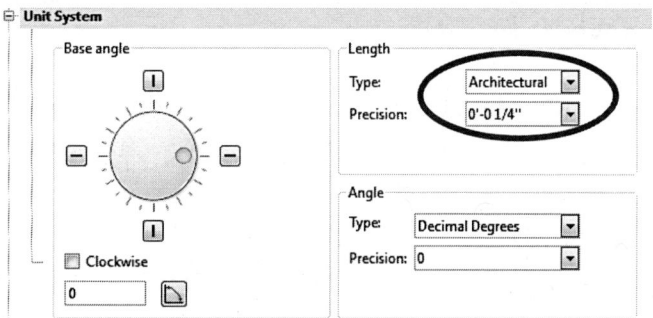

## Architectural Drawing Boundary

A drawing's boundary varies based on the size of the structure being drawn, but can easily be changed to fit a small storage shed or a large commercial building. In actuality though, by drawing outside the boundary all you've done is lose the ability to use the grid. We'll set up the drawing area for a D-Size sheet of paper plotted at 1/4"=1', which suits many residential architectural applications.

1. Select **Drawing Boundary** from the **Format** menu. Press **enter** to except the default of **0'-0",0'-0"** for the lower left corner.

2. For the upper right corner enter **1728,1152**. As mentioned previously, this creates an Architectural D-Size drawing area at 1/4"=1'. This was calculated by taking the reciprocal of the scale (1/4"=1' or .25"=12", 12/.25=48) and multiplying it (48) by the dimensions of a D-Size sheet of paper (36"X24").

```
Default: (0'-0",0'-0")
Options: OFf, ON or
Specify lower left corner»
Default: (1'-0",0'-9")
Specify upper right corner» 1728,1152
:
```

4. Zoom to the boundary by typing "**Z**" enter and "**B**" enter (these are keyboard shortcuts). Place the pick box in the upper right-hand corner of the drawing area. Note the coordinate display reports something like 170',96',0' for this location. If desired, set up a grid and snap at an interval you expect to use (e.g., 24") by right clicking on the **Grid** button in the status bar and selecting **Settings**. Turn on the **Grid** to view the drawing boundary. If the spacing is too tight, DraftSight will say "Grid too dense to display" in the command window. **Save** the template in a location recommended by your facilitator as **Architectural.dwt** (not .dwg).

## Architectural Drawing Layers

Typically, layers for an architectural drawing are related to objects in the drawing area. We'll set up a number of common layers used in architectural drawing.

1. Select the **Layers Manager** icon in the **Layers** toolbar.

2. Create the layers with the line styles shown in the figure below (review Ch. 8 if needed). Select colors that will show up well on your preferred background*. Be sure to click **OK** when finished.

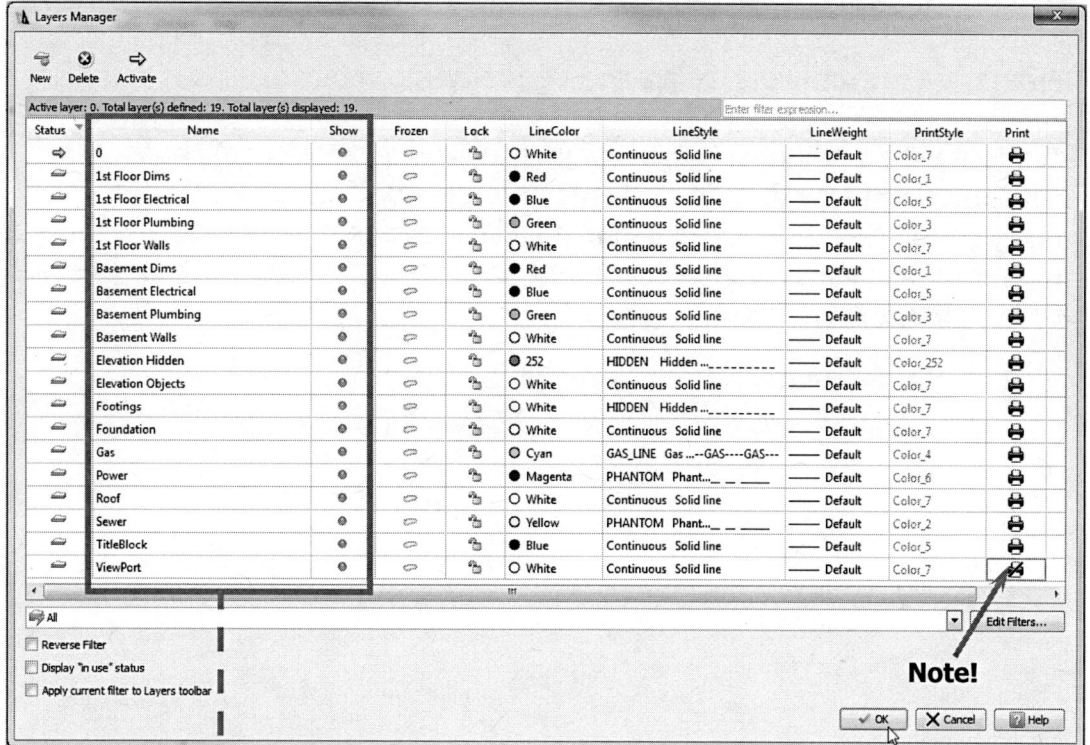

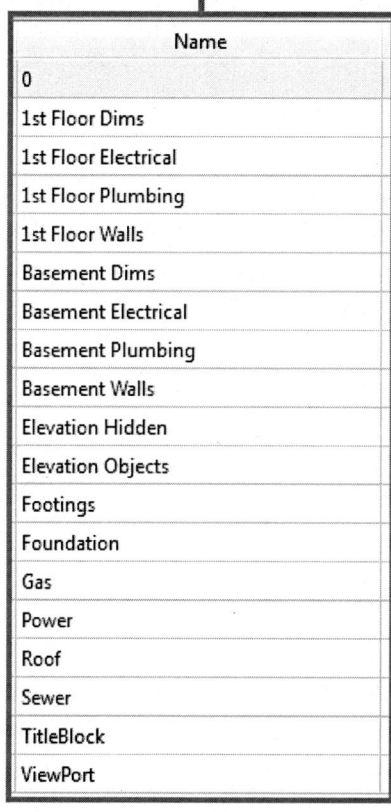

**Note!**

*Tip:* To change background color, go to the Tools Menu and select "Options". Pick the "Display" tab, then the "Colors" button. Click in the miniature drawing area and select the background color you desire from the color drop down menu.

3. **Save** the template in place you can access it (network drive or USB memory if not using your own personal computer).

## Setting-up an Architectural Text Style

The default text font in DraftSight can be difficult to read, and isn't very aesthetically pleasing. It is recommended that you change it:

1.  From the **Format** menu, select the **Text Style** command.

2.  If a font with a "hand-written" appearance is your preference, choose **Cityblueprint** from the **Text**, **Font:** drop-down . If you prefer a more neutral font, then Arial or Tahoma should be considered instead. It's really a matter of personal preference. You may even create multiple styles if desired by selecting the **New** icon.

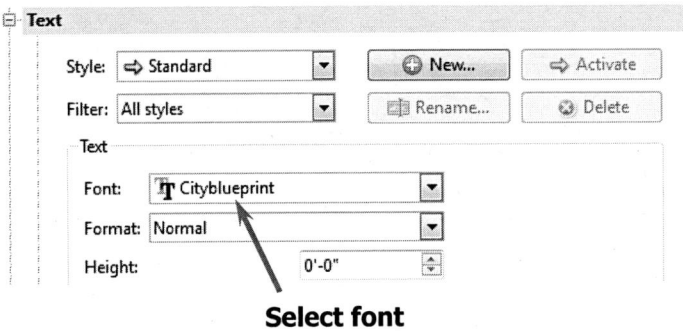

**Select font**

3.  Click **OK** when finished. **Save** the drawing template.

## Creating Architectural Dimension Styles

Perhaps the most tiring part of making a drafting template is creating the dimension styles. It is also perhaps the most necessary, since proper dimensioning is a must to communicate design intent. The following assumes that you are using a feet-inch unit format and drawing primarily at ¼"=1'.

1.  From the **Dimension** toolbar select the **Dimension Style** icon. Inside the *Options* window make the following changes:

2.  First, select the **Rename** icon and rename the Standard dimension style to "**Quarter**" (for ¼"=1').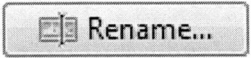

3. **Angular Dimensions**: check **Hide leading zeros**. Leave the format as-is unless you anticipate using surveyor units (in which case it is recommended you create a new dimension style for such.

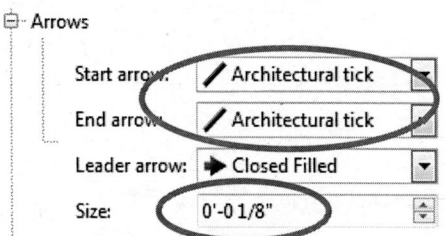

4. **Arrows**: Change to **Architectural tick** and the size to **1/8"**. Click the **Apply** button at the bottom of the *Options* window to save what you've done so far. Notice the updates in the preview window.

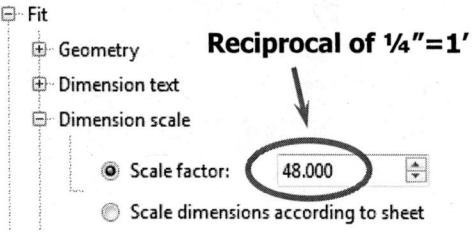

5. **Fit**: Enter the reciprocal of the drawing scale (**48**) in the *Scale* **Factor:** field. This effectively multiplies all other values (e.g., text height) by 48 so the dimensions will be legible when plotted at ¼"=1'.

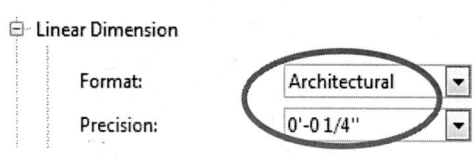

6. **Linear Dimension:** set the Format to **Architectural** and Precision at **1/4"**. Note that DraftSight assumes you want to hide the leading zeros when using architectural dimensioning.

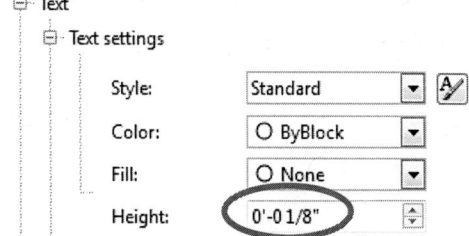

7. **Text, Text Settings:** Set the height to **1/8"**. For the **Text alignment** choose **Align with dimension lines**. Click the **Apply** button to save the changes made thus-far.

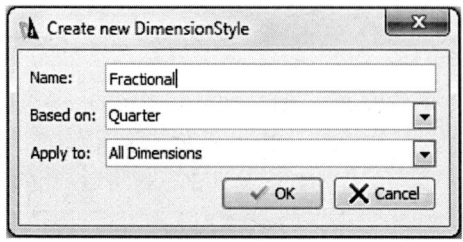

8. Create a new dimension style for objects too small for feet-inches and require better precision. These objects (e.g., cabinets) are typically measured in just inches. Select the **New** icon. Enter "**Fractional**" for the new style name. Press **OK**.

9. Go to **Linear Dimensions**. Change the format to **Fractional** and the precision to **1/16**. Press **Apply**.

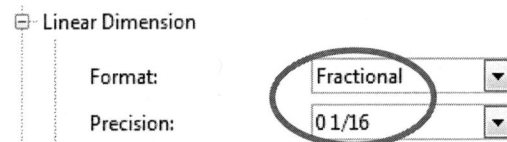

10. There are now two dimension styles.  On your own, create dimension styles for use with drawings plotted at **1/8"=1' and 1/2"=1'**. Name them "Eighth" and "Half" (Hint: Create a new style based on **Quarter** and go to **Fit**, **Dimension scale**, **Scale factor:**  change this value to the reciprocal of the new scale).  Click the **OK** button to save the changes and exit the *Options* window. **Save** the drawing template file.

## Creating an Architectural Title Block

The title block is an often overlooked part of drafting but contains vital information such as: contact information, date drawn, revision history, drawing scale, customer name and approvals.  Other than that, title blocks can be fairly personalized and are left to company preference.  In this section we'll start a generic architectural title block. Adapt it to your own needs as required.

1. With your new architectural template open and the **TitleBlock** layer active, initiate the **rectangle** command.  Enter "**f**" in the command window and fillet the rectangle's corners **.25"**, and "**w**" to set the width at **.12"**. Draw the rectangle from absolute coordinates **1,1** to **34,22** (this will give you a 1" margin when printing on an architectural D-Size paper which is 36" x 24").  **Zoom** in on the rectangle if necessary.

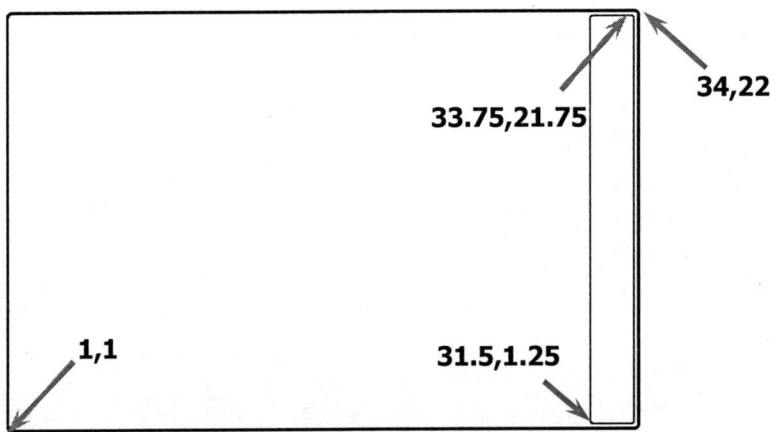

2. Draw another rectangle with fillets of **.12"** and a width of **.06"** from absolute coordinates **31.5,1.25** to **33.75,21.75**.  On your own divide this smaller rectangle vertically into five compartments. One should contain your company's logo and contact information.  The second should list the project's

title, file name, location and customer information. The third compartment should contain the sheet number, scale and sheet size (D). The fourth will contain the revision history. The fifth will contain approvals and dates. Use the example below as a guide (it has been rotated 90° for easier viewing, your text will be vertical on the drawing- or not- your choice).

**Tip:** The "X"s serve as placeholders, prompting you to enter required information. These lines are easy to edit, just double click them. In order to make title block entry even more seamless, research "attributes" in DraftSight's Help utility.

3. **Save** your drawing template. At the risk of sounding redundant, we'll now make a block of your title block. We'll learn more about blocks in the next module, but this will allow us to store the title block away and re-use it later.

4. Select **Define** from the **Draw** menu, **Block** cascading menu. The *Block Definition* window will appear.

5. Enter "**D-Size**" for the **Name**. Click on the **Select in graphics area** icon. The window will temporarily dismiss so you can use a window to select your title block. You should now see title block in the preview window. Select the **Convert to block option**. Leave everything else as it is and click **OK**.

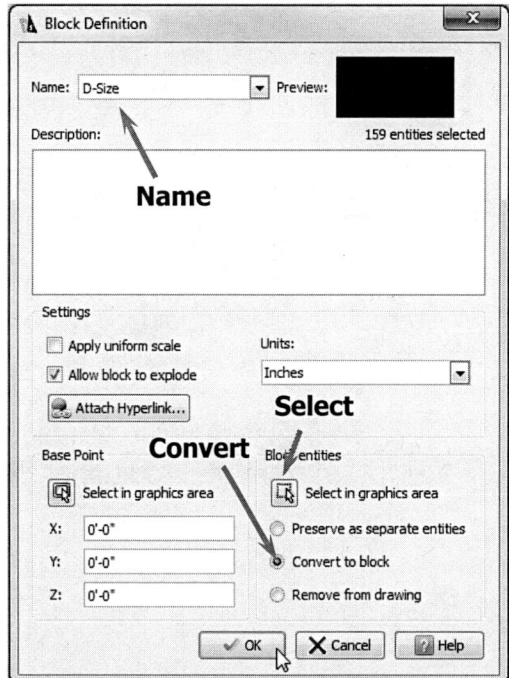

6. The title block disappears, but it can be brought back by choosing the **Block** command found in the Insert **menu**. Try it! **Save** your drawing template.

Note that the title block we created is full-scale. In order for an average house plan to fit inside, you would have to scale it up by a factor of 48 (at 1/4"=1'), or…. Module A3 will introduce you to sheet space.

## Module A1 Suggested Learning Exercises

1. Create a ½"=1' dimension style using fractional unit format for your drawing template. This could be used for section or detail views. Name it "Half-fractional".

2. Use your new drawing template to draw and dimension an architectural drawing from the Additional Exercises located in the Appendix.

## Module A2- Symbol Libraries

Objectives:
1. Create a block
2. Insert a block
3. Explode a block
4. Insert blocks from other drawings

A good symbol library is one of an architect's most valuable tools. Architectural drafting reuses many of the same components over and over again. These include plumbing fixtures, electrical symbols, windows, doors, appliances, furniture, shrubs etc. There is really no excuse for having to draw any of these more than once. DraftSight has the capability to store them in your drawing template for future use. These symbols are called "blocks".

## Creating Blocks

1. Start a **New** drawing using your architectural template (either a borrowed one or the one created in Module A1). In the drawing area, create the symbol for the kitchen range shown to the left using the **1st Floor Walls** layer. Estimate any missing measurements. Do not dimension the range.

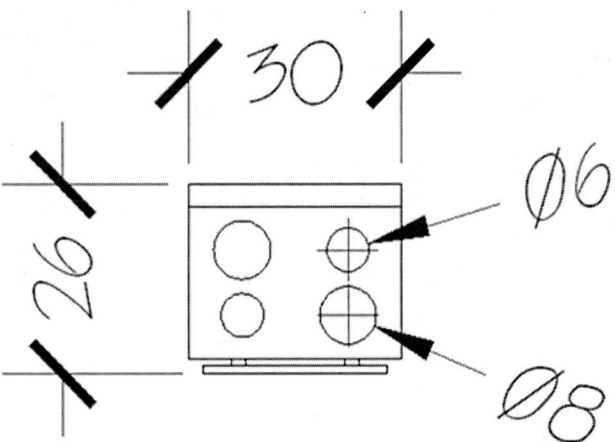

2. From the **Draw** menu and **Block** cascading menu, select **Define** (or just enter "block" in the command window). The **Block Definition** window should open.

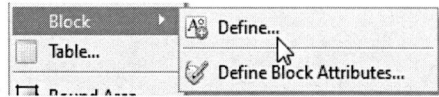

3.  Enter "**Range**" for the block name.  To select the **Base Point** click on the **Select in graphics area** icon under **Base Point**.  The window dismisses temporarily and allows you to select (use **ESnap**) the upper-left corner of the range.  To select the **Block entities** click on the **Select in graphics area** icon under **Block Entities**.  The window temporarily dismisses so you can select the entities that makes up the range.  Right-click or press **Enter** to return to the *Block Definition* window after selecting the objects.  Select the **Remove from drawing** option.  Press the **OK** button when finished. The range should disappear.

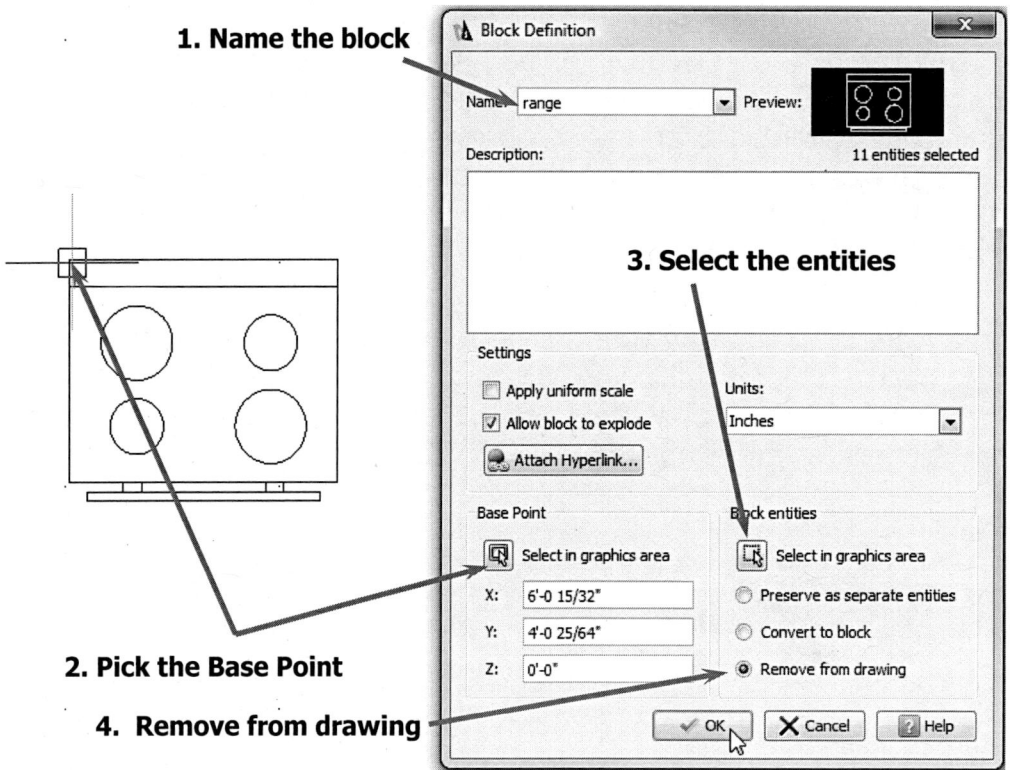

## Inserting Blocks

1.  The symbol of the range is gone, safely stored away in the drawing file for future use.  We will now retrieve it.  From the **Insert** menu, select **Block**. The *Insert Block* window should appear.

2.  Select "**Range**" from the **Name:** list.  Set the remaining values as shown in the figure on the next page. Press **OK** when finished.

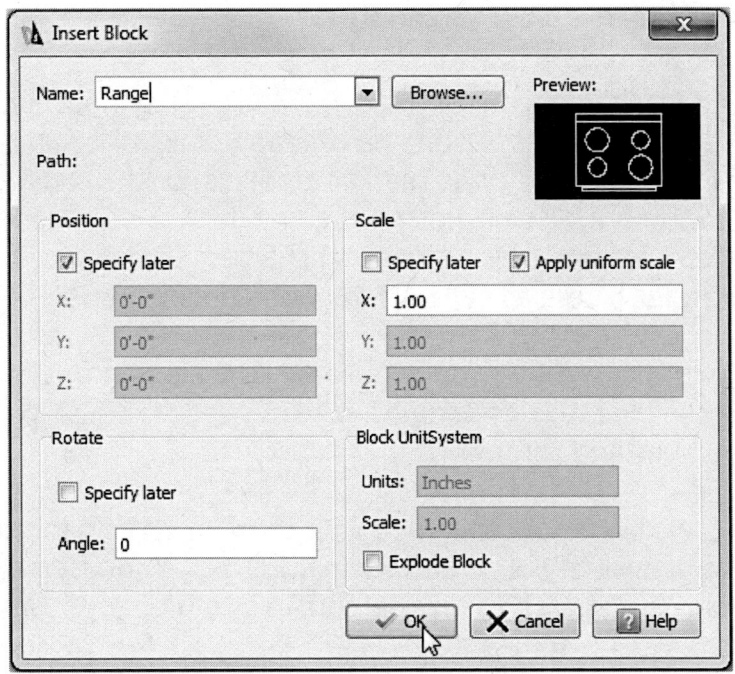

3. Select any point in the drawing area for the **destination**. Note the destination point is the same point as the base point defined earlier. Without any command active, select the block. How many entity grips does it have? The block now behaves as one entity, even though it is made of several. Note the grip as at the base point.

4. Finally, we'll "explode" the block, or return it to its original state. This should only be done if for some reason you need to edit the block. Select the **Explode** icon in the **Modify** toolbar and pick the range. Press **Enter**. Select the range using a window. Now how many grips does it have?

5. On your own, create the blocks of the refrigerator and dishwasher shown below. Practice inserting each of them, trying some of the options available in the *Insert Block* window. **Save** your drawing template file.

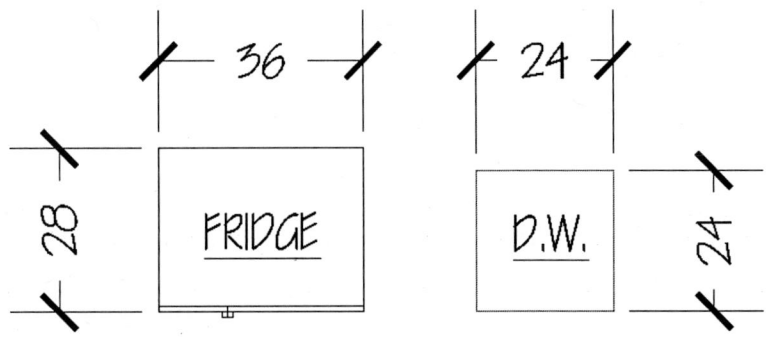

## Using Blocks from other drawings

You could spend many hours building a comprehensive symbol library on your own.  However, chances are someone has already drawn the symbols for you.  In fact many of the companies who market products for the construction industry provide CAD blocks on their websites for the architect.  User websites also provide CAD blocks for free or for a nominal charge.  Sometimes it may be necessary to transfer blocks as symbols from one drawing to another.

1. Open **Parkinglot.dwg** that you completed as an assignment in Chapter 5 (if you did not complete this drawing or have misplaced it, just sketch the plan views of the trees and shrubs).

2. In Chapter 5 we were not concerned with drawing objects to scale.  **Copy** one instance of each of your trees and shrubs into an unused portion of the drawing area.  **Scale** each to an appropriate size (i.e. approximately 12' in diameter for a tree, 6' for a shrub).

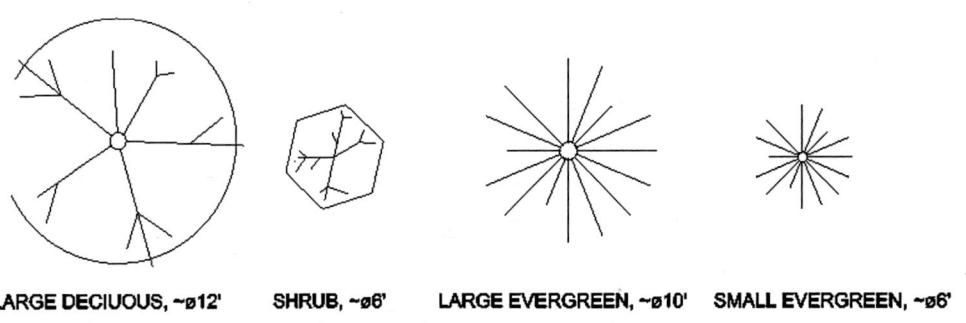

LARGE DECIUOUS, ~ø12'     SHRUB, ~ø6'     LARGE EVERGREEN, ~ø10'     SMALL EVERGREEN, ~ø6'

3. Create a **Block** of each type of tree/shrub.  Keep in mind these are plan views of the trees, and you'll need elevation views as well, so name them appropriately (e.g. "Large Deciduous Plan View").  Select the center of each tree/shrub for the **Base Point**.  **Save** the drawing and **close** it.

4. Start a **New** drawing using your architectural drawing template. Select **Block** from the **Insert** menu. Select the **Browse** button and find **Plarkinglot.dwg**. Click **OK** when finished.

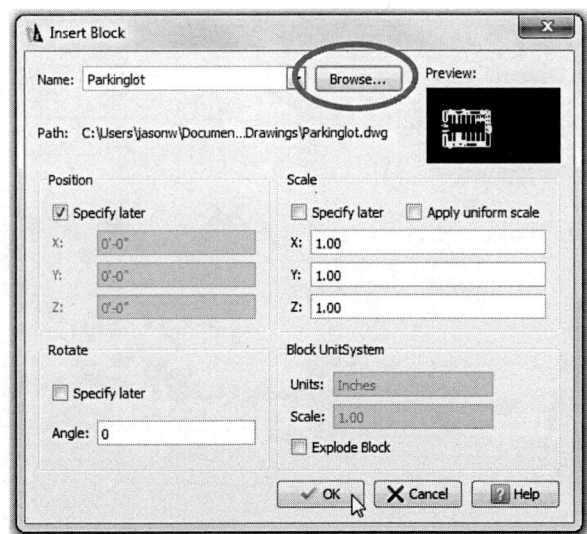

5. Place the block of the drawing anywhere in the drawing area, then delete it. Activate the **Elevation Objects** layer (DraftSight inserts blocks onto the active layer).

6. Select the **Block** command from the **Insert** menu. This time pick the **Name:** drop-down list. Note that all of the blocks from **Parkinglot.dwg** have now been absorbed by your drawing template. Proceed to insert and place a few of these, then delete them.

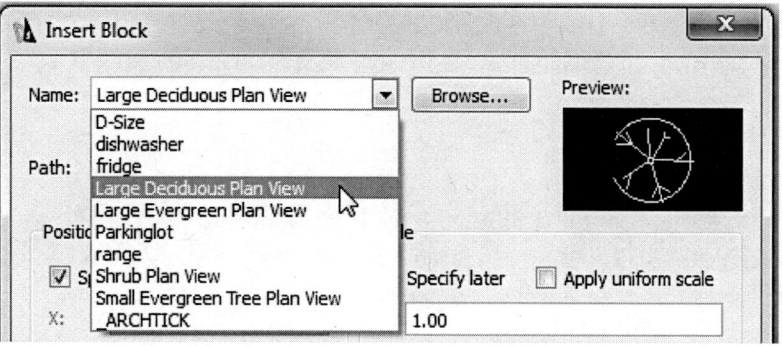

7. You can also delete blocks from the drawing entirely. You may have noticed a block called "Parkinglot" in the list of blocks. We don't need that anymore. Go to the **Clean** command in the **File** menu. Inside the *Clean* window, Select Parkinglot from the list of blocks and **Delete** it. **Close** the window. **Save** your drawing template.

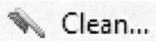 Clean...

8. Finally, if it is desirable to just grab one or two blocks from another drawing you can use **Copy** and **Paste** from the **Edit** menu instead of inserting the entire drawing. Try it!

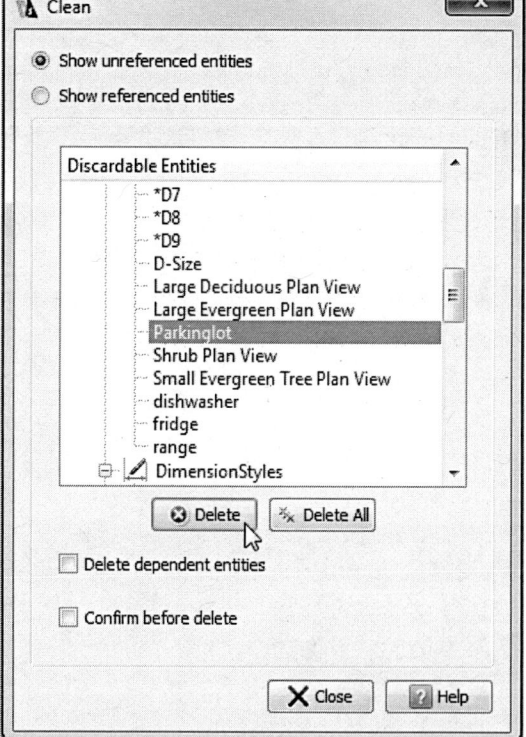

## Module A2 Suggested Learning Exercises

1.  Open the garage drawing from Unit 2. Delete one of the doors and two of the windows in the plan view.  Make blocks of the remaining door and window. Name them "**2-8 Door Plan View**" and "**4-0 Window Plan View**".  Insert the blocks to replace the missing door and windows.

2.  Do the same for the three electrical symbols created earlier in Garage.dwg. Name the symbols "**Outlet**", "**Ceiling Light**" and "**Wall Light**".

3.  Search the internet for free .dwg symbol libraries (for example **http://cben.net** ).  Find symbols of tree & shrub elevations and add these symbols to your architectural template and elevation views of the garage drawing.

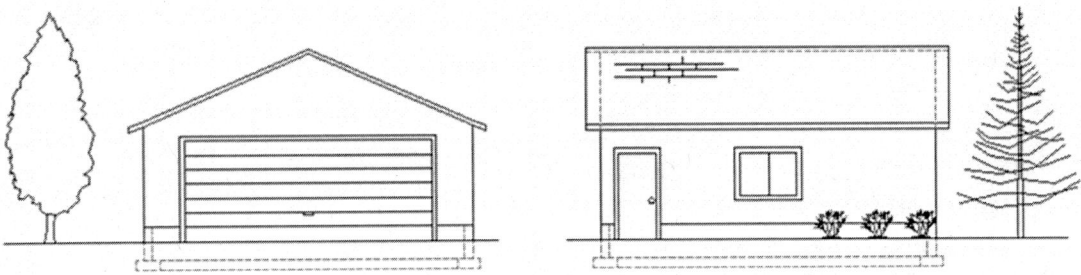

## Module A3- Advanced Architectural Techniques

Objectives:
1. Create and edit Polylines
2. Draw using Richlines (multilines)
3. Set-up a sheet space layout
4. Plot a drawing from sheet space
5. Create a window & door schedule

## Drawing and Editing Polylines

The **Polyline** command creates a series of lines that are tied to each other as one entity. One advantage of using polylines includes the ability to assign a line thickness; this comes in handy for drawing walls for house plans.

1. Start a **New** drawing using your architectural template. Activate the "**1st floor walls**" layer (or a similar layer).

2. Locate and select the **Polyline** icon in the **Draw** toolbar. Click in the lower left-hand corner of the drawing area for the **start point**.

3. Note there are several options presented in the command window (Arc, Halfwidth, Length, Undo, Width). Type "**w**" for **Width** and enter **4"** for both the start and end widths. Using polylines and coordinate entry methods, draw only the walls for the cabin floor plan shown below (a larger version can be found in the Appendix). The 4" wide polyline represents a 2x4 stud wall.

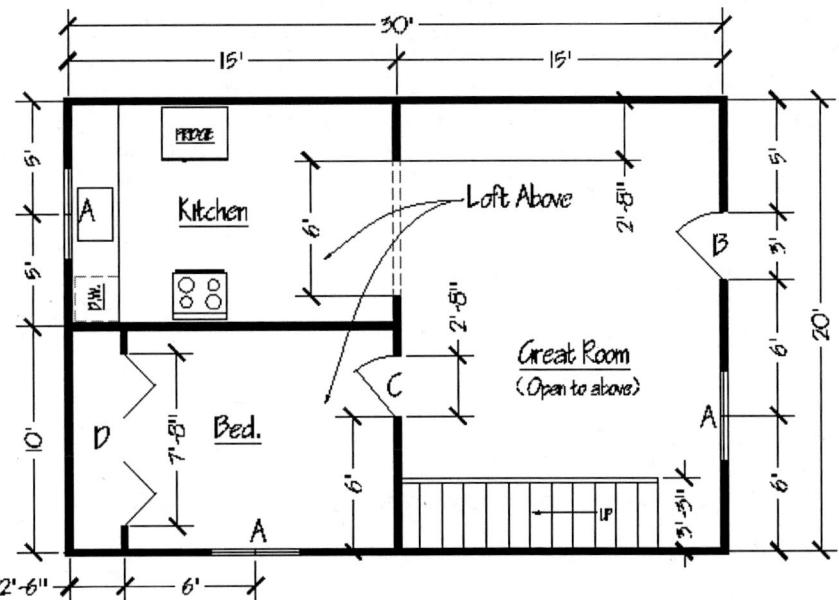

4. On your own, next to the cabin try sketching the pond shown at right using the **Polyline** arc option and 6" line width.  Note the **C̲lose** option to close the shape.

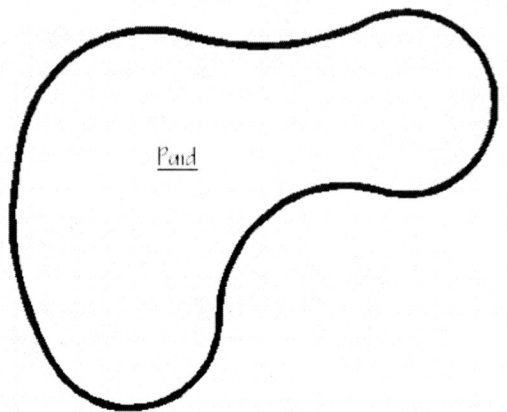

5. The companion command to Polyline is **Editpolyline**.  Select the **Polyline** command from the **Modify** menu, **Entity** cascading menu. Pick the sketch of the pond.

6. Note the many options available.  Of these **C̲lose**, **J̲oin** and **W̲idth** are perhaps the most useful.  **Close** is only available if editing an open polyline shape.  **Join** will combine two polylines provided their endpoints touch one another.  **Width** will allow you edit the polyline's width. Change the width of the polyline representing the pond by typing "**w**" entering **10** for the width.

7. Just for fun, try the **F̲it**, **S̲pline** and **D̲ecurve** options of the **Editpolyline** command.  Observe the effects on the sketch of the pond.

---

*Tip:* **Editpolyline** can be used to turn normal lines, curves, etc. into polylines. Try it!

---

8. Finally, using **Editpolyline** change the **exterior** walls of the cabin drawn previously such that they represent a 2 X 6 stud wall (6" wide polyline). **Save** the drawing as **Cabin.dwg**.

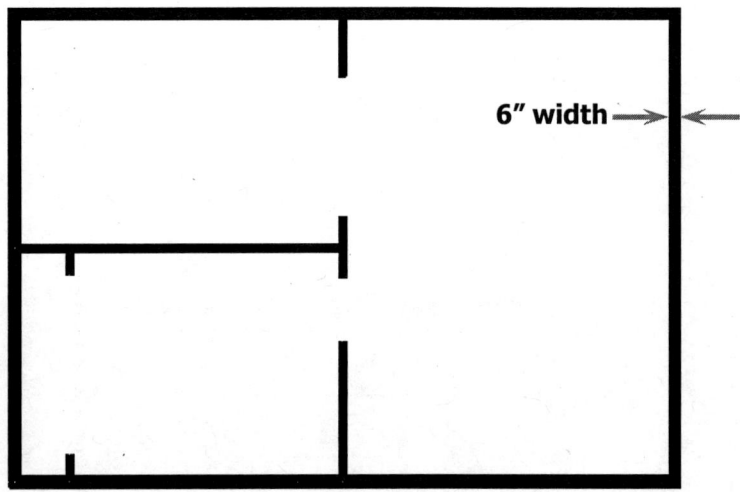

## Drawing RichLines (Multi-Lines)

Yet another way to draw plan views of walls is with the **RichLine** command. These are drawn just like regular lines, but a companion parallel line shows up to represent the inside (or outside) of a wall.

1. **Open** Cabin.dwg (if it isn't already) and **Zoom** in on an area of the drawing just above the floor plan started previously using polylines.

2. Select **RichLine** from the **Draw** menu.  Note the **Justification** option, it determines how the richline runs between the points you specify.  The possibilities are **bottom, top** and **zero** (middle). Also note the **Scale** option, the distance between the parallel lines that make up a multliline.  Specify a **Top** justification and a **scale** of **4**.

Active settings: Justification = Top, Scale = 1.00, Style = Standard
Options: Justification, Scale, STyle or
**Specify start point» j**

**Top Justification**

**Zero Justification**

**Bottom Justification**

**Scale**

Commence drawing the Cabin walls shown below using the dimensions from the previous section (note the **Close** option).  Try different justifications.

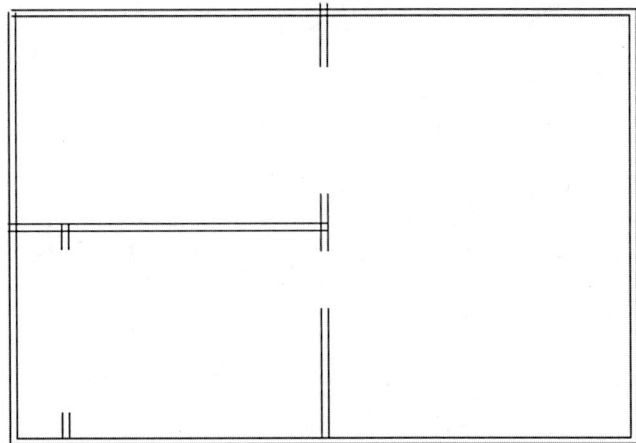

> **Tip:** If you find that you use multi-lines a lot, you can set up **RichLine Styles** to manage the different kinds (an idea similar to Text Styles and Dimension Styles). It is accessed from the **Format** menu.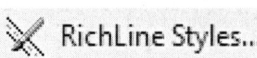

3. Next we'll join the interior walls to the exterior ones. Enter "**editrichline**" in the command window (there is not a menu item for this command at the time of this writing).

4. The ***Edit RichLines*** window should appear. Use the tools associated with the icons to clean-up the wall joints of your floor plan\*. Use the **Help** button if you need a detailed description of what each tool does. The figure below should serve as a guide.

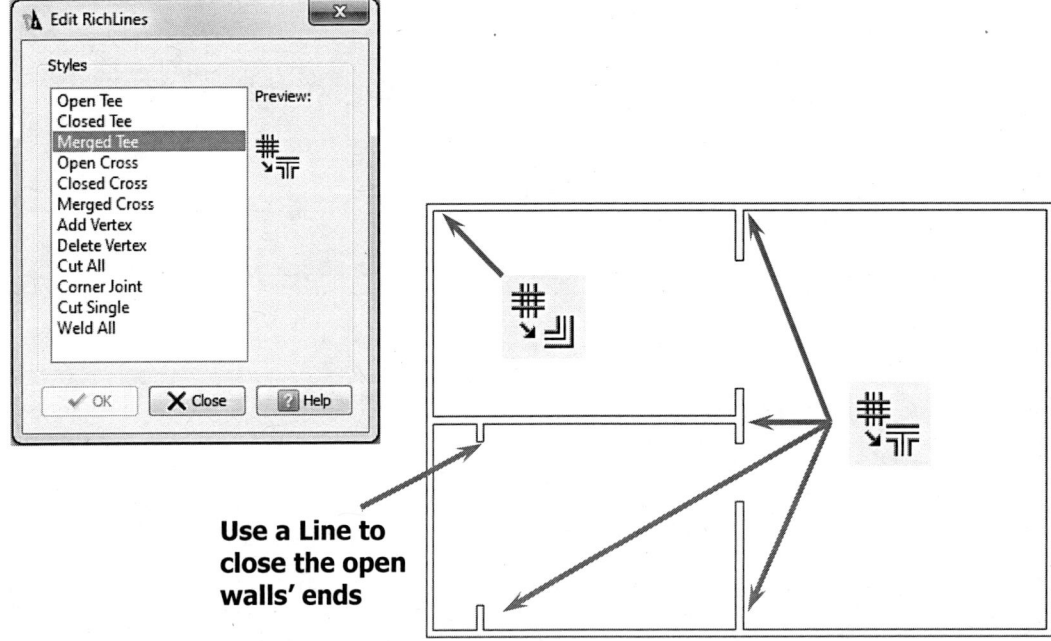

**Use a Line to close the open walls' ends**

5. Finally, finish the floor plan so it looks like the one in the figure at the start of this module. Use your blocks of the windows, doors and kitchen appliances. You may start with either the floor plan drawn with Polylines or RichLines, your choice. Dimension the floor plan on the 1$^{st}$ floor dims layer using the **half** dimstyle embedded in your drawing template. **Save** the drawing.

\* As of the publication date for this text, these tools were still in development. They might not work properly until a future update of DraftSight is released.

## Sheet Space

Now we'll set-up the cabin to plot in **Sheet Space**. This environment is a paste-up area of sorts that can be used to better manage plot scales, and as a place to add title blocks prior printing your drawings. In the Architectural drawing template done in Module A1 we created a title block. We'll print this title block with the cabin drawing.

1. **Open** Cabin.dwg (if it isn't already). Select the **Sheet1** tab at the bottom of the drawing area. Note the differences between **Sheet Space** and **Model Space**. The coordinate system icon had changed to a triangle, and there is a **viewport**, or a window back into **Model Space**.

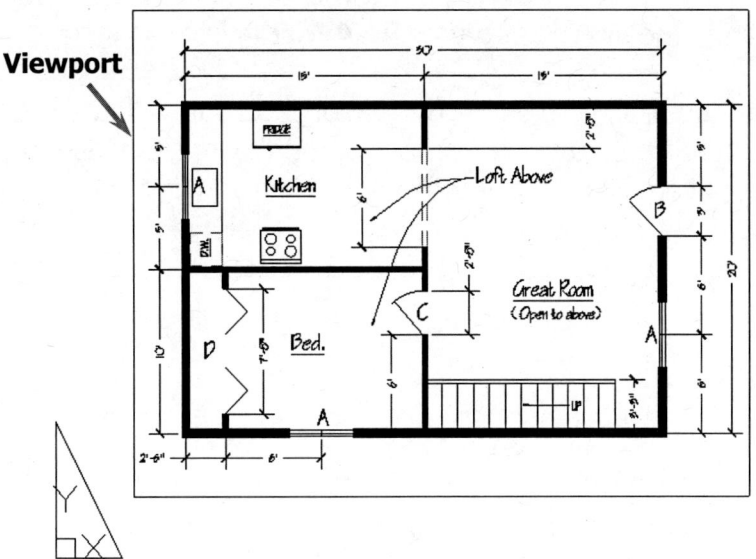

2. Your cabin didn't fit as nicely in the viewport as the one shown above. Double-click on the viewport to activate it. **Pan** and **Zoom** until just the cabin floor plan and its dimensions fit inside the viewport as shown below.

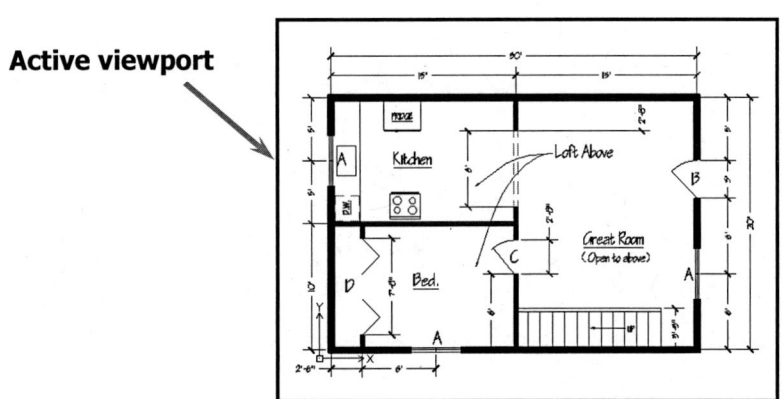

3. Double-click outside the viewport to deactivate it. Single-click on the viewport. Notice it has entity grips. Right-click and pick **Properties** from the pop-up menu (unless the **Properties** window is already open).

4. Find the ***Standard Scale*** field in the ***Properties*** window and select **1/2"=1'**.

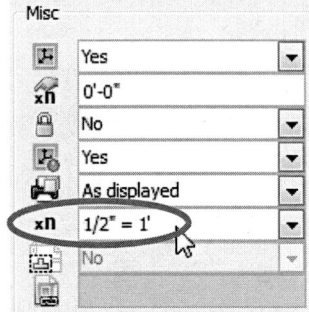

5. If necessary, resize the viewport using its entity grips so the entire cabin and its dimensions fit inside. **DO NOT ZOOM** when the viewport is active or you will have to reset the viewport's scale.

6. **Insert** your title block. **Move** the viewport to the left-center of the title block. Change the viewport to the **ViewPort** layer.

7. Fill out the title block and **Print** the drawing layout at **1:1** scale if you have access to a D-Size plotter. If not, or you don't want to waste a D-size piece of paper, print it **1:2** on a B-size printer. Your drawing should look similar to the one below.

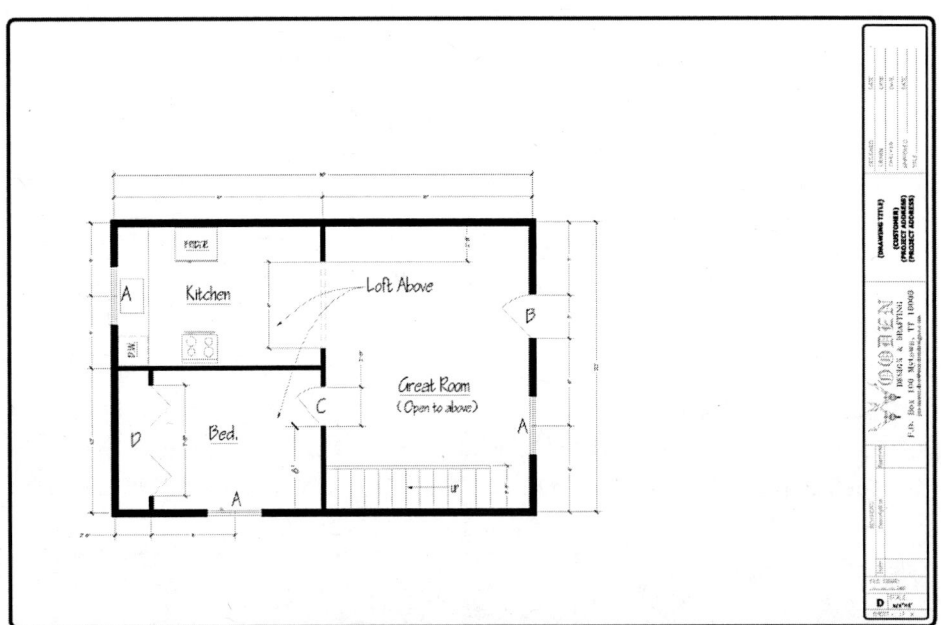

---

***Tip:*** Need to find the area of a floor plan or room? Go to the **Tools** menu, **Inquiry** cascading menu and select **Get Area**. Use **ESnap** to pick the points that define the area. Press **Enter**, the measured area appears in the command window. What is the area of the cabin?

---

## Creating a schedule using Table

An important part of construction plans is the materials schedule. Commonly created for doors and windows, the schedule lists the type, supplier, quantity and size of the purchased materials for the structure being drawn. While there are many ways to make a schedule (spreadsheets can be imported by choosing **Object** from the **Insert** menu for example), we'll take this opportunity to introduce the **Table** command.

1. With Cabin.dwg open, select the **Sheet1** tab. From the **Draw** menu, select the **Table** command. The *Insert Table* window should appear.

   Table...

2. Select the **View table styles** icon next to the **TableStyle** name field and change the text height to **.18**. For the insertion method, select **Set position**. Enter **4** for the number of **rows** and **columns**, and **1"** for the **width** and **height**. See below. Select **OK** when finished.

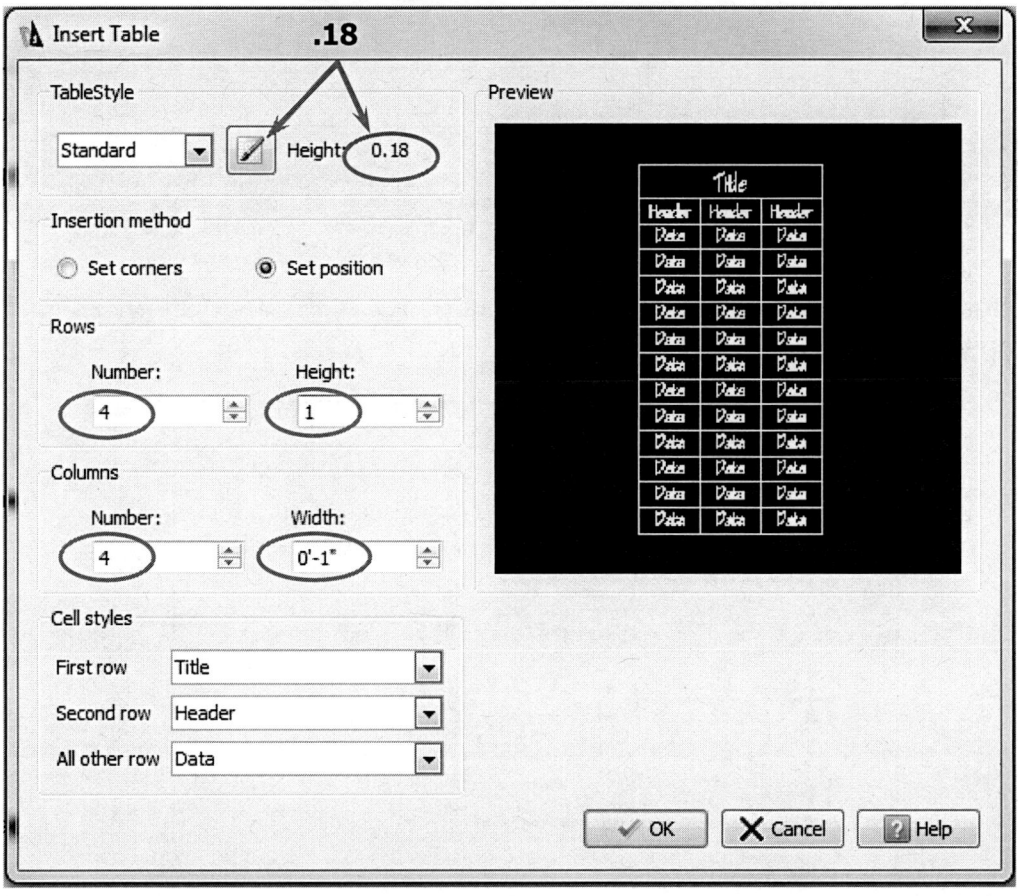

3. Place the table in the upper-right corner of the drawing. The ***Edit Note*** window should appear.  Type "**Window & Door Schedule**" for the title and press the **Tab** key.  Type "**Symbol**" to for the first header cell and press the **Tab** key. Continue to enter the information found in the graphic below.  Pressing the arrow keys will also take you from one cell to another.  If you exit the ***Edit Note*** window and find a mistake: click on the table, right-click and select **Table edit** from the pop-up menu and select a cell to change.

| Window and Door Schedule | | | |
|---|---|---|---|
| Symbol | Qty: | Description: | Supplier: |
| A | 3 | 4-0 X 4-0 Sliding window | Andersen |
| B | 1 | 3-0 x 6-8 Exterior Door | Therma-Tru |
| C | 1 | 2-8 x 6-8 Interior door | Waynesboro |
| D | 1 | 17-6 X 6-8 Bi-fold door | Colonial |

4. Use **EGrips** to resize the columns and to place the table as shown below.  Double-click on the viewport to activate it and place symbols corresponding to the schedule (e.g., "**A**", "**B**", etc.) near the doors and windows.  Return to **Sheet space** and plot the drawing layout at 1:1 scale on an 11 X 17 piece of paper.  **Save** the drawing.

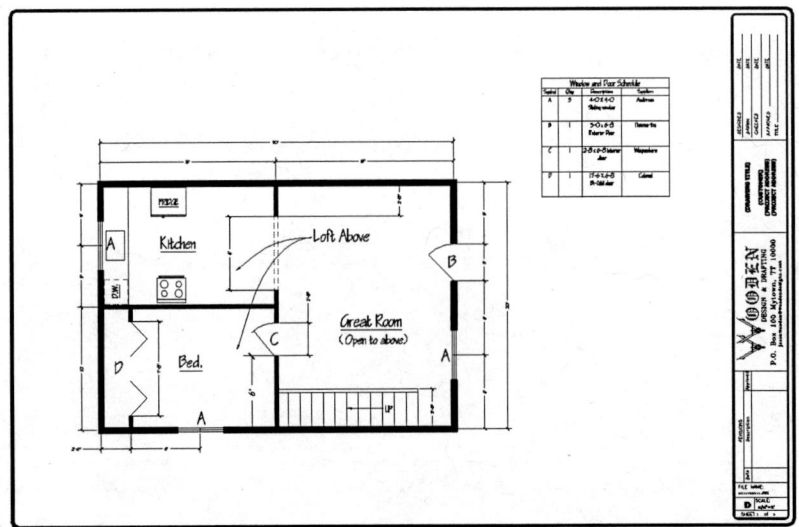

## Module A3 Suggested Learning Exercises

Open Garage.dwg from Unit 2 and do the following:

1. Create a "**viewports**" layer.  Configure this layer so that it will not plot.
2. Rename Sheet1 to "**Floor Plan**" and insert/create a B-Sized title block. Set the viewport to a scale of **¼"=1'**. Put the viewport on the viewport layer.
3. Fill in the title block appropriately.
4. **Pan** to center the floor plan and section view in the viewport.
5. Create a door and window schedule using **TABLE**.  Place it on the **Floor Plan** layout.
6. Create new sheets for the **elevations** and **isometric view** with title blocks.
7. **Print** all sheets.

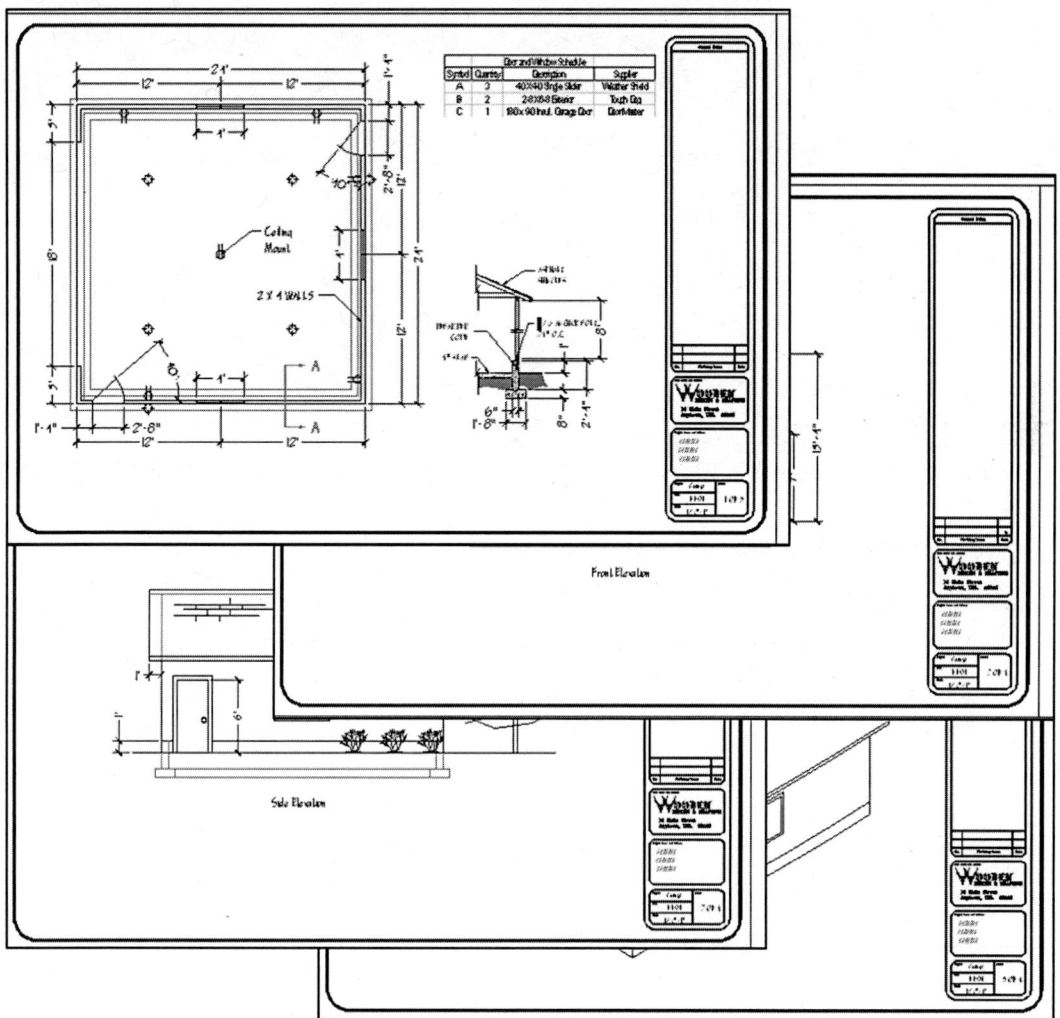

**NOTES:**

# Appendix

Answers to the crossword puzzles found in Chapter 1 and the end of Unit 2:

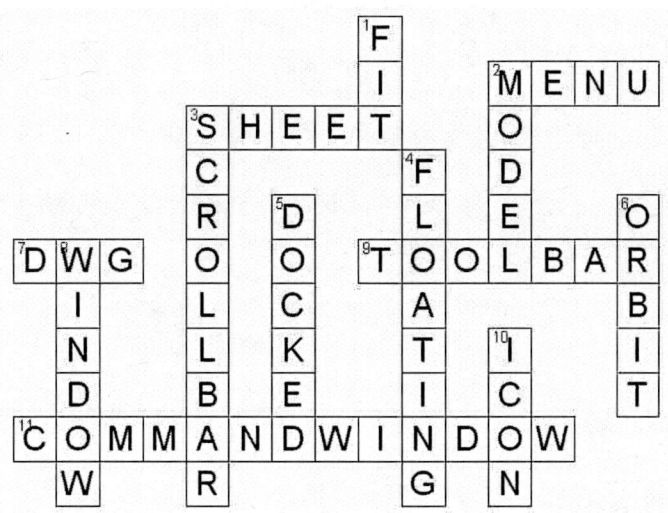

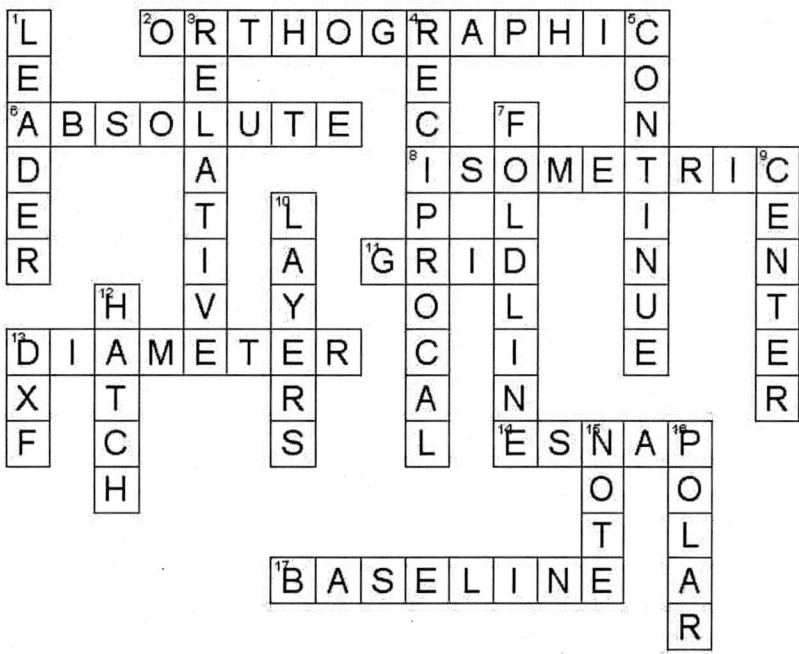

Additional Exercises

Mechanical

# Exercise M1- Coupe

# Exercise M2- Ring Nest

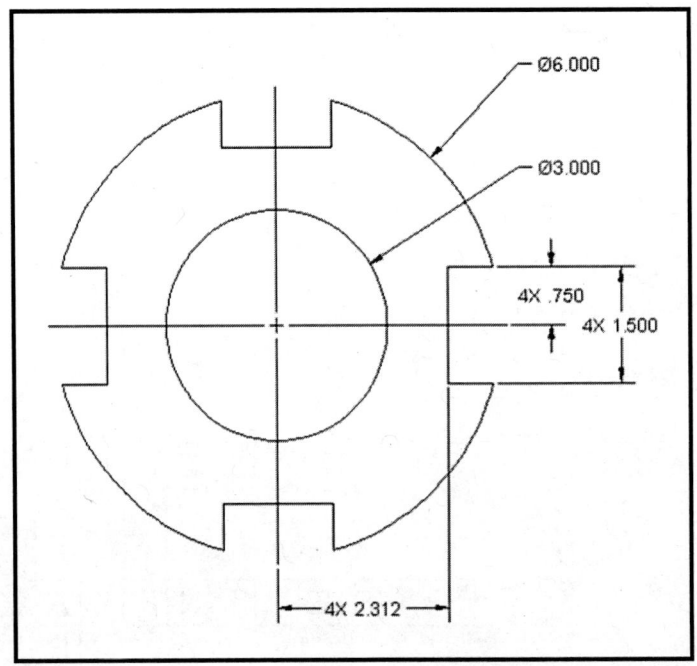

## Exercise M3- Gasket

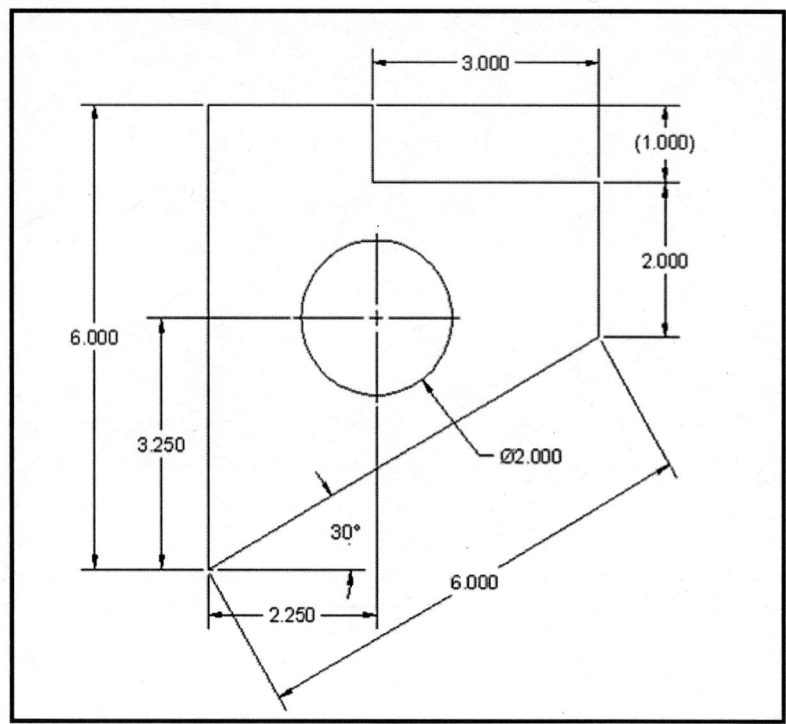

## Exercise M4- Guide Block

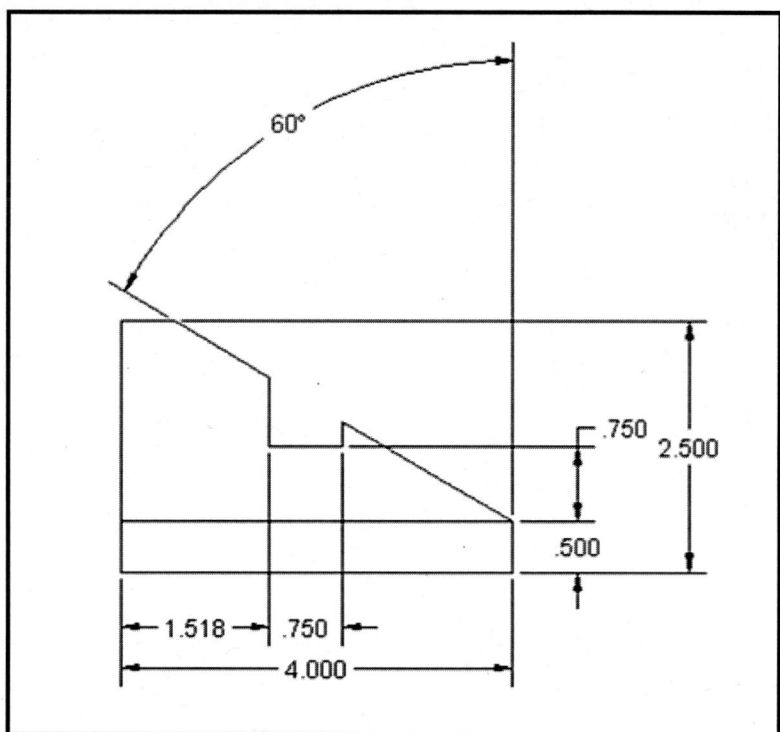

## Exercise M5- Motor Mount

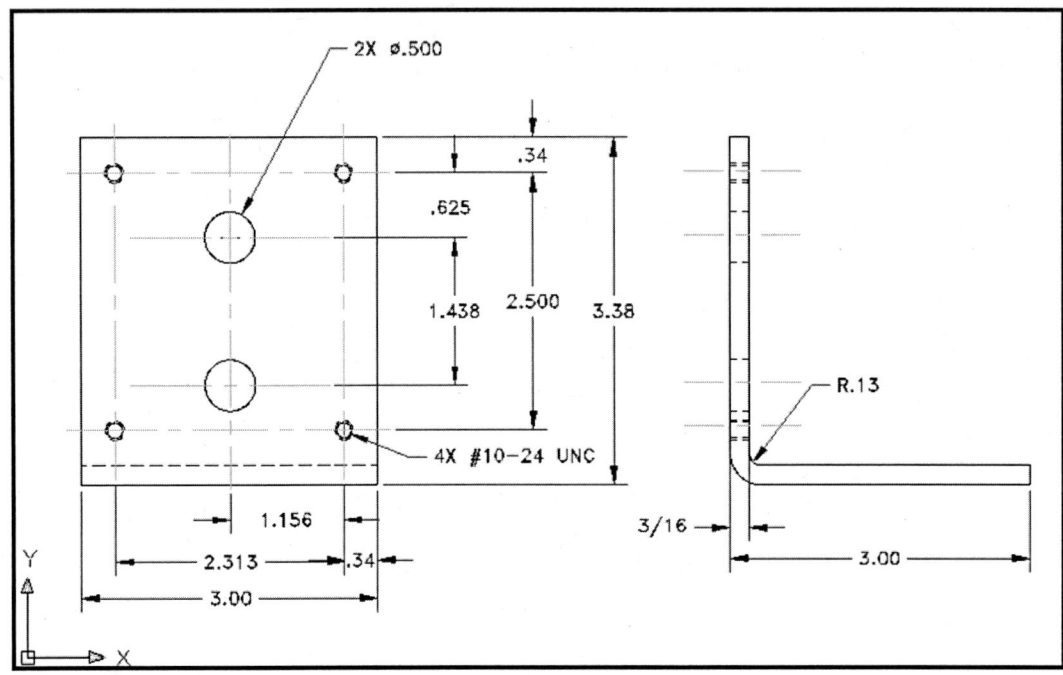

## Exercise M6- Tie Down

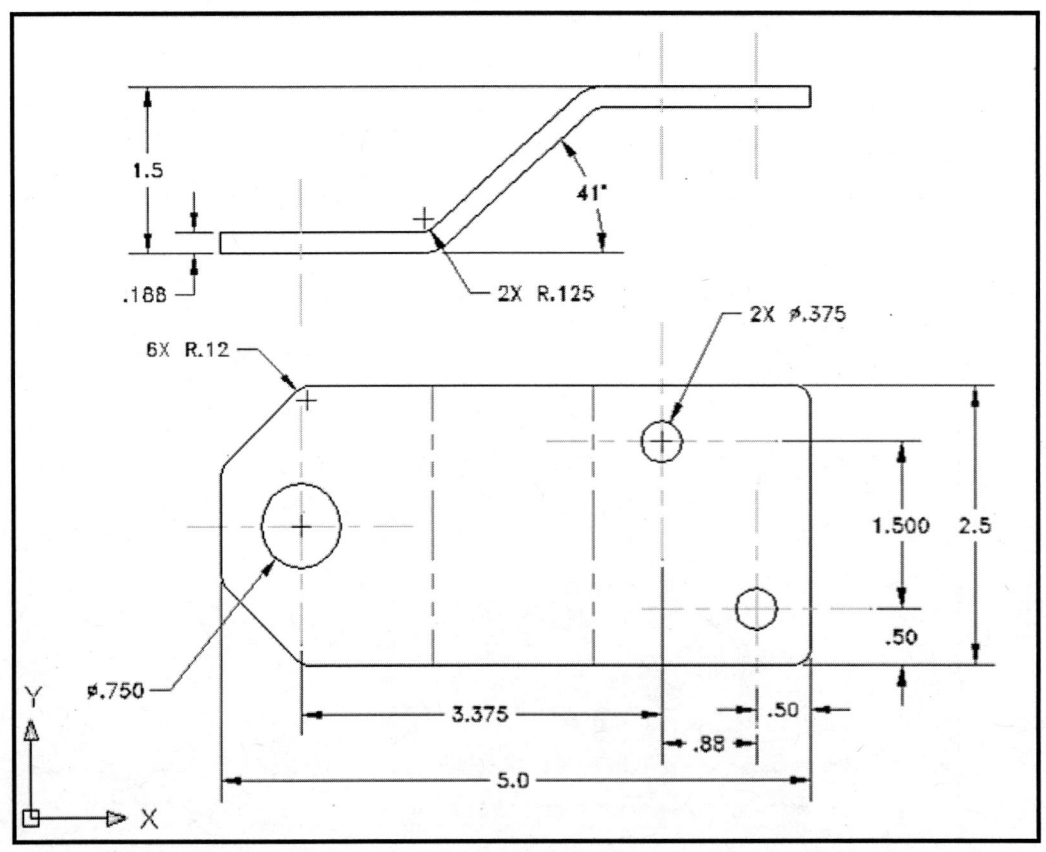

## Exercise M7- Lamp Base

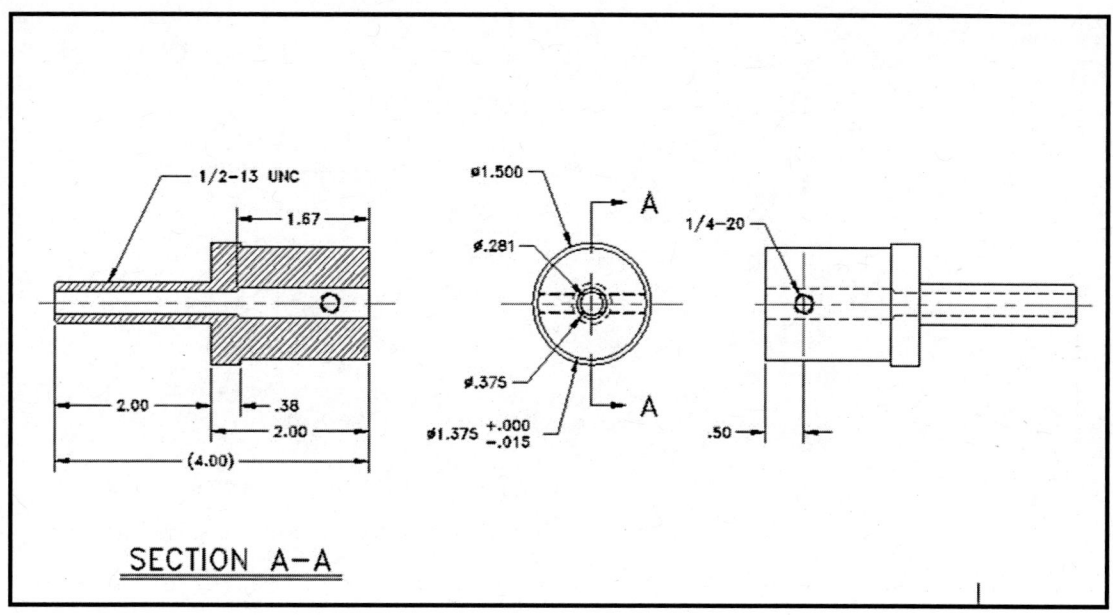

SECTION A-A

## Exercise M8- Flywheel Puller

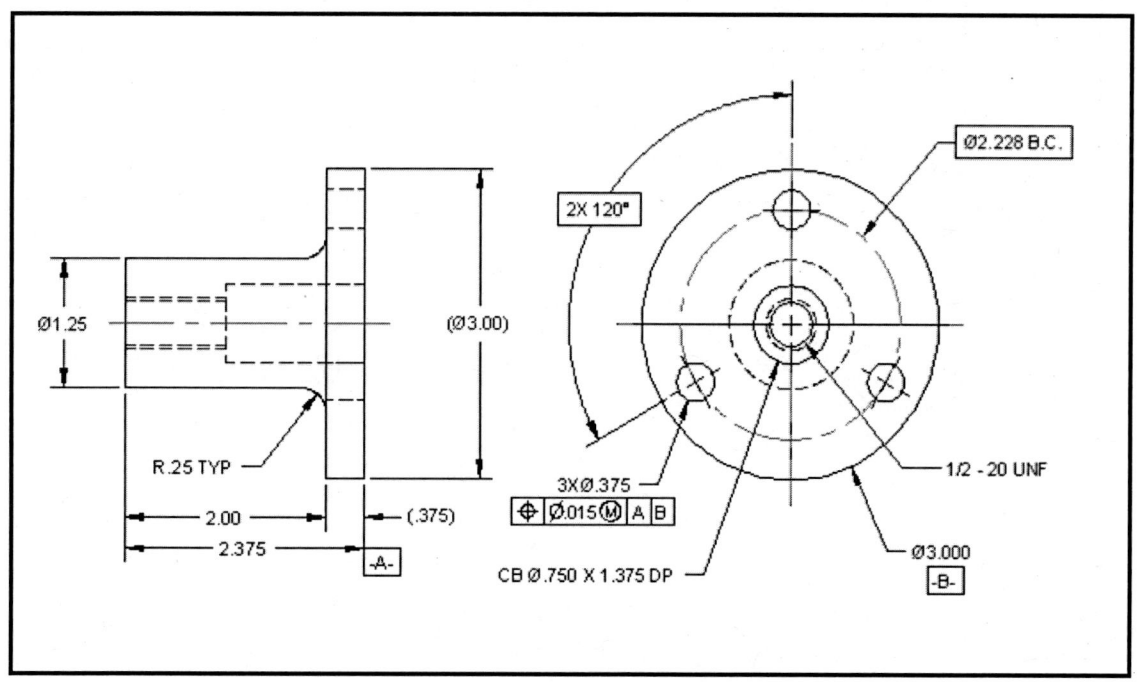

# Exercise M9- Yoke

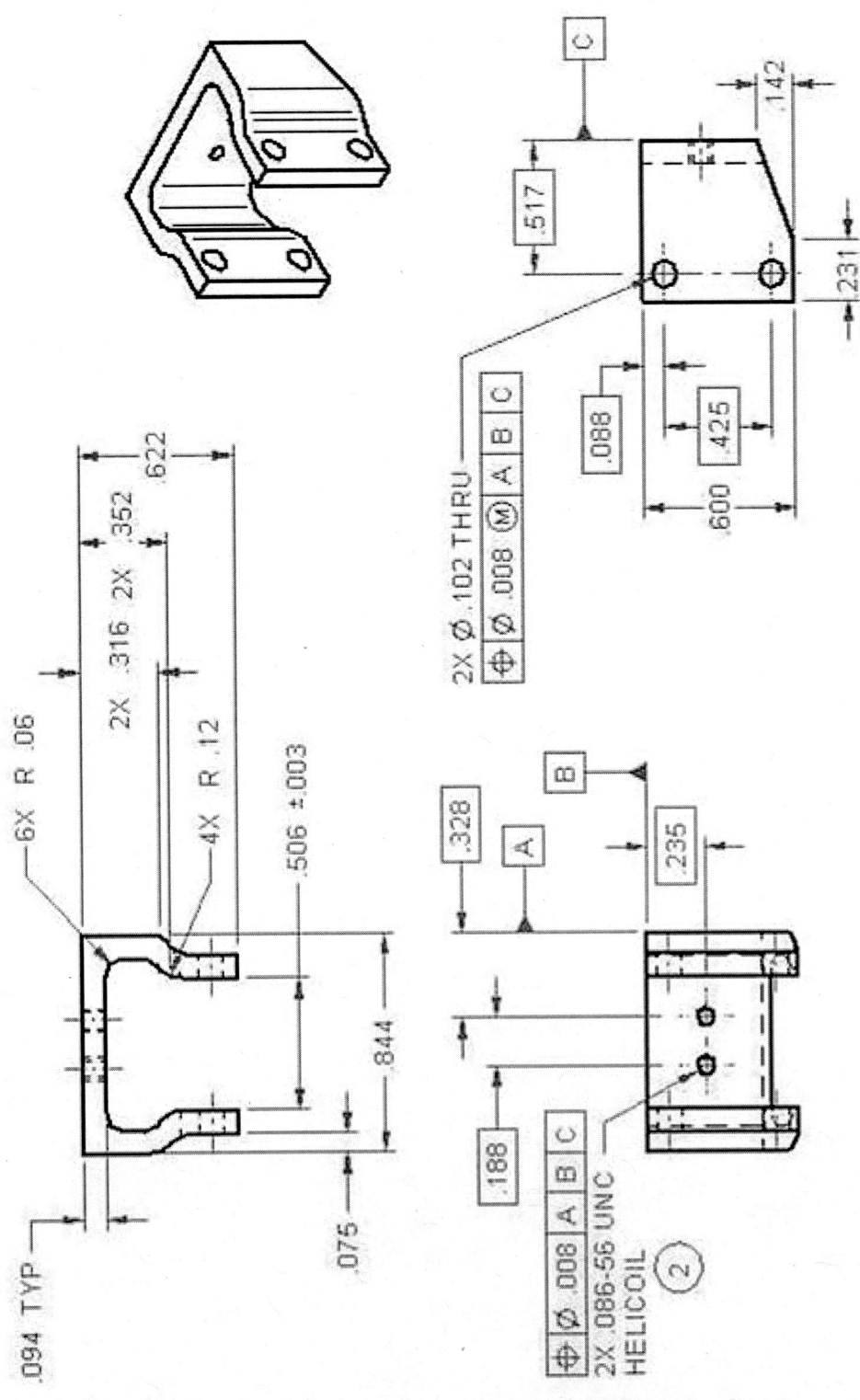

## Architectural

## Exercise A1- Floor Plan, Cabin

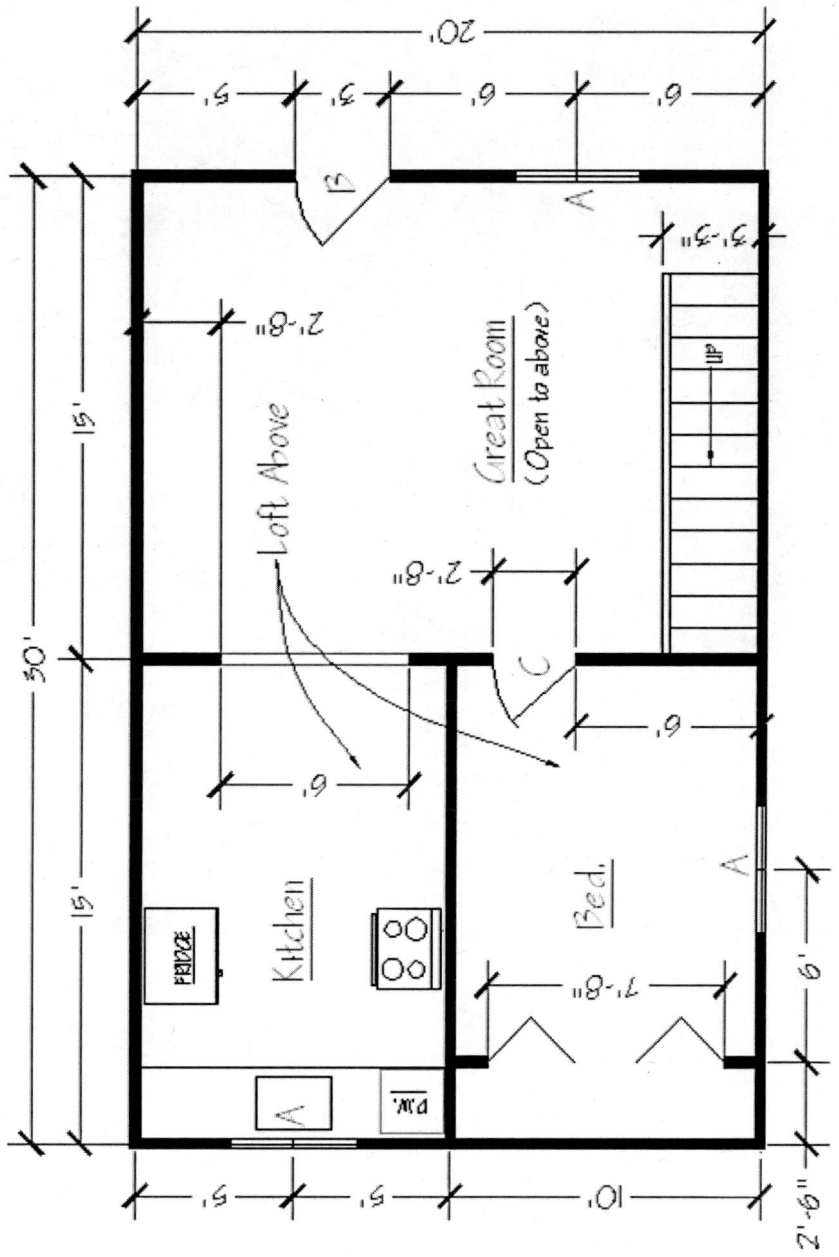

## Exercise A2- Plot Plan

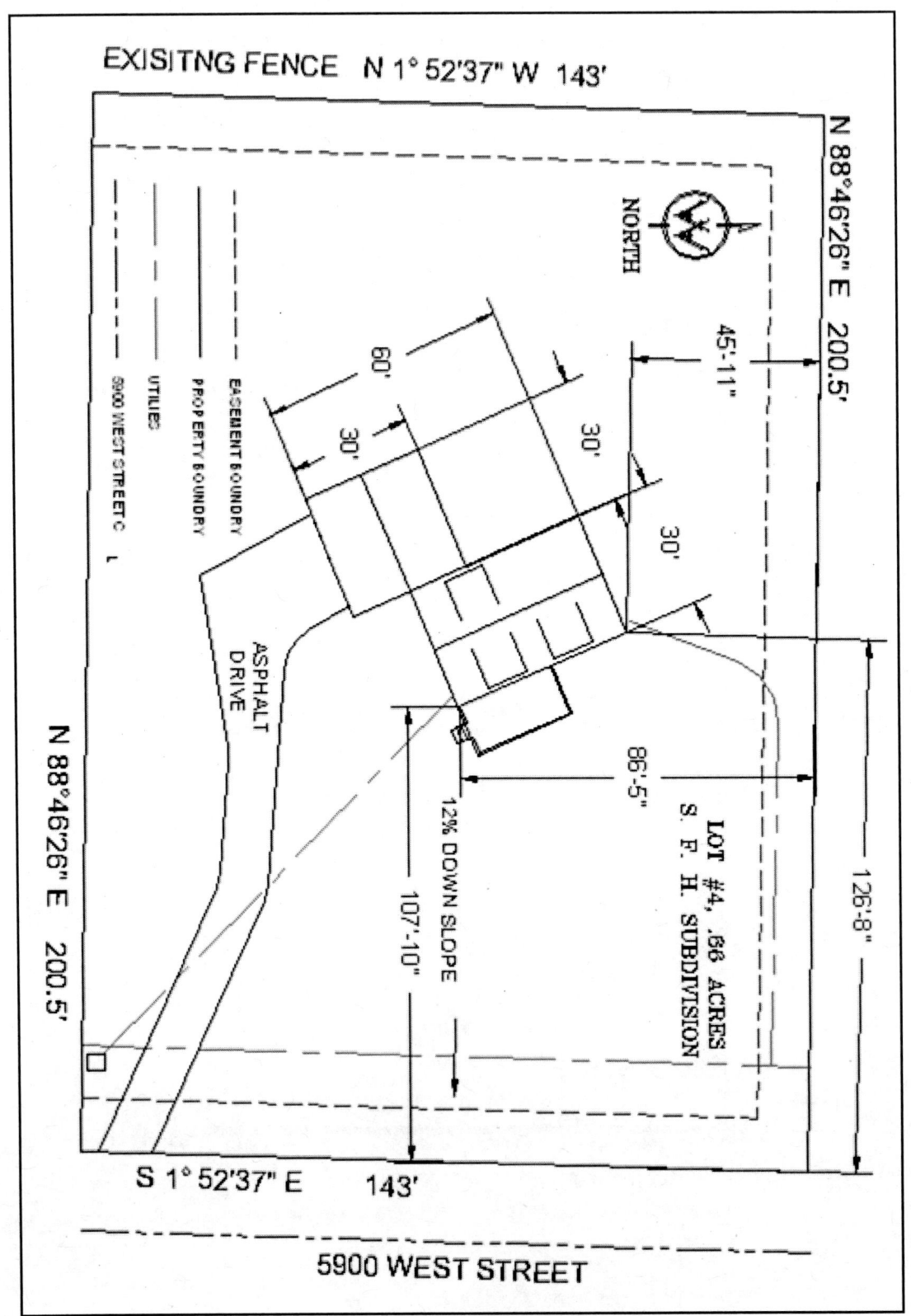

## Exercise A3- Playground

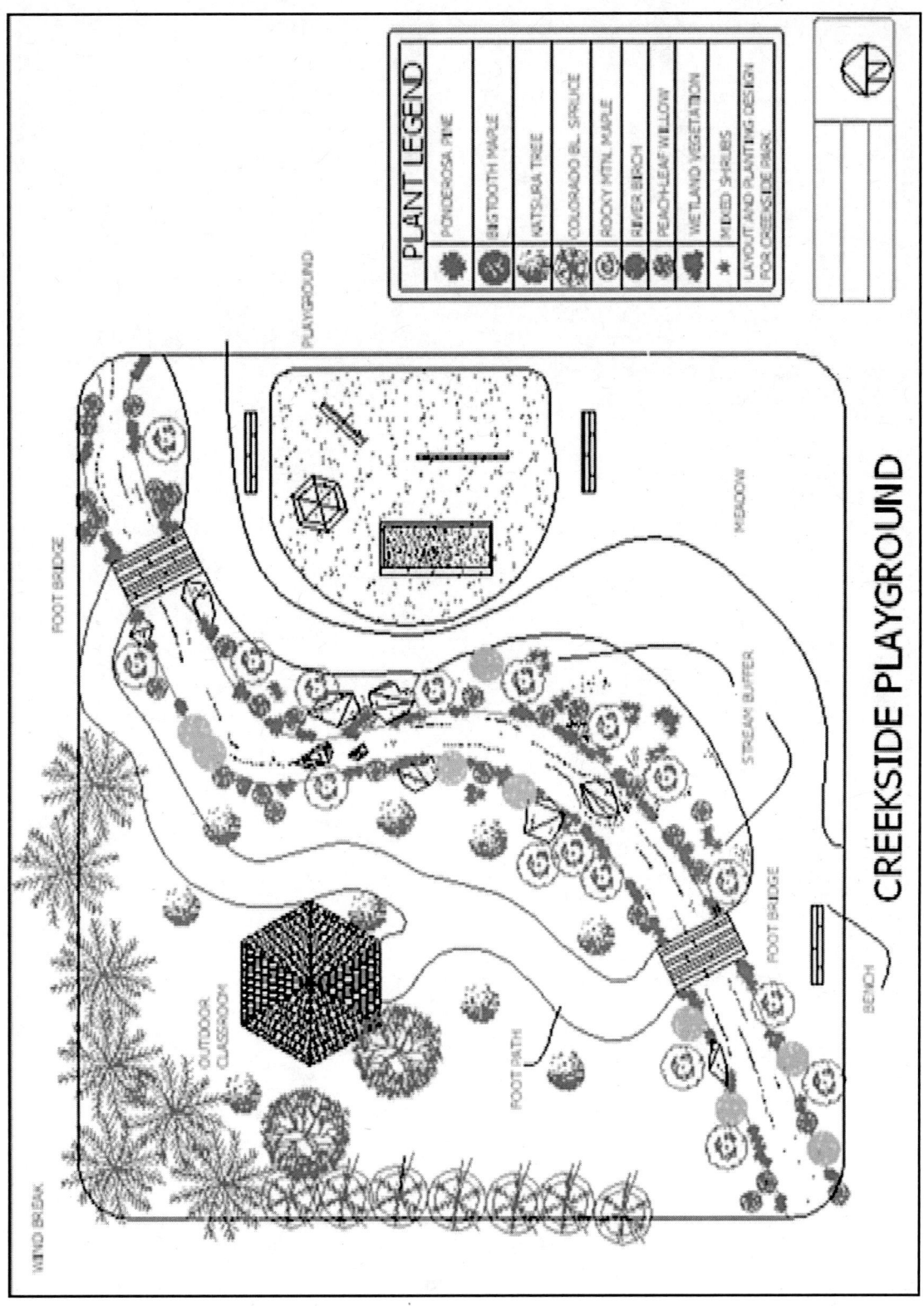

## Exercise A4- Parking lot with dimensions

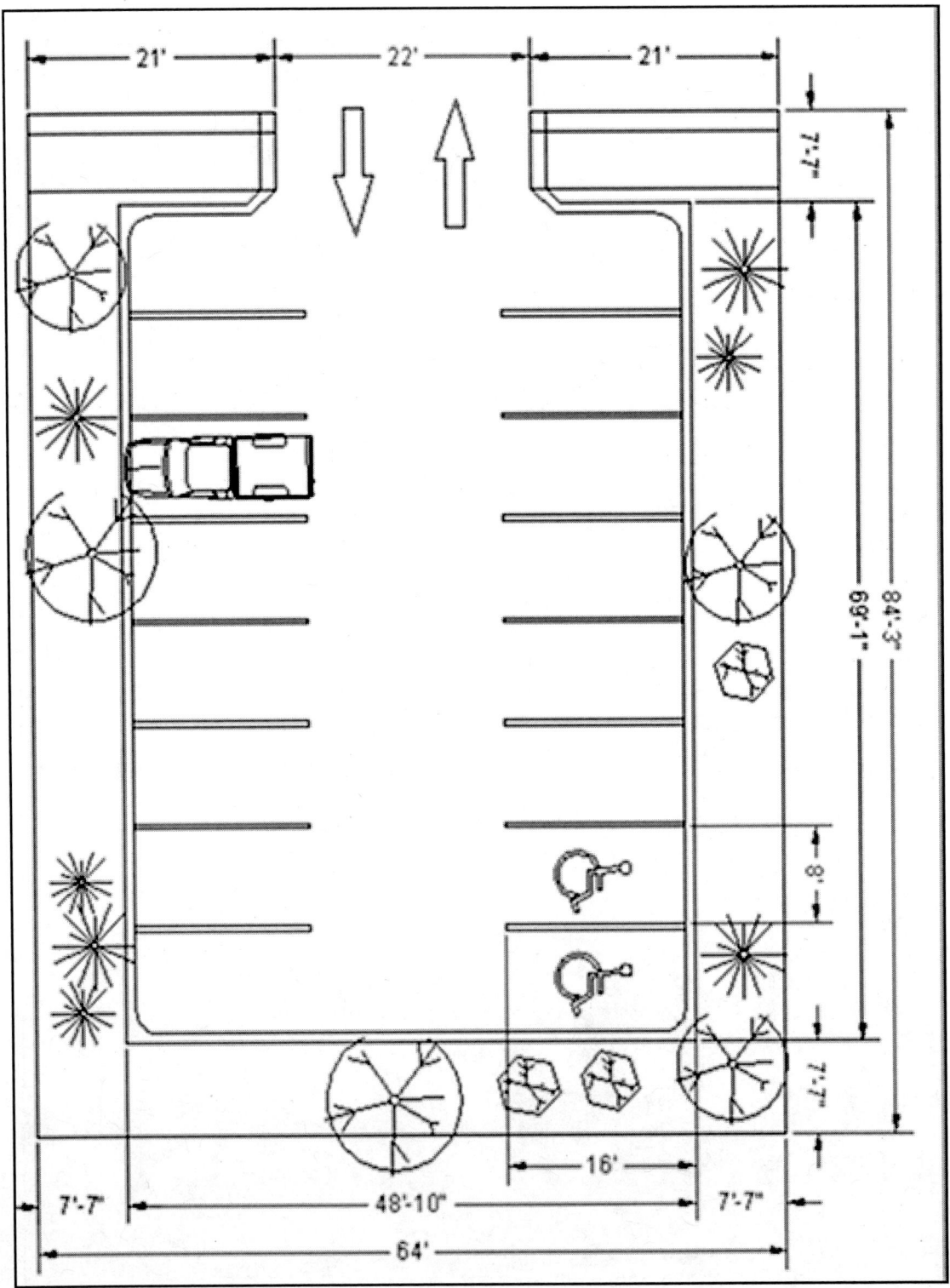

## Needs Assessment Instruments

# Pre-Class Survey

### *Please provide the following information:*

1. Name: _____     Date: _____

2. Age:  Under 18 ( )   18-29 ( )   30-49 ( )   50+ ( )

3. Status (check all that apply):
   ( ) Employed in drafting or closely related field (machining, construction)
   ( ) Currently not-employed
   ( ) Full-time student*
   *If checked, please list your current field of study _____

4. Experience Level (please rate yourself):

|  | No Experience | Beginner | Intermediate | Expert |
|---|---|---|---|---|
| Drafting: | ( ) | ( ) | ( ) | ( ) |
| Using Computers: | ( ) | ( ) | ( ) | ( ) |
| Computer Aided Drafting (CAD): | ( ) | ( ) | ( ) | ( ) |

5. CAD field of interest (check all that apply):
   ( ) Mechanical                    ( ) Civil/Structural
   ( ) Architectural                 ( ) GIS/Mapping
   ( ) Landscape Architectural       ( ) Electrical
   ( ) Interior Design               ( ) Other _____

6. "Based on past experience, I learn best... (Please check one item to complete the sentence.)
   ( ) ...while working as part of a group or team."
   ( ) ...on my own, occasionally relying on an instructor or other class members."

7. Ideally, who would be in charge of the learning that takes place in this class?
   ( ) Me                    ( ) The instructor

8. Please state why you are taking this class and what you expect to gain from it:

   _____

   _____

   _____

## Learning Contract

Please fill out and return to the class facilitator by the third class period.

I _____ (learner's name) contract for a grade of ____(choose one):

| Grade | Condition |
|---|---|
| A | Satisfactorily complete all applicable (mechanical or architectural) learning exercises found at the end of each chapter in Part A, and the exercises from least three modules found in Part B.  Score 90% or better on the reviews found at the ends of Units 1 and 2. |

| Ch.1____ | Ch.6____ | Ch.11___ |
|---|---|---|
| Ch.2____ | Ch.7____ | Mod.1___ |
| Ch.3____ | Ch.8____ | Mod.2___ |
| Ch.4____ | Ch.9____ | Mod.3___ |
| Ch.5____ | Ch.10___ | Unit 1 Rev.____<br>Unit 2 Rev.____ |

| Grade | Condition |
|---|---|
| B | Satisfactorily complete all applicable (mechanical or architectural) learning exercises found at the end of each chapter in Part A, and the exercises from least one module found in Part B.  Score 80% or better on the reviews found at the ends of Units 1 and 2. |

| Ch.1____ | Ch.6____ | Ch.11___ |
|---|---|---|
| Ch.2____ | Ch.7____ | Mod.1___ |
| Ch.3____ | Ch.8____ | Unit 1 Rev.____ |
| Ch.4____ | Ch.9____ | Unit 2 Rev.____ |
| Ch.5____ | Ch.10___ |  |

| Grade | Condition |
|---|---|
| P | Satisfactorily complete all applicable (mechanical or architectural) learning exercises found at the end of each chapter in Part A.  Score 70% or better on the reviews found at the ends of Units 1 and 2. |

| Ch.1____ | Ch.6____ | Ch.11___ |
|---|---|---|
| Ch.2____ | Ch.7____ | Unit 1 Rev.____ |
| Ch.3____ | Ch.8____ | Unit 2 Rev.____ |
| Ch.4____ | Ch.9____ |  |
| Ch.5____ | Ch.10___ |  |

Learner's Signature _____ Date: _____

Facilitator's Signature_____ Date: _____

## Course Evaluation

| To the learner: Please rate your class experience in the following areas and return to the course facilitator before the last day of class. | Excellent | Very Good | Good | Fair | Poor | N/A |
|---|---|---|---|---|---|---|
| 1. The overall quality of this course was: | | | | | | |
| 2. The extent to which my needs and objectives were met was: | | | | | | |
| 3. The extent to which my responsibilities were explained was: | | | | | | |
| 4. The helpfulness of the recommended text was: | | | | | | |
| 5. The fairness of the course grading procedure was: | | | | | | |
| 6. The helpfulness of suggested assignments was: | | | | | | |
| 7. The usefulness of examples given by the facilitator was: | | | | | | |
| 8. The facilitator's helpfulness in resolving questions was: | | | | | | |
| 9. The degree to which the class helped with my current employment: | | | | | | |
| 10. The extent to which I received my time and money's worth is: | | | | | | |
| 11. The odds I am going to continue with an advanced CAD class are: | | | | | | |
| 12. The chance I will take another adult-education course is: | | | | | | |

Thank you!  Your feedback is appreciated.  We hope our staff can serve you again soon. Please feel free to make additional comments in the space provided below:

_____

_____

_____

_____

_____

_____

**NOTES:**

# Index